quick & easy
KETOGENIC COOKING

time-saving paleo recipes and
meal plans to improve
your health and
help you lose weight

Maria Emmerich

VICTORY BELT PUBLISHING INC.

LAS VEGAS

First Published in 2016 by Victory Belt Publishing Inc.

Copyright © 2016 Maria Emmerich

ISBN-13: 978-1-628601-00-8

Front and Back Cover Photography by Hayley Mason and Bill Staley

Interior Design by Yordan Terziev and Boryana Yordanova

Meal Plans by Craig Emmerich

Printed in Canada

TC 0918

TABLE OF CONTENTS

Letter to
THE READER

If you feel overwhelmed with work, life, family, and responsibilities and cooking sounds like another job, please know, I am a busy working parent just like many of you. Before kids, I didn't understand the difficulty of finding time to prepare ketogenic meals, and when my nutrition clients would complain that they did not have time to eat healthy, I would think, "It is easy . . . I do it daily." I worked all the time and still was able to find time to put keto meals together. Now, though, I know how hard it can be.

On November 16, 2011, life threw me for a loop. My husband, Craig, and I received an e-mail telling us that we could pick up our two baby boys from Ethiopia. Three days later we were on a plane, and life was never the same. We arrived home in the U.S. on the night before Thanksgiving. Let's just say that Thanksgiving was anything but turkey and gravy. (If you would like to watch a video of our journey, you can find it here: http://mariamindbodyhealth.com/adoption-first-video-of-our-family/.)

It was the most magnificent yet the most difficult time of my life. All of a sudden I was responsible for a one-year-old and a toddler who were scared of everything new—and everything was new to them. I remember them crying the first time they were in the bathtub. They must have been thinking, "Why is this lady putting me in a huge hole and filling it with water?" They didn't have a bathtub at the orphanage.

Because every experience was new to the boys, I held Kai in a baby carrier at all times while holding Micah's hand. Try cooking with one hand! Yep, that was what I did. But it was important because the boys had never had such a sense of security before, and I needed to make up for them not having had anyone.

I'm not complaining—I would give anything to hold baby Kai in a carrier again—but it was an eye-opening experience for me to realize how hard it is to make healthy meals while prioritizing family. But it can be done. Even with all these challenges, cooking one-handed with another little one strapped to my chest, all while running a business, I did it. Which leads me to yet another reason why I love this book. Many of the recipes can be made with one hand!

I love cooking. There is nothing I adore more on a rainy day than spending it in the kitchen with the radio on. I say "rainy day" because on beautiful sunny days I prefer to be outside in my kayak or on my bicycle; sunny days are when my slow cooker is on (and there are many slow cooker recipes in this cookbook!). But I understand that we all have different passions, and that is why this cookbook rules! Even a novice cook can make these recipes. And if you prefer to be outside like I do, you will love the bonus chapter, which shows you how to smoke foods outside!

So that was my goal with this cookbook: to provide quick and easy recipes that anyone can make, no matter how busy you are and whether you're a novice cook or love to spend your free time in the kitchen. But most of all, I wanted to provide delicious, nutritious recipes that can help you get into and stay in ketosis and improve your health.

Maria

My
STORY

Until I was a sophomore in high school, I never thought much about my weight. That changed one day when I tried on my friend's cute jacket, thinking that we were about the same size. It quickly became obvious that the jacket was too small for me when one of my classmates started loudly singing "Fat Girl in a Little Coat" to the tune of "Fat Guy in a Little Coat" from the movie *Tommy Boy*. Everyone started laughing, and I was mortified.

That moment inspired me to make changes to improve my health. I started working hard to get enough exercise and eat what I thought were healthy foods, following the food pyramid and government guidelines, which meant lots of carbohydrates and whole grains. I studied exercise and nutrition in college and took pride in doing everything right when it came to my health—that is, I thought I was doing everything right.

Immediately after college, I developed severe irritable bowel syndrome and acid reflux. I couldn't even drink water without getting reflux. My doctor suggested medication for the symptoms, but I wanted to find a real solution. Then I remembered taking my dog, Teva, to the veterinarian when I was in high school. She'd been losing her hair in patches, and the first question the vet asked me was, "What are you feeding her?"

Not one of the doctors I'd seen over the years had asked me about my diet, and I started pondering why. Why are drugs, not nutrition, physicians' first choice of therapy? I dug deeper into this subject and eventually looked closer at a low-carb, no-grain diet. I decided to cut out most carbs and all grains, and my symptoms immediately began to improve. That was the first step on my path to a ketogenic diet, but I wouldn't take the next step for many years, and it took some difficult times to get there.

In 2007, I was working as a rock-climbing guide and loving it when the economy took a nosedive. My husband, Craig, lost his job, and our primary source of income vanished. With that loss, we had to put off our dream of adopting children. It was devastating: we had no money, no insurance, and a heavy burden on our shoulders that challenged our marriage in ways we couldn't have imagined.

But one of the things I love most about Craig is his perseverance—a trait we have in common—and we pushed back. I decided to become a nutritionist and started working for myself. I didn't have a lot of clients at first, so I started self-publishing books in my free time to help supplement our income. We also started tightening our budget, having "date night" at home and checking out movies from the local library. These prudent measures and our willingness to tighten our belts saved our finances and our marriage from devastation. And things got better. Craig got another job, and I took on more clients as a nutritionist. I loved helping my clients find better health through improved diet—something that I still found doctors never considered.

But in my work with people who had severe metabolic syndrome and diabetes, I found that their blood sugar levels weren't improving enough despite limiting carbs and sugars. I remembered learning in college that since the body can't store protein, it turns excess protein into sugar, and I decided it was time to limit not just carbs but also protein. In other words, I stumbled onto a low-carb, moderate-protein, high-fat diet—a ketogenic diet—and it made all the difference for my clients, and for me.

Maria Emmerich

Now that I am keto-adapted—my body burns fat, not sugar, for fuel—my life and my body are running better than they have in many years. My fitness and energy levels are through the roof, and I'm truly happy. Although I was never athletic growing up, now I am more active than the vast majority of the population. At the age of thirty-five, I run every single morning not because I have to but because I love it. I'm not training for a race or trying to lose weight. I just love it! I know, I'm weird, but it is who I am.

Eating a ketogenic diet hasn't changed my love of food—I've always loved to eat and I always will. But since we adopted two beautiful toddler boys in November 2011, I've had to reassess the way I cook. Quick and easy meals, especially ones I could make while keeping an eye on two active toddlers, became my priority. Meal planning became more important than ever so that I didn't have to spend time after work figuring out what to make for dinner that night. And of course, my meals had to appeal not just to Craig and me but to our boys, too.

Over the years I've found ways to create keto-friendly versions of classic dishes. As a young teenager I often cooked and baked for my family, and my signature dish was lasagna. Now my boys love my Skillet Lasagna (page 266). My family still enjoys all the foods I remember from growing up, just modified to be healthier. And faster!

I know that my priorities are also the priorities of so many families who need fast, easy, and healthy meals, and that's what led to this cookbook. I want you to enjoy tasty foods that fit within a real foods–based, low-carb, high-fat, ketogenic way of eating. It will enhance your health in ways you could never imagine.

In addition to 170 quick, easy, and delicious ketogenic recipes, which you'll find in chapters 5 through 15 and in a bonus section on smoking, this book is packed with lots of handy features to help you along your keto journey.

If you're new to keto, begin by reading the introduction to the ketogenic diet, which starts on page 10. Keep in mind, though, that this is a cookbook; if you're looking for more in-depth information about the science behind keto and how to adapt it to meet your individual needs, turn to page 379 in the Resources section for a list of other books that may prove helpful.

Part 1: The Ketogenic Kitchen

Part 1 is full of handy information and tips for keto cooks—both those who love to spend time in the kitchen and those who would rather be doing anything but cooking. Chapter 1 gives you the lowdown on key keto ingredients, including healthy fats and natural sweeteners, and walks you through stocking your fridge, freezer, and pantry with the right foods. In chapter 2, you'll find a list of the kitchen equipment I consider most essential, as well as some handy extras. Chapter 3 will help you navigate the world of eating keto by offering tips on saving time in the kitchen, planning ahead to ensure your success, and eating out at restaurants.

I know that even non-ketogenic meal planning can be tricky for a lot of people. To help you get started with keto, or to get back on track if you've hit some bumps, I've included meal plans in chapter 4: some for weight loss and healing and some for maintenance. The seven-day plans have corresponding shopping lists that make it easy to pick up everything you need for a successful week of healthy eating. If you're looking for dairy-free meals, two of the thirty-day plans are dairy-free.

Part 2: Easy Ketogenic Recipes

To help you navigate the recipes in this book, I have included a number of helpful features.

Icons
I've marked the recipes with a number of icons, as applicable.

First, there are icons highlighting those recipes that are free of eggs, nuts, and/or dairy, which are problematic for some people:

EGG-FREE   NUT-FREE   DAIRY-FREE

If a recipe isn't always free of a particular allergen but there's a substitution to make the recipe free of that allergen, you will see the word OPTION above the icon, like this:

I've also included icons for recipes that save you time and effort by putting your slow cooker to work or by utilizing a single pot or bowl.

Finally, if you are a visual learner like me, I've included the video icon whenever you can find a video of me making a particular recipe on my site, MariaMindBodyHealth.com.

Options

In many families, only one member follows a ketogenic diet. If this is the case at your house, I have included single serving options for many of my recipes. I've also included tips for busy people, indicating when recipes or parts of recipes can be made in advance and providing other strategies to help you get healthy meals on the table faster and more easily. And if you are a vegetarian, you'll want to look for the vegetarian options, in which I suggest ways to modify the recipes to make them work for vegetarians.

Keto Meters and Nutritional Information

Keto meters indicate where each recipe ranks on the keto "scale": high, medium, or low. Note that in a few cases, a dish's ranking can vary based on whether you include an optional ingredient or component, such as a keto salad dressing.

Finally, I have included nutritional information for each recipe, listing the total calories along with the fat, protein, carbohydrate, and fiber counts in grams and the total percentages of fat, protein, and carbohydrate. You'll find this information helpful as you fine-tune your personal keto targets for these macronutrients (see pages 18 to 19 for my general recommendations).

NUTRITIONAL INFO (per serving)				
calories	fat	protein	carbs	fiber
215	20.6g	4.6g	2.1g	0g
	87%	9%	4%	

Introduction to
THE KETOGENIC DIET

The ketogenic diet is a high-fat, moderate-protein, low-carb diet that has amazing health benefits. Though it was developed in 1921 by Dr. R. M. Wilder at the Mayo Clinic in Minnesota to treat patients with seizures, it was forgotten for close to seventy years when antiseizure medications came onto the market. Then, in 1994, an episode of *Dateline NBC* profiled Hollywood film director Jim Abrahams's son Charlie and the treatment of Charlie's seizures. Charlie didn't respond to seizure medications, so Jim, a frustrated father, went looking for other answers. He found the ketogenic diet, and with it, Charlie was soon seizure-free. The Abrahams family then started the Charlie Foundation to raise awareness of the ketogenic diet as an option for managing intractable epilepsy. Since then, the diet has received increasing media attention.

Specific Health Benefits of the Ketogenic Diet

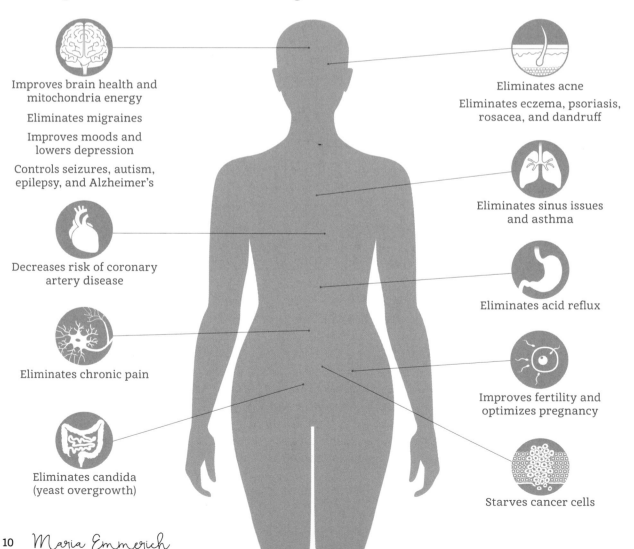

Improves brain health and mitochondria energy

Eliminates migraines

Improves moods and lowers depression

Controls seizures, autism, epilepsy, and Alzheimer's

Decreases risk of coronary artery disease

Eliminates chronic pain

Eliminates candida (yeast overgrowth)

Eliminates acne

Eliminates eczema, psoriasis, rosacea, and dandruff

Eliminates sinus issues and asthma

Eliminates acid reflux

Improves fertility and optimizes pregnancy

Starves cancer cells

Maria Emmerich

What Is the Ketogenic Diet?

There are two sources of fuel for the human body: sugar and fat. When the body burns fat, molecules called ketone bodies are created for use as energy in the brain and other tissue.

The goal of the ketogenic diet is to get the body to metabolize (burn) fat rather than sugar. Being a fat burner is referred to as being "keto-adapted" or "in ketosis," and it is the preferred metabolic state of the human body.

Too many people remain slaves to the belief that glucose is the only source of fuel for our bodies. As a result, they live in fear of running low on glucose. The truth is that fat is the ideal energy source and has been for most of human evolution. That's why we have all this fat on our bodies—to use for energy whenever we need it! We actually need only minimal amounts of glucose, most or all of which the liver can supply as needed on a daily basis.

The ketogenic diet is, at its core, a low-carb, moderate-protein, high-fat diet. It's probably pretty clear why it's low-carb and high-fat—the goal is to get the body to use fat for fuel, not sugar. You'll also need to hit your protein goal for each day. This ensures that you don't lose any lean mass (muscle). (For more specific information about the amounts of carbs, protein, and fat that are recommended on a ketogenic diet, turn to the section "How to Become Keto-Adapted," beginning on page 18.)

It's important to remember that when we say the ketogenic diet is low-carb, that doesn't just refer to white bread and candy. We all know that sugar is bad for us, but many people don't realize how many foods we think of as healthy turn into sugar in the body. Those foods include:

- Whole-wheat bread, whole-grain cereals, and oatmeal
- Bananas, mangoes, pineapple, and other high-carbohydrate fruits
- Potatoes, sweet potatoes, corn, and other high-carbohydrate vegetables
- Rice, wild rice, quinoa, and polenta

After all, starch—complex carbohydrates such as whole grains and root vegetables—is just glucose molecules hooked together in a long chain. The digestive tract breaks it down into glucose . . . also known as sugar!

In the past, I always followed a ketogenic diet myself, but I was more passive in my approach with my clients. I thought, "Of course they can eat spaghetti squash; they were eating white pasta, so changing to squash would be an improvement." But in many cases, insulin resistance and inflammation were still issues. My clients' metabolisms were too damaged to handle that amount of starch. Sure, our ancestors likely could eat root vegetables and more starch than the clients I see today, but our ancestors did not eat like we do in modern times. After years of consuming "food" filled with fructose, food dyes, MSG, pesticides, and all the other chemicals found in food products today, our cells are so damaged that we need a stricter approach.

Some people can eat a whole-foods diet filled with sweet potatoes and fruit and not be overweight, but this doesn't mean that they are healthy. I've had a handful of female clients who weighed around 115 pounds, had very high blood sugar levels, and had to be put on insulin. It's not just diabetics and people who want to lose weight who should limit their intake of both carbohydrates and protein; everyone should. We are all, in an evolutionary sense, predisposed to becoming diabetic.

The sad fact that carbohydrates and glucose are so cheap and readily available doesn't mean that we should depend on them as a primary fuel source or revere them. In fact, it is this blind allegiance to the carb paradigm that has driven so many people to experience the vast array of metabolic problems that threaten to overwhelm our health-care system. I can't believe that a large segment of the health and fitness community still defends carbohydrates and glucose as fuel sources with such tenacity.

I used to enjoy reading women's health and fitness magazines. Since my children came into my life, those days have been put on pause (at least until my kids are no longer demanding toddlers who prefer to sit on my lap whenever I open a book). I cherish these times, so I don't mind. But I did happen to pick up a women's health magazine recently while I was waiting for a weight-lifting class at my local fitness center, and I was shocked that I ever wasted my time reading it. Not only did the magazine push "healthy" whole grains, but it also pushed lean protein. No fat was included anywhere. This is the so-called "clean" diet that so many people adhere to while trying to lose weight. But fat is essential to our diet: our brains and cells are over 60 percent fat!

Why Is It Important to Burn Fat Instead of Sugar?

Too Much Sugar Damages Your Health

Eating too many carbs is associated with a lot of health problems, including diabetes, heart disease, obesity, and inflammation (which in itself is associated with many health problems, particularly autoimmune disease).

After we eat carbohydrates, if we're healthy, insulin transports glucose from the bloodstream into our cells, where it's used for energy. But if we've been taking in more glucose than our bodies need for a long time, we can become insulin-resistant—our cells stop responding to insulin. That means that after eating, our blood glucose stays high because the glucose can't make it into our cells.

Elevated blood sugar increases the risk of diabetes. The excess glucose also acts like tar in the bloodstream, clogging arteries and binding with proteins and fats (a process called glycation) to form damaging molecules called advanced glycation end-products (AGEs). It also causes inflammation and raises triglyceride levels, increasing our risk for coronary artery disease.

If the above information isn't bad enough, I have more bad news: when we're insulin-resistant, insulin levels continue to rise because the pancreas mistakenly believes, "If a little insulin is not working, we just need to make more!" This is not good. Insulin is very toxic at high levels, causing cellular damage, cancer, and plaque buildup in the arteries (which is why diabetics are more likely to have heart disease).

Sorry, but I have even more bad news: our cells become so damaged after a lifetime of cereal and skim milk for breakfast that not only does insulin resistance block glucose from entering cells, it also affects the absorption of amino acids. Amino acids are the building blocks of protein, and we need them to create muscle. So now we can't even maintain our muscles! If that isn't bad enough, our muscles become cannibals. Because the body thinks there is not enough available sugar—remember, the glucose from what you eat isn't getting into your cells—it starts consuming valuable muscle to make more glucose. The result: we lose muscle. Additionally, since insulin stops the production of the fat-burning enzyme lipase, now we can't even burn stored fat! We can work out all we want, but if we continue to eat oatmeal before workouts, we will never be fat burners.

And now comes even more bad news: because of everything our bodies have been through, thyroid disorders can occur. When the liver becomes insulin-resistant, it can't convert the thyroid hormone T4 into T3, so we may get those unexplained thyroid problems that continue to lower our energy and our metabolism.

That's what's going on inside our bodies. What does it feel like on the whole to be a sugar burner?

Sugar Burners Are Hungry, Tired, and Overweight

A sugar burner can't easily access stored fat for energy, which means we always need to be topping up our energy by eating. I know, the runner's magazine you are reading says that your body burns glucose for energy, which is why marathoners eat a huge pasta dinner the night before a race and have oatmeal for breakfast. I did that for years and ran some pretty good marathons, but I was also overweight and had a lot of joint pain. I essentially wanted a glucose IV drip hooked up to my veins because I was always hungry or "hangry" (hungry + angry). When I went two, three, or four hours without food, or even—dare I say it—skipped a meal, the people around me needed to watch out! I was the definition of a suffering sugar burner.

A sugar burner relies on a short-lived source of fuel for energy. You can store only about 50 to 90 grams of glucose in your liver, which really isn't a lot. You can also store glucose in your muscles, but that amount varies quite a bit from person to person (trained athletes usually have larger storage sites if they train with carbohydrates). Overall, you can't store very much glucose in your body, unless you count the grams of glucose in the snacks in your pockets.

Because there's not a lot of storage space for glucose, the excess glucose you consume is converted to fat for storage. And unfortunately, sugar burners end up gaining a lot of body fat. When you eat, blood sugar rises, and what goes up must come down. As blood sugar falls, you get hungry and lethargic and crave more carbohydrates. Exercise becomes too darn difficult, and the sad cycle continues.

The "Healthy" Diet of a Sugar Burner (Spoiler: It's Not Healthy)

Let's look at a hypothetical situation.

It is Monday morning, and you are running late. You have already adopted a grain-free lifestyle, so, as you run out the door, you grab a gluten-free granola bar made with dried fruit and nuts.

No time for breakfast means no time to pack a lunch, either, so at noon, you run to the health food store to grab a gluten-free quinoa and beet salad and a kombucha (a fermented beverage for digestive health) to drink. Meetings at work run late, so you nosh on a banana to tide you over until dinner.

You weren't able to plan dinner, either, so you stop at the grocery store on your way home for an organic roast chicken and a container of mashed sweet potatoes.

Does this sound like you? Are you feeling better with your diet, but the scale isn't moving? Of course it isn't. You are still a sugar burner. You may be reading this and thinking, *There was no sugar in this day of eating,* but look again. It was filled with sugar.

The dried fruit in the granola bar is glorified candy. The quinoa in the salad is a starch, and just 1 cup becomes about 9 teaspoons of sugar in your blood. But did you really have just 1 cup? Probably not. The beets are also sugar. One cup of cooked beets becomes another 3 teaspoons of sugar in your blood.

Am I driving you nuts? I hope I am, because if you are eating "clean" and are still frustrated with your weight, you must realize which foods are converted to sugar in your blood.

Sugar is demonized on television commercials and in health magazines (and rightly so), but these critics take a wrong turn when they recommend eating a banana when you have a sugar craving. Guess what? Your sugar craving may have gone away, but only because you ate sugar! Bananas are sweet for a reason. It is the same with kombucha; it tastes sweet because there is sugar in it.

No, eating a banana isn't the same as eating a Kit Kat bar; however, the prevailing definition of insanity is doing the same thing over and over again while expecting a different outcome. I'm not judging you: I was guilty of this myself. I would eat dried prunes for lunch thinking that they were fat-free and filled with fiber (to keep me full). How brilliant was I? Fifty-pounds-overweight brilliant; that's how smart I was!

Maybe you read that example and thought, *I don't eat that way.* I know that diet is way too high in carbohydrates for me. Well, let's dive into another typical day of "healthy" eating that I often hear about in my office. I had a client come in the other day who described what her diet was on "good" days: an egg-white omelet with two organic chicken sausages for breakfast; for a snack, 18 homemade vegan nut-flour crackers; lunch was sautéed turkey in chicken broth; and dinner was chicken with a ton of low-starch vegetables. Puzzled? She was eating way too much protein, which was being converted to glucose and keeping her a sugar burner. She also didn't eat any healthy fats. As well, she often had "bad" days of eating because cravings got the best of her. And it didn't come as a surprise to me that her hair was falling out.

What It's Like to Be a Fat Burner

If that's what being a sugar burner is like, what's it like to be a fat burner?

Our bodies evolved to depend on fat for the majority of our energy needs. In a keto-adapted body, fat tissue releases a bunch of fatty acids four to six hours after eating and during fasting, and our muscles burn these for energy. That means your body always has a source of energy—body fat—on hand, so you rarely feel hungry.

There's so much more fat available on our bodies for fuel than there is glucose. For example, let's imagine a very lean man with 12 percent body fat who weighs 160 pounds. He has over 19 pounds of fat to burn for fuel, but the amount of glucose stored in his muscles and liver is limited to about 500 grams. Think about this: Would you rather have 19 pounds (8618 grams) of energy or 500 grams of energy? It's no contest!

And because your body is burning fat for fuel, you're likely to lose weight. And all those health problems related to sugar that we talked about earlier? They all improve on a ketogenic diet—blood sugar stabilizes, we become more insulin-sensitive, inflammation decreases, and we're less at risk for diabetes, heart disease, and other health problems.

I hope this information and the testimonials that follow encourage you to transition to a ketogenic lifestyle. If you're ready to start, get out your camera and take a "before" photo, because in a month, you will be shocked at the difference in your body, both inside and out.

VEGETARIANS

If you are a vegetarian, you can succeed on a ketogenic diet. Remember, this is not a high-protein diet; the body coverts excess protein into sugar, just like carbohydrates, via gluconeogenesis, so the focus is on low carbs, moderate protein, and high fat.

Look for this vegetarian icon marking vegetarian recipes throughout this book; even more recipes have a vegetarian option. See the Special Diets chart starting on page 385 for these recipes, which include the following:

Cheesy Grits 302

Creamy Cilantro-Lime Pasta 303

Eggs Gribiche 193

Easy Tomato Soup with Grilled Cheese 218

Easy as Portobello Pizza Pie 306

Mushroom Alfredo 246

Mushroom Ragu 300

Pan-Fried Smoked Cauliflower Steaks 372

Pizza Muffins 162

Pizza Sticks 304

Upside-Down Pizza 264

CHRONIC PAIN: *"One year ago, I began my journey with Maria. I was a few weeks shy of 65. Despite the efforts of several specialists, I still had uncontrolled severe chronic pain. The cause of the pain is inoperable. My cervical spine is ribbon thin in several places. Attempts at adjusting pain meds were unsuccessful. I was facing using 6 to 8 different medicines for the rest of my life. I was taking close to 20 pills per day. Those pills barely took the edge off. I was never comfortable. No one had to remind me to take the medicine. Since starting eating Maria's way, I rarely use pain meds. If I have pain, it is usually because I have had a really active day! That's quite a change from using a walker and a cane.*

Pain management was my primary goal in changing my eating habits. Other benefits that have come are a 45-pound weight loss, more energy, improved balance, and food cravings have stopped. Even after a year, I still notice health improvements. I'm a lifer—no plans to switch back to another way of eating."

—Pam

DEPRESSION: *"I was diagnosed 8 years ago with what they figure to be lifelong depression and PTSD. From the first day I was on meds, I looked forward to the day that I would find a way to stop them. Just never wanted the chemicals in my body but had to respect that I needed help and knew no other way to get better. I had healed a little before working with Maria. Had been able to discontinue antidepressants but not the anxiety meds. Then I found Maria. In just a few months I have found an inner peace I never knew was possible. Thank you for lighting the way. I am overjoyed to be healing."*

—Pam

HEART DISEASE: *"The day I have been so nervous about has come. . . . The results of my lipid profile and cardiac calcium scan were in the mail. My triglycerides were 93!!!!!! The lowest they have EVER been and all my other labs were better than I expected. Plus there was no identifiable plaque in my heart or arteries, and the 'age' of my arteries was 39! Could this really be true?? (I am 65.) Holy schmoly—the LOW CARB, MODERATE PROTEIN, AND HIGH FAT way of eating works!!!! Doing the happy dance today!!!! Thanks Maria!!! I bless the day I was led to you!!!"*

—Barbara

WEIGHT LOSS AND MORE: *"I've lost 99 pounds eating keto. I'm now weaning off of fibromyalgia pain medication because this diet reduces inflammation and helps with my pain more than meds, so why take them? My husband lost 70 pounds, got off his CPAP at night, said goodbye to migraines, cured his acid reflux, and normalized his blood pressure. My oldest daughter lost about 20 pounds. My middle daughter has lost almost 50 pounds and reversed ADHD, oppositional defiance disorder, sleep apnea, migraines, and undiagnosable tummy troubles (her doctor assumed she was lying!). My youngest didn't need to lose any weight but no longer gets bloated after she eats, and it doesn't take her 2 full weeks to get better after being sick anymore. Ketogenic living has completely changed our family for the better."*

—Amanda

PREGNANCY: *"I just had a baby 8 weeks ago and followed Maria's way of eating (WOE) the whole time. I had the best, easiest pregnancy I ever had! I had very minimal morning sickness and less fatigue than with the others. I had no swelling and my blood pressure was perfect. I never experienced that extreme discomfort that so many women complain of. I 100% attribute a great pregnancy to Maria's WOE. I gave birth naturally to a very healthy 7-pound, 5-ounce baby boy. I'm actually sad he's the last one because my pregnancy was so wonderful."*

—Lisa

ASTHMA, IBS: *"After a milestone birthday, I vowed I would embrace TMW ('The Maria Way') and begin my journey of a keto-adapted lifestyle. Two days after starting eating TMW, I'm down 9.8 pounds!*

I realize this is drastic, but being a sedentary person in general, I promised to also exercise at least 4 to 5 days a week. Being a female, other factors played into the drastic results, but I can attest to the fact that all the research you've done has helped a great number of people, and in this very short few days of eating TMW, I'm feeling good, have energy, and am in ketosis, a fat-burning mode that I could never even stay in while eating those pre-packaged crummy foods!

I suffered from IBS but so far, I've not had any issues! I have had asthma since I was 4 years old, and I am now "cured!" I wanted to thank you for all your efforts putting your books together and the recipes . . . keep them coming! Cheers to you and thank you for helping me change for the better!!!"

—Kathya

MIGRAINES AND SEIZURES: *"I have had weight issues since I was a child. I had tried many of the weight loss diets from Weight Watchers to SlimFast to the Cabbage Soup diet. But when a friend of mine told me about Maria's blog, I thought I would check it out. I was having migraines and was having mini seizures three, sometimes four times a month. Since I have cut out not only grains but all flours except almond and coconut flour and have gone completely ketogenic, not only do I not have any migraines, but I've not had any seizures.*

The reason for my long dialogue is to say that I understand you being questionable about it, but I'm telling you that it works. I along with countless others on Maria's Facebook page and other fans of Maria's blog will tell you it works too. Thank you, Maria, for showing us the right way to being healthy."

—Jolena

How to Become Keto-Adapted

1. Cut way down on sugar.

The first obvious step to becoming keto-adapted is to cut out sugar, and when I say sugar, I also mean starch. Remember, complex carbohydrates are just glucose molecules hooked together in a long chain. The digestive tract breaks them down into glucose, just as it does sugar. So a complex-carbohydrate diet filled with sweet potatoes (or whatever starch you choose) is really a sugary diet.

With the ketogenic lifestyle, the only reason to eat carbohydrate is that it provides some fiber to feed gut flora. For that, you need only about 10 to 20 grams per day, or even less if you're eating naturally fermented foods, which replenish gut flora.

To stay in nutritional ketosis and reap all its health benefits, most people need to consume less than 30 grams of total carbs a day. Some people can go as high as 50 grams a day, and some high-end athletes can even get close to 100 grams, but for the vast majority of people, less than 30 grams a day is the best goal. People with metabolic issues such as diabetes or prediabetes will have to stick to less than 20 grams a day, and for extreme cases (or to help break a stall), limit yourself to 10 grams a day of total carbs.

Another estimate is to get 5 percent of your calories from carbs. You can use this equation to calculate that:

(calories x 0.05) / 4 = carb grams

Everyone is different, so it's important to stay under your particular limit. (Test your ketones to make sure you stay in ketosis—see page 22 for more.) This may seem like an awful uphill battle, but it really isn't that hard. In this book you'll find foods such as Spring Popovers (page 146), Cinnamon Roll Minute Muffins (page 152), and Zucchini Tortillas (page 212) that can help make the transition easier. I recommend eating them with fatty meats and spoonfuls of coconut oil in order to get the proper percentages of fat, protein, and carbohydrates. My favorite breakfast is my keto "bread" dipped (or should I say drenched!) in my Minute Hollandaise (page 129). I often pass my poached eggs to my husband, Craig, and just eat the hollandaise. I understand that my bread does not taste like French bakery baguettes, but add a ton of organic butter to it and you will want to become keto-adapted, too! You will feel so good that you will never again look at those baguettes with longing.

2. Hit your protein goal.

When it comes to protein intake on the ketogenic diet, moderate protein based on your lean body mass is a goal to hit.

A good general rule is to get 0.8 times your lean body mass in grams of protein a day. Your lean body mass is your body weight without your body fat, so if you weigh 175 pounds and have 40 percent body fat, your lean body mass is 105 pounds (175 x 0.6) and your daily protein goal should be about 84 grams a day (105 x 0.8)

You want to make sure to hit this protein goal each day or at least average it out over the course of the week (some days higher, some lower).

ADDING MORE FAT TO YOUR DIET WITH MCT OIL

If you don't like fatty cuts of meat, you can add medium-chain triglycerides (MCTs) to your diet in the form of MCT oil. MCTs are composed of fatty acids—the building blocks of fats—and they prompt our bodies to produce more ketones, which is essential to being keto-adapted.

Medium-chain triglycerides are different from long-chain triglycerides. The body uses MCTs quickly; they are not stored in fat cells, and any extra are converted to ketones. This is why I am very specific with my food recommendations, even salad dressings. It is always best to make your own dressings—because it's easy, but more so because you can make them with MCT oil rather than olive oil, which is a long-chain triglyceride and will not turn into ketones.

In addition, people who have malnutrition or malabsorption syndromes are treated with MCTs because they do not require energy for absorption, utilization, or storage. On rare occasions, MCT oil can cause nausea in high amounts, so be cautious and start out slowly.

3. Eat lots of healthy fats.

Finally, there's fat. In order to become keto-adapted, you need to turn up your healthy fat intake to push yourself over the adaptation divide as quickly as possible. But once keto-adapted, you should reduce your fat intake in order to use more body fat as fuel (instead of dietary fat). The amount of fat you need to eat per day will depend on your caloric needs. Just subtract your protein and carb calories from your day's total calories and the rest of your calories come from fat. So if you're aiming for 1,200 calories and you have 20 grams of carbs and 80 grams of protein (totaling 400 calories), the remainder would be 800 calories or 89 grams of fat.

(total calories – (carb grams x 4) – (protein grams x 4)) / 9 calories per gram of fat = fat grams per day.

4. Adjust nutrients and supplements as needed.

People who are transitioning to a low-carb diet like the ketogenic diet sometimes complain of side effects such as headaches, dizzy spells, lightheadedness, fatigue, and cramping. These symptoms aren't universal, but when they do occur, the nutrients discussed below can help.

Cravings are one of the major effects most people notice when they start to transition to keto. Ironically, one benefit of becoming keto-adapted is that the desire for carbohydrates and sugar disappears, but this can take time. If you find yourself gravitating toward carbs on the weekends, whether it is a beer or a piece of pizza, remember: cheating will stop you from becoming keto-adapted (or kick you out of ketosis if you're in it). Supplements can help deter those nasty cravings, which set me back for years! I would do well during the week, but then I would give in on weekends. I never was truly keto-adapted until I added in supplements to get rid of cravings and help me stay the course.

Sodium. People who have metabolic syndrome have a lot of insulin circulating in their blood most of the time. You don't need to be overweight for this to happen. I have had clients who were underweight and still had extreme blood sugar issues. This excess insulin does many wicked things to your body, one of which is causing fluid retention. I had a client who was extremely obese, and her weight would fluctuate by up to 20 pounds daily because of water retention. Yep, 20 pounds of water retention!

One sign of water retention is pitting edema in your lower legs. To test if you have pitting edema, press your finger into the tissue of your shin bone. If your finger leaves an indentation, you have pitting edema. Many overweight people complain of this sensation late in the afternoon or after being on their feet for a long time. What's happening is that excess water is gathering in the lower legs and soaking into the soft tissues. During sleep, when the body is horizontal, the fluid is redistributed into the upper body, so come morning, the pitting edema has gone away, but it returns as the day goes on. This happens to everyone with insulin issues—it is just more noticeable in those who are overweight.

One of the first effects of transitioning to keto is a rapid improvement in insulin sensitivity and a corresponding fall in insulin levels. As insulin levels fall, the kidneys begin to release fluid promptly. One common complaint I get from clients is that they are up in the night urinating more than usual. This effect goes away eventually, and when you release that excess fluid, fat oxidation becomes easier, but there is some bad news, too.

As the extra water goes, it takes with it essential sodium. When sodium levels fall below a certain point, which can happen quite fast, you may experience some undesirable side effects, such as headaches, low energy, dizziness, and cramping.

At first, you might notice that if you stand up quickly, you get dizzy or feel faint. This is because you are dehydrated! But just drinking water isn't going to work, as it would on a high-carb diet. You need more sodium. Salt is not the evil nutrient that doctors warn us about. You've got to start thinking differently. Just as it's important to understand that eating more fat lowers your risk of heart disease, it is important to understand that a well-formulated low-carb diet requires a lot more sodium.

You can add more salt to your food or take sodium tablets. But my favorite way to get more sodium is to consume homemade bone broth (page 132). It is so easy to make—you can even do it in a slow cooker! Bone broth not only contains sodium, it also delivers a ton of minerals and electrolytes. Commercial broth does not convey these benefits. Bone broth takes a few days to make, but I often make a huge batch in the pot that Craig used to use for home brewing (this was years ago . . . yes, we have come a long way on our journey!). I freeze the broth in small containers, and it keeps for a long time. If you don't want to make your own bone broth, you can use store-bought bouillon, but please watch out for MSG and gluten. Not all brands are healthy.

Here are some other things to be aware of about sodium:

- If you get fierce headaches when starting out on a low-carb diet, add sodium. Eliminating all packaged foods eliminates a lot of sodium from your diet.

- Even if you don't have side effects like pitting edema or headaches, you will need extra water and sodium to counter the loss of fluid.

- In addition to drinking homemade bone broth or store-bought bouillon, I suggest that you replace your regular salt with Celtic sea salt or Himalayan salt. These natural salts are harvested from ancient sea beds or made by evaporating seawater with high mineral content and contain about 70 percent of the sodium of regular salt (which has been processed until it is pretty much pure sodium chloride). They also contain other minerals and micronutrients found in mineral-rich seas, including iodine. I greatly prefer the taste of these salts to regular salt; they are well worth the extra bucks. Make sure that you don't use Morton's sea salt, which often has dextrose (a type of sugar) added as an anticaking agent and is devoid of iodine and other nutrients. After a few months of using natural sea salt, you will find that if you go to a relative's house or to a restaurant, regular table salt will have a chemical-like taste.

Potassium. If you don't want to lose lean muscle, pay attention! Because you lose a lot of sodium through the diuretic effect of a low-carb diet, you will eventually lose a lot of potassium as well. Keeping your potassium level up helps safeguard your lean muscle mass as you lose weight. Also, like low sodium, low potassium can cause cramping and fatigue. A deficiency also causes low energy, heavy legs when walking up stairs, salt cravings, dizziness, and moodiness. Causes of low potassium include dehydration from diarrhea, sweating, and low-carb diets that include too much protein and not enough salt.

You can replenish your potassium by taking 200 milligrams of potassium supplements a day. You can also add potassium-rich foods to your diet, such as avocados; paprika and red chili powder; cocoa powder and unsweetened baking chocolate; fish such as pompano, salmon, halibut, and tuna; and dried herbs such as chervil, parsley, basil, dill, tarragon, ground turmeric, saffron, and oregano.

Magnesium. Most people who have metabolic syndrome or high blood pressure or are overweight, insulin-resistant, or diabetic are deficient in magnesium. Your body needs 54 milligrams of magnesium to process just 1 gram of sugar! That creates a high demand for magnesium. No wonder it is one of the most common deficiencies I see in clients. About 70 percent of people don't get the minimum recommended daily intake of magnesium.

As your cells grow resistant to insulin, you can't store magnesium; therefore, it passes out of your body through urination. Magnesium in your cells relaxes your muscles, so if your magnesium level is too low, your blood vessels will constrict rather than relax, which will raise your blood pressure and decrease your energy level.

It is not entirely necessary to get a blood test to see if you are deficient in magnesium because the fact is that most people are deficient. Being keto-adapted helps, but it's not always enough. I will always take magnesium supplements. Magnesium helps repair muscles, naturally relaxes blood vessels and tight muscles, and is a miracle cure for migraines and many other ailments. Good magnesium levels help regulate potassium levels as well. Magnesium is necessary for the production of fatty acids and proteins. It's also important for the proper function of muscles and nerves, for metabolism and energy, and for bone development.

How to Know If You're Keto-Adapted: Testing for Ketones

When you burn fat, your body produces ketone bodies, which are what the body uses for fuel. There are three different types of ketone bodies: acetoacetate, which is found in the urine; acetone, which is found in the breath; and beta-hydroxybutyrate (BHB), which is found in the blood.

There are three ways to test your ketones, each of which has its pluses and minuses.

Testing Your Urine

PRODUCT: Ketone urine test strips

PROS: Cheap

CONS: Not as reliable once you're keto-adapted (see below); drinking lots of water can affect results

Our bodies excrete excess ketones in two ways: through the urine or through the breath. When you test for ketones in your urine, you typically see higher levels in the early stages of keto-adaptation because your body isn't using ketones for fuel yet. After you are fully keto-adapted (which takes two to four weeks or so), you will see fewer ketones in your urine because your body will be using more ketones for fuel instead of excreting them.

Urine test strips are also very susceptible to changes based on your state of hydration. The more hydrated you are (and we should all be drinking more water with a ketogenic lifestyle, since the foods we eat have less water), the lower your ketone level on the urine test strip will be.

Testing Your Breath

PRODUCT: Ketonix Breath Analyzer

PROS: Low long-term cost ($99 up front with no ongoing cost); accurate at testing acetone; easy to do

CONS: Doesn't always correlate directly to blood ketones; alcohol consumption can give a false positive; drinking lots of water can affect results

Breath ketone testers test your breath for acetone. This is what some people call "keto breath." Testing your breath for acetone gives you a good idea of how much your body is turning fat into fuel, but it doesn't correlate directly to the BHB in your blood—which is the most accurate measure of the ketones being produced in your body.

Testing Your Blood

PRODUCT: Blood meter (I like the Precision XtraBlood Glucose and Ketone Monitoring System best)

PROS: Very accurate

CONS: Expensive in the long term, $4 or more per strip; requires finger prick for blood

Testing your blood for ketones measures the amount of BHB in your blood and thus how much energy (in the form of ketones) is really available to fuel your body. The higher the number, the more your body is using ketones for fuel. This is the best indicator of your true state of ketosis. The optimal range is 1–5 (2–4 is great for weight loss).

When to Test Ketones

Testing in the morning before you eat anything will give you the best idea of your body's ongoing state of ketosis. In general, ketones are the lowest of the day at this time. A decent ketone level (1.0) at that time indicates that a state of ketosis is being maintained throughout the day.

Ketones go up during the day if you are eating a good keto diet, especially after you eat a very ketogenic meal (such as one that includes MCT oil). They also go up after intense exercise. Oils that contain MCTs (such as coconut oil) increase ketones. In the evening, you'll generally have a higher level, maybe the highest for the day (2.0 to 3.0 is great).

It's up to you how long you keep testing your ketones. It's important when you're first starting out on a ketogenic diet so that you can tell when you've gotten into full nutritional ketosis. But once you're in ketosis, you certainly don't have to keep testing forever. However, it can be a useful tool to help you figure out if certain foods kick you out of ketosis—test one hour after eating the food you're wondering about.

What Is a Good Ketone Level?

Ketosis is defined as a blood ketone (BHB) range of 0.5 to about 5.0 millimoles (mmol or sometimes mM). This is the range in which the body is using ketones for its primary fuel source. The ideal range for weight loss and healing is about 2 to about 4 mmol.

More is not better when it comes to ketones. Many studies have shown that sustaining levels above about 4 to 5 mmol does not provide any additional benefit, and in some people, too high a ketone level—10 or higher—can lead to a state called diabetic ketoacidosis (DKA) and in extreme cases can lead to death. But this level of blood ketones is seen only in people with severe beta cell (pancreas) issues, such as type 1 diabetics. Dr. Peter Attia, cofounder of the Nutrition Science Initiative, said it best in his blog post "Ketosis-advantaged or misunderstood state? (Part I)" (found at eatingacademy.com/nutrition/ketosis-advantaged-or-misunderstood-state-part-i):

> A person with a normal pancreas, regardless of how long they fast (including the fellow I reference above who fasted for 382 days!) or how much they restrict carbohydrates, can not enter DKA because even a trace amount of insulin will keep B-OHB [blood ketone] levels below about 7 or 8 mM, well below the threshold to develop the pathologic acid-base abnormalities associated with DKA. Let me reiterate, it is physiologically impossible to induce DKA in anyone that does not have T1D [type 1 diabetes] or very, very, very late-stage T2D [type 2 diabetes] with pancreatic "burnout."

PART 1

The Ketogenic Kitchen

Ingredients

CHAPTER 1

Healthy
FATS

When you are keto-adapted, healthy fat is your fuel source. You need to eat lots of healthy fat to keep your fuel reserves full.

Saturated fats like MCT oil, coconut oil, butter, ghee, tallow, and lard are your best choices: they are stable and anti-inflammatory, they protect against oxidation, and they have many other important health benefits. When it comes to fats to include in your high-fat lifestyle, the higher the amount of saturated fatty acids (SFAs), the better. Grass-fed and organic sources are always best if you can get them.

MCT stands for "medium-chain triglycerides," which are chains of fatty acids. MCTs are found naturally in coconut oil, palm oil, and dairy; MCT oil is extracted from coconut or palm oil and contains higher, concentrated levels of MCTs. Unlike coconut oil, MCT oil stays liquid even when refrigerated.

Consuming fats with an abundance of MCTs is of particular benefit because MCTs, unlike long-chained triglycerides, are easy for your body to turn into ketones. *Note:* Whenever you find MCT oil alongside other oil choices in a list of ingredients for one of the recipes in this book, it's always preferable to use MCT oil because of its ability to produce ketones. However, to make the recipes as accessible as possible, I always give second-best oil choices as well.

Below is a list of the best oils and fats to use with their SFA and polyunsaturated fatty acids (PUFA) content. (PUFAs should be avoided; compare the PUFA content of these good fats with that of the bad fats on page 30.)

97% SFA | less than 1% PUFA

MCT oil (such as the SKINNYFat brand):*

- Has a neutral flavor
- Works in savory dishes
- Can be heated using a low to moderate heat source (no higher than 320°F)

92% SFA | 1.9% PUFA

Coconut oil:

- Has a strong coconut flavor
- Works great in sweet dishes and exotic Thai dishes
- Can be heated
- Can also be used on the skin

82% SFA | 2% PUFA

Palm kernel oil:**

- Has a neutral flavor
- Works great for baking
- Can be heated

75% SFA | 3% PUFA

Suet:

- Great for frying
- Harder to work with than beef tallow (which is rendered from suet)

*MCT oil can be found at most health food stores, but if you have trouble finding it, you can use avocado oil, macadamia nut oil, or extra-virgin olive oil instead, keeping in mind that avocado oil is the most neutral-flavored of the three. I prefer cooking with the SKINNYFat brand of MCT oil because, unlike coconut oil, it doesn't have a distinct coconut taste that can overwhelm dishes. I also use SKINNYFat because I've found that, unlike other MCT oils, it does not cause the stomach upset that can occur when first adding MCT oil to your diet.

**Be sure to purchase sustainably sourced and processed palm kernel oil. There are ecological concerns associated with some palm oils—for instance, its production can endanger gorillas—so make sure to know the source.

65% SFA **2%** PUFA

Ghee/Clarified butter:

- Great for heating and frying (smoke point of 475°F vs. 350°F for butter)
- Great flavor (ghee has a unique nutty/caramelized flavor)
- Very stable

60% SFA **3%** PUFA

Cocoa butter:

- Has a mild coconut flavor
- Works great for sweet and savory cooking
- Can be heated

60% SFA **3%** PUFA

Butter:

- Adds wonderful flavor
- Very versatile and easy to use
- OK for low heat (for higher heat, see Ghee/Clarified butter)

57% SFA **7%** PUFA

Buffalo tallow:

- Very flavorful
- Great for frying
- Adds a unique flavor

51% SFA **2%** PUFA

Beef tallow:

- Adds a rich flavor
- Great for frying

47% SFA **7%** PUFA

Mutton tallow:

- Has a unique flavor
- Good for frying and heating

43% SFA **13%** PUFA

Duck fat:

- Adds great flavor to foods
- Works great for frying savory foods
- OK to heat

41% SFA **12%** PUFA

Lard:

- Has a mild flavor
- Works great for frying sweet or savory foods
- Can be heated

40% SFA **10%** PUFA

Bacon fat:

- Adds great flavor
- OK to heat

30% SFA **21%** PUFA

Schmaltz:

- OK to heat
- A bit higher in PUFA than others

15% SFA **10%** PUFA

Macadamia nut oil:

- Has a mild nutty flavor
- Works great in salad dressings
- Use in nonheat applications, such as salad dressings

14% SFA **9.9%** PUFA

Extra-virgin olive oil:***

- Has a strong olive flavor
- Works great in Italian salad dressings
- Use in nonheat applications, such as salad dressings

11% SFA **10%** PUFA

Avocado oil:

- Has a mild, neutral flavor
- Works great in savory and sweet dishes as well as exotic Thai dishes
- Can be heated

10% SFA **14%** PUFA

Hazelnut oil:

- Has a mild hazelnut flavor
- Works great in sweet dishes and exotic Thai dishes
- Use in nonheat applications, such as salad dressings

8.2% SFA **17%** PUFA

Almond oil:

- Has a mild, neutral flavor
- Works great in sweet dishes and exotic Thai dishes
- Use in nonheat applications, such as salad dressings
- Can also be used on the skin

8% SFA **9%** PUFA

High oleic sunflower oil:

- Has a mild flavor
- Works great for sweet dishes and exotic Thai dishes
- Use in nonheat applications, such as salad dressings

***Extra-virgin olive oil is a good fat to include in a ketogenic lifestyle, but only when it's used cold, such as in salad dressings. Do not use extra-virgin olive oil for cooking; heat causes the oil to oxidize, which is harmful to your health.*

ADDING MCT OIL TO YOUR DIET

Here is a sampling of recipes in this book that are great ways to add MCT oil to your diet. However, please note that if you are trying to lose weight, I do not recommend that you drink your calories; chewing food signals hormones to tell us we are satisfied.

 116
Caesar Dressing

 145
Dairy-Free Chocolate Shake

 263
Easy Corned Beef "Hash"

 120
Easy French Dressing

 193
Eggs Gribiche

 112
Fat-Burning Immersion Blender Mayo

 240
King Crab Legs with Garlic Butter

 135
Olive Salsa

 130
Simple Chimichurri Sauce

 220
Simple Salade Niçoise

 245
Slow Cooker Chimichurri Chicken

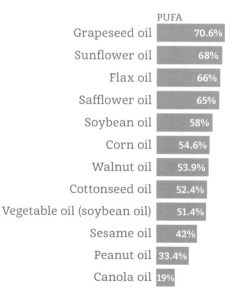 343 344 345
3 ice cream flavors: Coffee, Hibiscus Berry, or Chai

Bad Fats

There are two kinds of fats that should be avoided: trans fats and polyunsaturated fatty acids (PUFAs).

Trans fats are the most inflammatory fats. They are among the worst substances we can consume for our overall health. Many studies show trans fats increase the risk of the heart disease and cancer. Here is a list of trans fats to avoid at all costs:

- Hydrogenated or partially hydrogenated oils (check ingredient labels)
- Margarine
- Vegetable shortening

PUFAs should also be limited, as they are prone to oxidation, which is damaging to health. Many oils are high in PUFAs. Here is a list of the most common:

PUFA

Oil	PUFA
Grapeseed oil	70.6%
Sunflower oil	68%
Flax oil	66%
Safflower oil	65%
Soybean oil	58%
Corn oil	54.6%
Walnut oil	53.9%
Cottonseed oil	52.4%
Vegetable oil (soybean oil)	51.4%
Sesame oil	42%
Peanut oil	33.4%
Canola oil	19%

Natural SWEETENERS

I get questions almost daily about sweeteners. They usually come in the form of "Why do you use 'artificial' sweeteners? And can I use coconut sugar or Sugar In The Raw [a brand of turbinado sugar] instead?"

First off, nothing that I recommend is artificial. Erythritol is found in many fruits and vegetables and in fermented foods, and just as you can find sugarcane fields and honey in nature, you can find the stevia herb and grow it in a pot in your own home if you want to. Both are as natural as honey or maple syrup, yet they can be consumed without the negative effects of other common natural sweeteners because they are low on the glycemic index; that is, they have less effect on blood sugar.

The truth is that commonly used natural sweeteners such as honey, maple syrup, and agave all increase blood sugar. When blood sugar rises, it not only causes inflammation but also will take you out of ketosis, which is why I do not allow those sweeteners and prefer natural sweeteners that don't raise blood sugar.

I listened to a great radio program on NPR that discussed how generations past often had dessert after dinner—a slice of pie or something else special made from scratch by the mother. The nutritionist on the show talked about how mothers often felt that their role was to create a nurturing and well-kept home, which meant home-cooked meals and tasty baked treats. So what is the issue with having sugar now, and why are we seeing such a rise in metabolic syndrome not only in adults but in kids, too?

The thing is, we no longer have just a small piece of pie after dinner. It starts with breakfast. I grew up on cereal and skim milk, which is what many people eat for breakfast today. Did you know that there is more sugar in a cup of skim milk than there is in four Starbursts? Then for a snack, we grab a granola bar, which has the same sugar content as a candy bar! Lunch almost always includes sugary things that didn't exist in the past—like pudding, Jell-O, Gatorade, or juice. Sugar used to be a treat, but now it is a staple in the standard American diet.

In 1960, the average American consumed 2 teaspoons of sugar per day. In recent years, that amount has increased to over 65 teaspoons (1⅓ cups) every day! Today fructose consumption accounts for approximately 10.2 percent of total calories—empty calories, I might add. (Fructose is a particular concern when it comes to health; see page 32 for more information.)

Since even natural sweeteners like sugarcane, honey, agave, and maple syrup all raise blood sugar levels, I recommend sticking to other natural sweeteners that are more keto-friendly.

THE HEALTH EFFECTS OF FRUCTOSE

Americans aren't just eating too much sugar. We're eating too much of a particular kind of sugar: fructose. Fructose is even more damaging to health than other kinds of sugars. There are two big reasons why.

AGEs. One of the big contributors to the aging process and the development and perpetuation of degenerative diseases is advanced glycation end-products (AGEs). These are are formed through glycation, a chemical reaction in which sugars, the breakdown products of sugars, or free radicals from oxidative damage bind with proteins. AGEs form a sort of a crust around our cells. Many studies have shown that this crust is linked with a wide range of diseases, including diabetes, Alzheimer's, heart disease, asthma, stroke, cataracts, glaucoma, polycystic ovary syndrome (PCOS), and autoimmune disease.

So what role does fructose play here? Studies have shown that fructose enables glycation reactions at ten times the rate of glucose!

Nonalcoholic fatty liver disease. Fructose can be metabolized only by the liver. It's a complicated process, but in the end, it's often turned into triglycerides, a kind of fat. These triglycerides frequently stay in the liver, and with enough fructose, all the resulting triglycerides cause nonalcoholic fatty liver disease. That can lead to liver inflammation and, eventually, cirrhosis. Nonalcoholic fatty liver disease is also associated with metabolic syndrome and heart disease.

I see so many children with fatty livers, and it's because they're drinking sodas and juices and consuming too much fructose! Here's an interesting fact: 8 ounces of Welch's 100 percent grape juice (no sugar added, just grape juice) contains more fructose than a 12-ounce can of Mountain Dew!

In his book *Cholesterol Clarity*, Jimmy Moore illustrates the connection between fructose and fatty liver disease with this ultra-clear analogy: "One way to remember that eating carbohydrates leads to an increase in blood and liver fat is to compare it to the French delicacy foie gras, a 'fatty liver' created by force-feeding carbohydrate (corn or, in Roman times, figs) to a goose. The same thing happens in humans."

Unfortunately, Americans ingest a lot of fructose, most frequently in the forms of sucrose (table sugar), which is 50 percent fructose and 50 percent glucose bonded together; high-fructose corn syrup (HFCS), which is about 55 percent fructose; and honey, also 55 percent fructose. Agave syrup is 90 percent fructose—not a health food!

In traditional cultures, fruit was a seasonal food, consumed in summer when people were most active. They didn't have trucks shipping in fruit from other countries or factories squeezing out all the juice for a sweet drink and eliminating the fiber that helps us feel full. Eating an orange is fine, but drinking six of them in an 8-ounce glass is too hard on children's livers. Different types of fruit have different levels of fructose, too. Avocados are very low in fructose, whereas tropical fruits like bananas are very high.

What can you do? Avoid fructose, first of all. That means avoiding not just juices and soda but also honey, agave, and coconut sugar, all of which have high amounts of fructose. The next best thing you can do for your liver is to increase the amount of antioxidants you consume. Antioxidants are natural defenses against oxidative stress and may reverse or protect against advanced liver damage.

Keto-Friendly Natural Sweeteners

Here is a list of all the natural sweeteners that I recommend:

- Stevia, liquid or powdered (with no additives)
- Stevia glycerite (thick liquid stevia)
- Blended name-brand sweeteners, such as Swerve
- Erythritol (including Sukrin granulated and icing sugar)
- Monk fruit
- Yacón syrup
- Xylitol

More information on all of these begins below.

GLYCEMIC INDEX OF SWEETENERS	
Stevia with no additives	0
Stevia glycerite	0
Swerve	0
Erythritol	0
Monk fruit	0
Yacón syrup	1
Xylitol	7
Agave	13
Maple syrup	54
Honey	62
Table sugar	68
Splenda	80
HFCS	87

Stevia

Stevia comes in a powdered or liquid form, as well as a thick liquid form called stevia glycerite (discussed below). Because stevia is so concentrated, many brands, such as Stevia In The Raw, add bulking agents to powdered forms of stevia, such as maltodextrin, to make it useful for baking. STAY AWAY from those products. Sugar has a glycemic index of 52, whereas maltodextrin has a glycemic index of 110!

Years ago, when I first started writing recipes, I used products that contained maltodextrin and probably ate a dessert that contained maltodextrin every day. When I realized how bad it was and removed maltodextrin from my diet, I lost seven pounds in a week!

Look for products that contain just stevia or stevia combined with another natural and keto-friendly sweetener.

Stevia Glycerite

Stevia glycerite is a thick liquid form of stevia that is similar in consistency to honey. Do not confuse it with liquid stevia, which is much more concentrated and has a bitter aftertaste. Stevia glycerite is about 200 percent as sweet as sugar, making it a bit less sweet than pure liquid or powdered stevia. I prefer to use stevia glycerite because unlike the powdered or liquid form of stevia, it has no bitter aftertaste. Stevia glycerite is great for cooking because it maintains flavor that many other sweeteners lose when heated. However, when used for baking it usually needs to be combined with another sweetener because it doesn't caramelize or create bulk.

Erythritol

I find it interesting that some people are reluctant to try alternative sweeteners like erythritol and xylitol. Many think they are artificial sweeteners due to their chemical-sounding names.

While this is typically a good instinct when looking at ingredient labels, in this case it is not warranted. I think that it is somewhat similar to calling salt "sodium chloride." Salt is mainly sodium chloride, but the perception is very different if we say "put some sodium chloride on my eggs" instead of "put some salt on my eggs." Or it's like calling maple syrup what it really is, concentrated xylem sap.

Erythritol is a sugar alcohol or polyol. It is found naturally in some fruits and fermented foods. Erythritol doesn't increase blood sugar or insulin levels. Almost all of it is absorbed before it reaches the colon, so it doesn't cause stomach upset the way other sugar alcohols can. It also has no calories.

The process of making erythritol involves fermenting glucose (typically from vegetables) to create a sweet-tasting end product. When using good non-GMO vegetables, this process is just as natural as making maple syrup. Erythritol is generally available in granulated form, though sometimes you can find it powdered. If you purchase a granulated product, such as Sukrin or Wholesome! All-Natural Zero, I suggest that you grind it to a powder before using it. Erythritol tends not to dissolve well in foods when used in granulated form, giving foods a granular texture.

Monk Fruit

Also known as luo han guo or lo han kuo, monk fruit is cultivated in the mountains of southern China. Mogrosides, chemical compounds extracted from the fruit, are 300 times sweeter than sugar, similar to stevia. But unlike stevia, mogrosides don't have a bitter aftertaste. Monk fruit comes in pure liquid form and in powdered form.

Again, be a detective and watch the ingredients. Since it is 300 times sweeter than sugar, the powdered form of monk fruit is typically bulked up with another sweetener to make it measure cup for cup like sugar, so watch out for things like maltodextrin. Choose a brand that has keto-approved added sweeteners, such as erythritol.

Swerve (and Other Blended Sweeteners)

Swerve is a natural sweetener made from non-GMO ingredients. It contains two natural sweeteners, erythritol and oligosaccharides, both of which have zero calories. Erythritol naturally occurs in small amounts in vegetables and fruits. It has zero impact on blood sugar and contains no artificial ingredients or preservatives.

Swerve works well as an all-purpose sugar substitute because it measures cup for cup with table sugar. I use the powdered form of Swerve (the one labeled "confectioners") because it dissolves readily when cooking or baking with it.

Other blended sweeteners also have great flavor and give good results in baking. Blending multiple natural sweeteners gives these products a better overall flavor and sweetness. Some great examples are Pyure (erythritol and stevia), Norbu (erythritol and monk fruit), Natvia (erythritol and stevia), Lakanto (erythritol and monk fruit), and Zsweet (erythritol and stevia). All of these options can be used in a 1:1 ratio for sugar.

Yacón Syrup

Yacón syrup is a thick syrup that is pressed from the yacón root and has a flavor reminiscent of molasses. It has been consumed for centuries in Peru.

You wouldn't want to use yacón syrup on its own, mainly because it is very expensive but also because it has some fructose in it. A small jar lasts us four to six months. I use a tablespoon here and there to improve the texture and flavor of my sauces; it's ideal for giving my sweet-and-sour sauce that perfect mouthfeel or giving my BBQ sauce that molasses flavor profile. Using this in a small amount keeps the sugar to one gram or so per serving.

Xylitol

Xylitol is a naturally occurring low-calorie sweetener found in fruits, vegetables, and certain hardwoods. Xylitol produces a lower glycemic response than sucrose or glucose, so it has a minimal effect on blood sugar and insulin. It is not as low on the glycemic index as erythritol (the base of a sweetener like Swerve), but sadly erythritol doesn't work in recipes such as low-carb hard candies because it does not melt down properly (it crystallizes as it cools). Also, some people prefer the taste of xylitol to erythritol. Xylitol comes in granulated form.

Here are some more benefits of xylitol:

- It has 40 percent fewer calories than sugar.

- Researchers found that kids who consistently chewed xylitol gum had 40 percent fewer ear infections than those who did not.

- Xylitol keeps pregnant women's teeth healthy, especially during the third trimester, when teeth are especially soft.

- Chewing xylitol gum or mints protects teeth against the bacteria that causes cavities.

- If you drink acidic sports drinks frequently, eat carbohydrates often, or spend hours dehydrated and breathing through a dry, acidic mouth, as athletes and teenagers do, you are at greater risk for tooth decay. Xylitol inhibits cavities by denying plaque bacteria the fuel (sugar) it needs to erode tooth enamel.

- Studies show that a consistent daily use of at least six to eight grams of xylitol can reduce cavities by as much as 80 percent. If you already have gum disease or cavities, these problems can be reversed. Regular use of xylitol (along with a grain-free diet and increased consumption of fat-soluble vitamins A, D, E, and K) can stop things from getting worse.

Though xylitol has many good qualities, it tends to kick some people out of ketosis. If you use this sweetener in baking or cooking, monitor your ketones closely and stop using it if you find that you're no longer in ketosis.

Cooking and Baking with Keto-Friendly Sweeteners

If you are new to the ketogenic lifestyle, you will likely find the level of sweetness in the recipes in this book perfect for a transition into a sugar-free life. As you continue on your journey, foods will start to naturally taste sweeter. When that happens, you may want to reduce the natural sweetener in a recipe to adjust the sweetness to your taste.

Also, if you are new to using keto-friendly natural sweeteners, I suggest that you blend them to get the best-tasting, well-rounded sweetness. Many times these natural sweeteners can be bitter on their own, and I find that blending them creates a fantastic end product. For example, I often add a touch of stevia glycerite to my dessert recipes to give them a more rounded sweetness. You are welcome to add a touch of stevia glycerite to any recipe that calls for sweetener, even the crispy fat bombs. In baking recipes, stevia glycerite adds flavor without affecting the baking process.

Whenever a recipe requires a powdered sweetener instead of a liquid sweetener, my go-to choice is Swerve (see page 34), which is available in granular and powdered form. I always use the powdered, or confectioners', form of Swerve because it creates a smoother texture in the finished product and gives better overall results in baking and cooking. That said, you can always pulverize a granular form of erythritol, such as Wholesome! All-Natural Zero, in a blender or coffee grinder to get the same powdered texture.

If a specific natural sweetener or type of natural sweetener (such as powdered or liquid) is called for, as is the case with the crispy fat bombs (pages 326 to 329), then substitutions cannot be used; if a different sweetener is used, the recipe simply will not work. For example, in those recipes where the sweetener has to melt, some sweeteners won't work, so in those instances it's important to use what's called for.

If you see the words "or equivalent" following a sweetener in an ingredients list, such as "¼ cup Swerve confectioners'-style sweetener or equivalent amount of liquid or powdered sweetener," you are free to use any keto-friendly sweetener of choice, liquid or powdered. For example, you could use liquid stevia, stevia glycerite, monk fruit, Zsweet, Wholesome! All-Natural Zero, or xylitol. To learn how to substitute one keto-friendly sweetener for another, refer to the following section.

Sweetener Conversions

Swerve, the sweetener I use most often, can be used 1:1 as a replacement for table sugar. Erythritol is 30 percent less sweet than table sugar, so add 1 teaspoon of stevia glycerite for every cup of erythritol used. If you use stevia, a little goes a long way; you need only a few drops of liquid stevia or ¼ teaspoon of powdered stevia to sweeten a dish. Monk fruit measures cup for cup like sugar. See the handy conversion charts on the next page for guidance.

HOW TO SUB ONE KETO-FRIENDLY SWEETENER FOR ANOTHER

1 cup Swerve = 1 cup powdered erythritol + 1 teaspoon stevia glycerite

1 cup Swerve = a few drops of liquid stevia

1 cup Swerve = a few drops of pure liquid monk fruit

1 cup Swerve = 1⅓ cups powdered erythritol

1 cup Swerve = 1 teaspoon powdered stevia (with no additives)

1 cup Swerve = 1 cup powdered monk fruit blend

1 cup Swerve = 1 cup xylitol

1 cup Swerve = 1 teaspoon stevia glycerite

1 cup Swerve = 2 cups yacón syrup

HOW TO SUB KETO-FRIENDLY SWEETENERS FOR GRANULATED SUGAR

	CALORIES	SWEETNESS	CONVERSION PER CUP OF SUGAR
Swerve	0	100% as sweet as sugar	1 cup
Stevia glycerite	0	200% as sweet as sugar	2½ teaspoons
Stevia, powdered	0	300% as sweet as sugar	1½ teaspoons
Stevia, liquid	0	250% as sweet as sugar	2 teaspoons
Erythritol, powdered	0 to 0.2 per gram	70% as sweet as sugar	1 cup *(plus 1 teaspoon stevia glycerite for sweetness*)*
Yacón syrup	2 per gram	50% as sweet as sugar	2 cups
Xylitol	2.4 per gram	100% as sweet as sugar	1 cup
Monk fruit (liquid)	0	300% as sweet as sugar	1½ teaspoons
Monk fruit (powdered blend)	0	100% as sweet as sugar	1 cup

If using erythritol in a recipe that calls specifically for powdered sweetener, omit the stevia glycerite and use 1⅓ cups of powdered erythritol per cup of sugar.

Sweeteners I Do Not Recommend

Honey

Honey may be less refined and more natural than table sugar, but it is still high in calories and fructose. One teaspoon of natural honey contains 22 calories—that's actually more calories than sugar, which as 16 calories per teaspoon. The biggest problem with honey, however, is that it is roughly 50 percent fructose. (For more on the problems with fructose, see page 32.)

Sure, honey does provide some nutritional benefits that are lacking in table sugar. Honey contains niacin, riboflavin, thiamine, vitamin B6, and other minerals. But it has only trace amounts of these; honey doesn't even come close to the U.S. Department of Agriculture's recommended daily standards of these minerals and vitamins. So, although these trace vitamins and minerals might make honey a slightly better choice than table sugar, it's still not a healthy food. Despite the fact that several websites claim honey to be some kind of miracle food, most of these statements are unproven. If you still think honey is worth using in your baked goods because of the vitamins, let me put it another way: only 2 percent of honey contains vitamins and minerals! And, in most cases, store-bought honey doesn't contain pollen, one of the key elements of honey that is claimed to have health benefits.

Honey without pollen is a watered-down, synthetic scam. The majority of honey on supermarket shelves is made with an ultra-filtering process that involves heating the honey to high temperatures and using high levels of pressure to force it through exceptionally small filters to eliminate pollen. Why do they do this? So the manufacturers can hide where they are getting the honey from. And why would they want to conceal the honey's source? Well, because most of the honey comes from Chinese markets that are responsible for allowing dangerous antibiotics and ample amounts of heavy metals to enter imported honey products. Makes you want to throw away those athletic "honey gel packs," doesn't it?

You might be thinking, *Okay, Maria, then I will only buy honey from my friends who make their own.* In that case, remember that by weight, a homemade batch of honey is 82 percent sugar. Half of that sugar (41 percent of the total weight) is fructose, and the honey still contains only trace amounts of vitamins and minerals.

Your body doesn't care whether you ingest honey or table sugar; once they enter your bloodstream, you produce an abundance of insulin. To your body, sugar is sugar. All types of sugar should be consumed cautiously, even honey.

Agave

Do you think that substituting granulated sugar with a sticky goo called agave is a better choice because agave is expensive and sold in the health food aisle?

No, it isn't! Sugar is about 50 percent fructose, whereas agave is 90 percent fructose. Don't be fooled when you see that agave is low on the glycemic index. Many diabetics are told that agave is a better option for them for this reason. Despite this fact, agave's high amount of fructose makes it a very unhealthy choice because of the correlation between fructose and higher levels of glycation and between fructose and nonalcoholic fatty liver disease (see page 32).

Coconut Sugar

When I was out with some girlfriends recently, one of them asked, "Maria, what are your thoughts on coconut sugar? I see so many claims that it is healthy."

Coconut sugar has become very popular in the past few years. It is derived from the coconut palm tree and is hyped as being more nutritious and lower on the glycemic index than sugar. Coconut sugar is made using a two-step process:

1. A cut is made on the flower of the coconut palm, and the liquid sap is collected into containers.

2. The sap is placed under heat until most of the water in it has evaporated.

Coconut sugar does retain some of the nutrients found in the coconut palm. It is difficult to find exact data, but according to the Philippine Department of Agriculture, coconut sugar contains several nutrients. Most notable of these are the minerals iron, zinc, calcium, and potassium, along with some polyphenols and antioxidants that may also provide some health benefits. The reason it is lower on the glycemic index is that it also contains a fiber called inulin, which may slow glucose absorption.

Even though coconut sugar does contain some nutrients, you'd have to eat a ridiculous amount to really derive any benefits. You would get a lot more nutrients from nonsweet foods. Coconut sugar has the same amount of empty calories as table sugar.

So again, you may be thinking, *Okay, Maria, if I want to sweeten something a little, I will use coconut sugar since it seems less harmful than honey.* No! Let me surprise you with a tidbit: even though I see claims all over the Web that coconut sugar is commendably fructose-free, 70 to 80 percent of it is made of sucrose, which is half fructose (and half glucose)! This essentially means that coconut sugar supplies the same amount of fructose as regular sugar, gram for gram.

Sucralose (Splenda)

Sucralose, also known by the brand name Splenda, is a popular artificial sweetener. It is best known for its former claim to be made from sugar (which the manufacturer got in trouble for and abandoned). It is 600 times sweeter than table sugar.

Splenda is not actually calorie-free. Sucralose does have calories, but because it is 600 times sweeter than sugar, very small amounts are needed to achieve the desired sweetness; but this is only when you use the true form (liquid sucralose). Splenda, however, is bulked up so it can be used in place of granulated sugar. The first two ingredients in Splenda are dextrose and maltodextrin, which are carbohydrates that are not free of calories. One cup of Splenda contains 96 calories and 32 grams of carbohydrates, which is substantial, especially for those with diabetes, but is overlooked due to its labeling as a no-calorie sweetener.

Sucralose has also been found to inhibit the absorption of zinc and iodine, which are essential for proper thyroid function. It is also linked to decreasing good gut bacteria, which exacerbates irritable bowel syndrome.

Artificial Sweeteners

Artificial sweeteners, such as aspartame, acesulfame potassium, neotame, saccharin, sucralose, and advantame, put stress on your metabolism, diminish the liver's ability to filter toxins, and affect overall health. They also can upset the balance of gut flora, which is essential for good health and immune function. Stay away from all artificial sweeteners.

Other High-Sugar Sweeteners

Be a detective and read those labels! Sugar is hidden in most products. Avoid foods whose ingredients label includes anything ending in "-ose" or the following sugars: agave nectar, beet sugar, brown rice syrup, brown sugar, cane crystals, corn sweetener, corn syrup, corn syrup solids, dehydrated cane juice, dextrin, dextrose, fructose, fruit juice concentrate, glucose, high-fructose corn syrup, honey, invert sugar, lactose, maltose, malt syrup, maple syrup, molasses, palm sugar, raw sugar, saccharose, sorghum, sorghum syrup, sucrose, syrup, treacle, turbinado sugar, xylose.

Undesirable Sugar Alcohols

Also stay away from the undesirable sugar alcohols, such as maltitol and sorbitol. Sugar alcohols have become popular as "sugar replacements" in foods such as protein bars, but they can cause gastrointestinal issues and will raise blood sugar levels.

HERBS AND SPICES

Fresh herbs like parsley, rosemary, oregano, and basil and spices like black pepper, nutmeg, and turmeric powder play a big role in a ketogenic kitchen because they are the most nutrient-rich plants you can consume. For example, everyone thinks that spinach is the perfect food, but fresh oregano has eight times the amount of antioxidants! Sure, we wouldn't eat a cup of oregano as we would a cup of spinach, but it shows that even a little bit of the herb provides a huge benefit.

Instead of consuming fruits and starchy veggies that have fructose and raise blood sugar quickly, I suggest overhauling your fridge and pantry so they're full of herbs and spices, and use them often. Not only will it enhance the flavor of your foods, it will also provide many more vitamins, minerals, and phytonutrients than any fruit or vegetable.

The graphs below give you an indication of just how nutrient-packed herbs and spices are. As you can see, there is more potassium in coriander than in a banana, and it comes without all the inflammatory sugar.

Vitamin C (mg per 100 g)

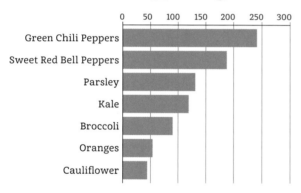

Vitamin E (mg per 100 g)

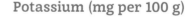

Calcium (mg per 100 g)

Potassium (mg per 100 g)

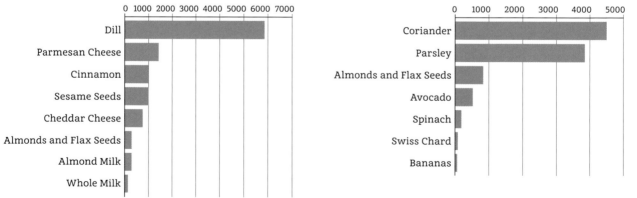

The Medicinal Power of Herbs and Spices

Here are some of the herbs and spices that I love and use often, as well as a sampling of recipes in this book that use them. In addition to the specific recipes listed below, add any of these herbs and spices to homemade salad dressings and appetizers!

Basil

- Relieves gas and stomach pain
- Try Goat Cheese Panna Cotta with Crispy Prosciutto and Fried Basil (page 296) or Slow Cooker Laotian Chicken and Herb (Larb) (page 250).

Black pepper

- Relieves indigestion
- Try Basted Rib-Eye Steak (page 276) or almost any other recipe.

Note: Make sure to use fresh ground pepper in order to get the full benefits. Also, because heat can destroy the healthy properties of pepper, I suggest you add it to a dish at the end of cooking.

Cayenne

- Improves circulation
- Try Grilled Chicken with White BBQ Sauce (page 248) or Homemade Sriracha (page 124).

Cilantro

- Detoxifies the body of heavy metals
- Try Cilantro Lime Sauce (page 115) or Slow Cooker Chicken Fajitas (page 244).

Cinnamon

- Lowers blood pressure and blood sugar
- Try Cinnamon Roll Minute Muffins (page 152), Frozen Snickerdoodle Cream Bites (page 332), or Chai Ice Cream (page 345).

Cloves

- Antimicrobial
- Try Slow Cooker Osso Buco (page 274).

Dill

- Treats heartburn, colic, and gas
- Try Cucumber Salad (page 224), Spring Popovers (page 146), or Dill Dip (page 178).

Fenugreek

- Flushes out toxins
- Try Slow Cooker "Butter" Chicken with Naan (page 252).

Ginger

- Reduces nausea
- Try Teriyaki Jerky (page 186), Cilantro Lime Sauce (page 115), or Dad's Tenderloin Bites (page 188).

Mint

- Helps relieve sore throats, irritable bowel syndrome, and indigestion; is very anti-inflammatory
- Try Grilled Lamb Chops with Mint Aioli (page 282) or Crème de Menthe Shake (page 144).

Oregano

- Soothes stomach muscles
- Try Pizza Spice Mix (page 111) or Pizza Muffins (page 162).

Rosemary

- Rich in antioxidants; helps pull calcium into bone broth
- Try Basted Rib-Eye Steak (page 276) or Slow Cooker Osso Buco (page 274).

Sage

- Antibiotic and antiseptic
- Try adding sage to taste to Chicken Alfredo (page 246) for additional health benefits.

Thyme

- Relaxes respiratory muscles
- Try Simple Slow Cooker Bone Broth (page 132) or Grilled Chicken with White BBQ Sauce (page 248).

Turmeric

- Anticancer properties
- Try Curry Braised Cucumbers (page 311) or Seasoned Salt (page 109).

Vanilla

Most people use vanilla extract rather than the whole bean because the extract is easy to find, convenient to use, and affordable. For this reason, I have made vanilla extract the first option in the recipes in this book and list a vanilla bean as a second choice. That said, I urge you to get into the habit of using vanilla beans. Vanilla beans are high in phenolic compounds, which are potent antioxidants and are also antimicrobial and anti-inflammatory.

Vanilla extract is made by infusing vanilla beans in alcohol for an extended period. The process of infusion does not allow antioxidants to seep into the extract. The chart at right shows how vanilla stacks up against other foods in terms of oxygen radical absorbance capacity (ORAC) value, which is used to measure a food's antioxidant properties.

Vanilla was traditionally used as an aphrodisiac and is reputed to help patients with erectile dysfunction and loss of libido. Because of its calming properties, it is thought to help reduce inflammation due to fever, and because of its high antioxidant content, it may also be effective at fighting off the free radicals that can lead to cancer.

ANTIOXIDANT VALUES OF FOODS SORTED BY ORAC VALUE	
ITEM	ORAC value
Sumac, bran, raw	312,400
Spices, cloves, ground	290,283
Sorghum, bran, hi-tannin	240,000
Spices, oregano, dried	175,295
Spices, rosemary, dried	165,280
Spices, thyme, dried	157,380
Spices, cinnamon, ground	131,420
Spices, turmeric, ground	127,068
Spices, vanilla beans, dried	122,400
Spices, sage, ground	119,929
Spices, szechuan pepper, dried	118,400
Acai, fruit pulp/skin, powder	102,700
Sorghum, bran, black	100,800
Rosehip	96,150
Sumac, grain, raw	86,800
Spices, parsley, dried	73,670
Sorghum, bran, red	71,000
Spices, nutmeg, ground	69,640
Spices, basil, dried	61,063
Cocoa, dry powder, unsweetened	55,653

In addition to giving skincare products an amazing scent, vanilla is also great for:

- *Healing wounds:* Historically, vanilla was used to help heal wounds, and we now know that it has anti-inflammatory properties that may help soothe inflamed skin.

- *Keeping skin young-looking:* As shown in the chart above, vanilla is a great source of antioxidants, which help protect skin from environmental dangers that can accelerate aging.

- *Treating acne and skin infections:* Vanilla can help reduce skin infections and the bacteria that cause acne.

- *Providing B vitamins:* There are a lot of B vitamins in vanilla, including vitamin B6 and niacin, which is a key nutrient in the maintenance of healthy skin. Thiamin, riboflavin, and pantothenic acid are also found in vanilla.

EGGS

I love eggs because they are an inexpensive and convenient keto food, even for vegetarians. Eggs are my favorite food, but I was such a bonehead when I was younger that I would use only the whites! Even in college, when money was tight, I would toss those beautiful yellow yolks in the garbage. How sad and detrimental those fat-free lies are. Yolks contain choline, healthy fats, and serious flavor!

But choosing eggs, whether at a grocery store or a farm, involves examining what the chickens have been fed, how they are living, and how the eggs were harvested. Choosing high-quality eggs will make your cooking more appetizing and nourishing, as well as more beautiful. While the majority of eggs on the market are not specialty eggs, an increasing number of outlets now offer organic, free-range, pastured, and omega-3 enriched eggs. Understanding the differences between the labels will help you choose eggs of the highest quality.

How to Choose the Healthiest Eggs

The common egg question: how to choose? This often confused me in the past. Here are some things to consider.

Size
Smaller eggs tend to have thicker shells than larger eggs and are less likely to become contaminated by bacteria.

Shell color
Since we have been ingrained with the idea that whole-grain foods are "healthier," we tend to think that brown foods are more nutritious than white. But brown eggs are not inherently higher in quality than white eggs; the only difference is in the hens laying the eggs. Do not choose eggs based on the color of their shells.

Egg grades
The USDA grades eggs as AA, A, and B. Grade AA eggs have thick, firm whites and high, round yolks. This grade of egg is virtually free of defects and is best for frying, poaching, and other cooking presentations where the appearance of the egg matters. Most eggs sold in supermarkets are grade A. These eggs are the same quality as grade AA except that the whites are categorized as "reasonably" firm. There is little to no difference in taste and no difference in nutritional value. Most grade B eggs are sold to restaurants, bakeries, and other food institutions and are used to make liquid, frozen, and dried egg products.

Egg labels
- *Natural:* This label has no real meaning; there's no official definition of "natural" when it comes to food.
- *Vegetarian:* This label means that the hens are fed a corn-based diet, which is usually genetically modified (unless otherwise noted). But chickens are omnivores, not vegetarians. Sadly, marketing has gotten us so confused about what to buy that these eggs cost almost a dollar more than "regular" eggs lacking this label.
- *Omega-3 enriched:* Again, marketers understand that consumers are confused, so they overprice these eggs. Regular eggs already are a good source of omega-3s, particularly if the hens are allowed to roam on pasture and enjoy a diverse natural diet, so this label is really just a marketing tactic used to get consumers to spend more. I suggest skipping this as a priority when egg shopping.
- *Cage-free:* All this label really means is that the hens are not caged, but most of them never see daylight. The purveyors are not obligated to let the hens outside, there are no mandatory inspections, and there are no guidelines on what the birds can be fed. Yet you still pay as much for these eggs as you do for organic eggs.
- *Free-range:* To guarantee that you eat truly free-range eggs, purchase eggs from pastured hens.
- *Certified organic:* These hens are kept in barns rather than cages. The hens are fed an organic, pesticide-free vegetarian diet and are not given antibiotics or hormones. This label is regulated with government inspections. Be conscious of antibiotic and hormone use. The USDA prohibits the use of hormones for egg production. Also, the use of therapeutic antibiotics is illegal unless the laying hens are ill. However, since this law isn't always enforced, the only way to ensure that the hens that laid the eggs were antibiotic-free is to purchase organic eggs.
- *Pasture-raised:* Pastured hens often eat diets that include greens, seeds, worms, and bugs, which is a "Paleo" chicken's diet. Studies have shown that eggs from pastured hens may have more omega-3 fatty acids, vitamins, and minerals.

Always look for the USDA shield when purchasing eggs from a store. Claims on egg packaging that bears the USDA shield have been verified by the United States Department of Agriculture.

Purchasing Eggs from Farmers

Many people believe that eggs from a farmer are automatically superior in taste and nutritional content. However, make sure to ask the farmer how the eggs are handled and what the hens eat. Are they fed GMO corn and soy, or are they free-ranging on grass, bugs, and worms? The problem with backyard eggs is that most of these chickens are fed a soy-based feed. All commercial chicken feed is soy-based. Also, many of these eggs do not undergo strict USDA inspection to ensure their safety. So asking questions about antibiotic and hormone use is your best defense.

I love to buy eggs from my trusted neighbor. Although I could ride my bike to pick them up, I get eleven dozen a week, so I have to drive since they won't all fit in my bike basket!

Raw Eggs

Although there is a small risk of salmonella in pastured eggs, it's far better to eat raw eggs from pastured hens than from any other source. The salmonella threat is amplified when the birds are raised in a contaminated and crowded environment, which is usually not the case at small farms that use organic practices, and where the chickens are raised in hygienic and roomy coops and have access to sunlight while they explore for their natural food.

If you are concerned, I advise washing pastured eggs in soapy water. If there is salmonella present, it is typically because the shell has chicken feces on the surface. When cracked, the shell would contaminate the raw egg. But salmonella is extremely rare in pastured eggs.

Egg Substitution

The only keto egg substitution I suggest in recipes is gelatin. Chia and flax are not recommended because they can affect the way estrogen acts in the body and because of their high total carbohydrate count.

Sea
SALT

When first adopting a ketogenic lifestyle, many people experience a decrease in sodium and need to add more salt to their diet. (See page 20 for more information on why this is, how to tell if you're experiencing a sodium deficiency, and what to do about it.)

What Type of Sea Salt Should I Use?

Not all salts are created equal. Most ordinary table salts are refined, bleached, and processed to the point that they lose nearly all their minerals, and often anticaking agents—including sugar!—are added. I recommend cooking with Himalayan or Celtic sea salt, which are either harvested from ancient sea beds or made by evaporating seawater with high mineral content. About 70 percent of their nutritional content is sodium—they contain about the same amount as table salt. The other 30 percent is made up of minerals and micronutrients (including iodine) found in mineral-rich seas.

In addition to prizing sea salts for their nutritional value, I greatly prefer their taste to that of table salt, which can taste like chemicals. (Incidentally, do not use Morton's "sea salt," which is devoid of iodine and nutrients.)

FRUITS

People often say, "Everything in moderation." But for someone who has extreme metabolic syndrome, that mantra can be just as damaging as telling an alcoholic the same thing about having a glass of wine.

Animals have learned how to become fat and become thin, and they do it in a tightly regulated way. Hibernating mammals double their weight and body fat in the fall in preparation for winter by consuming large amounts of fruit (for instance, bears eat a ton of berries). In the process, they develop all the features of metabolic syndrome. They get fat. Their visceral fat (fat around the internal organs) goes up. They get fatty liver. Their blood triglycerides go up. They become insulin-resistant. It's a process that their bodies go through because they're consuming too much fructose in the form of fruit. And once upon a time, humans experienced starvation in the winter, and it benefited us to go through this process in the fall just as it does hibernating mammals. But we don't fast in the winter anymore, and we eat fruit all year long.

I'm often asked, "Can I have fruit on a ketogenic diet?" Before I answer that, I want you to think about strawberries in the wild. We have a wild strawberry and raspberry patch in our yard. The strawberries are about the size of the tip of your thumb and are quite tart. My boys adore picking the tiny wild berries.

If you buy strawberries at, say, Sam's Club, on the other hand, they are often larger than golf balls and taste like candy. And even that isn't sweet enough for most people.

I've seen children applauded for eating strawberries covered in maple syrup—for eating fruit instead of junk food.

Do not eat fruit in abundance believing that it is a "free food." I just finished reading a book called *The Heavy*, by Dara-Lynn Weiss, which is a memoir of a mother trying to help her seven-year-old daughter lose weight. The mother went to a dietitian who assigned colors to foods to help her daughter understand which foods she could eat without guilt, which foods she had to eat in moderation, and which foods she should not eat. Fruit was a food that she could eat without guilt. So when the daughter wasn't losing weight, the mother desperately fed her only fruit for breakfast. Since she was always hungry on this fat-devoid diet, her mother would give her fruit for snacks, too. No wonder the poor girl was always hungry! I loved and hated this book at the same time. I loved it because it discusses what I see daily in clients and it reminded me of how I mistakenly followed that type of diet. I hated it because I wanted so desperately to call this mother and help her stop creating an eating disorder in such a young child.

A lot of Americans are ingrained with the idea that they should be eating an apple a day, so they pick up a big Golden Delicious and feel like they are "doing their body good." In her book *Eating on the Wild Side*, Jo Robinson reviews a 2009 study that examined 46 overweight men with high cholesterol and triglycerides who agreed to participate in an eating experiment. Half of them stayed on their regular diets, serving as a control group. The other half added a Golden Delicious apple to their fare. The goal was to determine whether eating an apple a day would reduce the risk of cardiovascular disease. At the end of the study, the men who ate an apple a day had higher levels of triglycerides and LDL cholesterol than they did before the study began. The conclusion was that the Golden Delicious apples were too low in phytonutrients to lower the men's bad cholesterol and were too high in sugar, causing an increase in triglycerides.

NOT FUN FACTS: The blueberries found in blueberry muffin mixes, cereals, and baked goods are dried REAL blueberries, right? Nope! Those little blue bites of tasty goodness are nothing but hydrogenated oils, artificial colors, and sugar.

Even my boys giggle at the berries in the store. They look like they are on steroids!

And as if grapes weren't already naturally super sweet, there's now a variety called Cotton Candy Grapes that have been bred to have twice as much sugar as regular grapes.

We need to update the recommendation of eating nine servings of fruits and vegetables for maximum health. I have a few issues with this suggestion. First, a few years ago, I read that most kids actually do get the recommended number of servings of fruits and vegetables. Are you shocked? Yep, it's because they eat french fries, onion rings, and ketchup. Sad, but it does fit the guidelines. Will you reap any benefits by eating seven to nine servings of these foods? Absolutely not.

Second, eating three bananas a day isn't a good idea, either. Studies show that the produce we consume today is relatively low in phytonutrients and much higher in sugar than it was in Paleolithic times. The fruits and vegetables in modern supermarkets have far fewer nutrients than those in the wild. Consumers want fruit that tastes sweet. The sad part is, we think it is a good thing when our kids eat massive amounts of fruit. The more palatable our produce becomes, the less beneficial it is for our health. The most beneficial phytonutrients have a bitter, sour, or astringent taste.

So, when I'm asked if I eat fruits, I jokingly say, "Of course! I eat avocados, olives, cucumbers, tomatoes, and coconuts!" (See the list of keto-friendly fruits on page 59; what's on it will surprise you!)

FRIDGE, FREEZER, AND PANTRY

Here at a quick glance is what you can usually find in my fridge and pantry on any given day, followed by much longer lists of keto-friendly foods. When buying food, choosing the highest-quality organic foods is always best.

What's in My Fridge?

I love listening to podcasts on long bike rides. One of my favorites is *The Splendid Table* on National Public Radio. In one segment, "Stump the Cook," a listener calls in and lists five ingredients that they have in their fridge. Then the host, Lynne Rossetto Kasper, has to create something that the listener would actually eat. If I called in, I would list these five things that are always in my fridge:

- Homemade mayo (page 112)
- 11 dozen eggs (a dozen hard-boiled)
- Healthy fats (such as organic grass-fed butter, lard, beef tallow, and duck fat)
- Vanilla beans
- Package of ground beef, thawing

I'm not sure if I would enjoy anything made with all these ingredients mixed together!

I also have supplements, such as probiotics, and keto bread in my fridge at all times. (You can find my recipe for keto bread on my site, MariaMindBodyHealth.com [search for "keto-adapted bread"], or in my previous cookbook, *The Ketogenic Cookbook*.)

What's in My Freezer?

- Homemade bone broth (page 132)
- ½ organic grass-fed cow from farmer (buying in bulk helps save money)
- Liver
- Beef or veal marrow bones (for roasting instructions, see page 272)
- Frozen herbs (harvested during the summer from my organic garden)
- Dairy-free/nut-free ice creams (pages 342 to 348)
- Orange Cream Push Pops (page 337)
- Wrapped portions of smoked meats for easy dinners (see the section on using a smoker, starting on page 360)

Healthy Fats

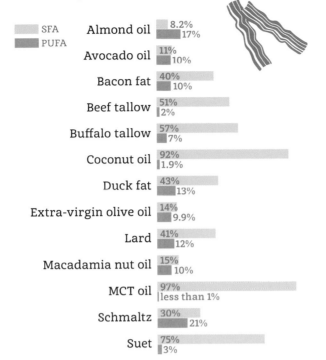

	SFA	PUFA
Almond oil	8.2%	17%
Avocado oil	11%	10%
Bacon fat	40%	10%
Beef tallow	51%	2%
Buffalo tallow	57%	7%
Coconut oil	92%	1.9%
Duck fat	43%	13%
Extra-virgin olive oil	14%	9.9%
Lard	41%	12%
Macadamia nut oil	15%	10%
MCT oil	97%	less than 1%
Schmaltz	30%	21%
Suet	75%	3%

If not dairy-sensitive:

Butter

Cheese

Cream

Cream cheese

Crème fraîche

Ghee

Sour cream

Proteins

Wild Meats
Bear

Boar

Buffalo

Elk

Rabbit

Venison

Farmed Meats
Beef

Goat

Lamb

Pork

Fish
Ahi

Catfish

Halibut

Herring

Mackerel

Mahi mahi

Salmon

Sardines

Snapper

Swordfish

Trout

Tuna

Walleye

Whitefish (cod, bluegill)

Seafood/Shellfish
Clams

Crab

Lobster

Mussels

Oysters

Prawns

Scallops

Shrimp

Snails

Poultry
Chicken

Chicken liver

Duck

Game hen

Goose

Ostrich

Partridge

Pheasant

Quail

Squab

Turkey

Eggs
Chicken eggs

Duck eggs

Goose eggs

Ostrich eggs

Quail eggs

50% — FATS
50% — PROTEIN

Percentage of total calories from fat

Percentage of total calories from protein

0%
Percentage of total calories from carbs in all meat cuts (with the exception of some seafood/shellfish; see page 55)

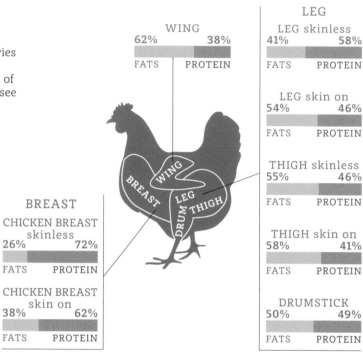

WING
62% FATS — 38% PROTEIN

LEG
LEG skinless
41% FATS — 58% PROTEIN

LEG skin on
54% FATS — 46% PROTEIN

THIGH skinless
55% FATS — 46% PROTEIN

THIGH skin on
58% FATS — 41% PROTEIN

DRUMSTICK
50% FATS — 49% PROTEIN

BREAST
CHICKEN BREAST skinless
26% FATS — 72% PROTEIN

CHICKEN BREAST skin on
38% FATS — 62% PROTEIN

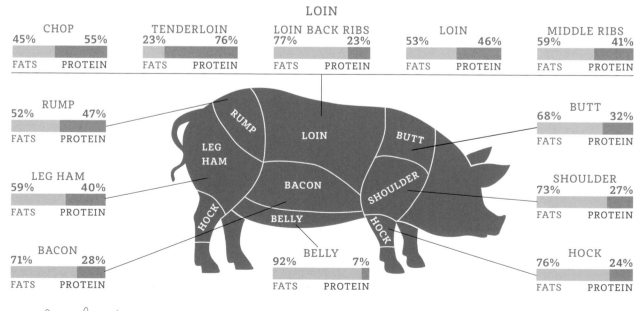

LOIN

CHOP
45% FATS — 55% PROTEIN

TENDERLOIN
23% FATS — 76% PROTEIN

LOIN BACK RIBS
77% FATS — 23% PROTEIN

LOIN
53% FATS — 46% PROTEIN

MIDDLE RIBS
59% FATS — 41% PROTEIN

RUMP
52% FATS — 47% PROTEIN

LEG HAM
59% FATS — 40% PROTEIN

BACON
71% FATS — 28% PROTEIN

BELLY
92% FATS — 7% PROTEIN

BUTT
68% FATS — 32% PROTEIN

SHOULDER
73% FATS — 27% PROTEIN

HOCK
76% FATS — 24% PROTEIN

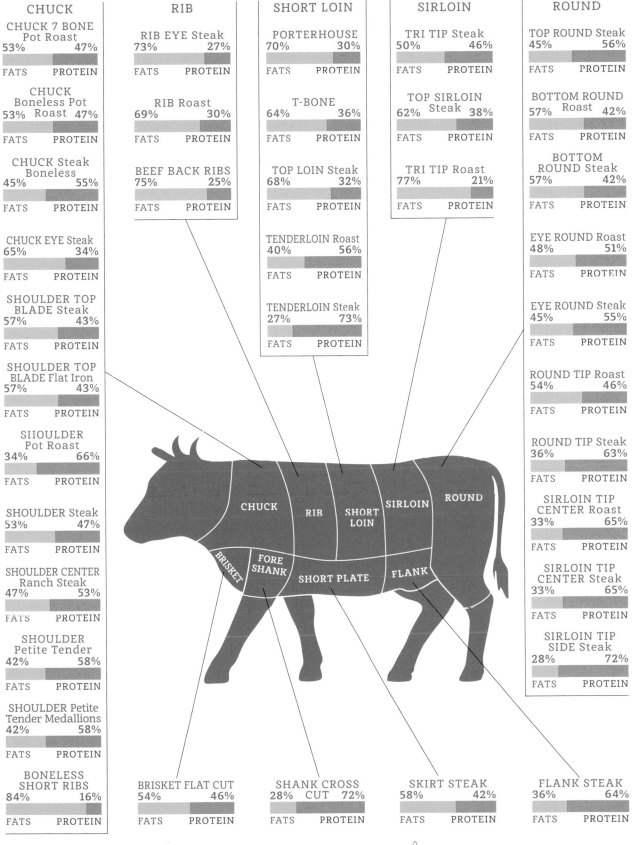

CHUCK

CHUCK 7 BONE Pot Roast
53% FATS | 47% PROTEIN

CHUCK Boneless Pot Roast
53% FATS | 47% PROTEIN

CHUCK Steak Boneless
45% FATS | 55% PROTEIN

CHUCK EYE Steak
65% FATS | 34% PROTEIN

SHOULDER TOP BLADE Steak
57% FATS | 43% PROTEIN

SHOULDER TOP BLADE Flat Iron
57% FATS | 43% PROTEIN

SHOULDER Pot Roast
34% FATS | 66% PROTEIN

SHOULDER Steak
53% FATS | 47% PROTEIN

SHOULDER CENTER Ranch Steak
47% FATS | 53% PROTEIN

SHOULDER Petite Tender
42% FATS | 58% PROTEIN

SHOULDER Petite Tender Medallions
42% FATS | 58% PROTEIN

BONELESS SHORT RIBS
84% FATS | 16% PROTEIN

RIB

RIB EYE Steak
73% FATS | 27% PROTEIN

RIB Roast
69% FATS | 30% PROTEIN

BEEF BACK RIBS
75% FATS | 25% PROTEIN

SHORT LOIN

PORTERHOUSE
70% FATS | 30% PROTEIN

T-BONE
64% FATS | 36% PROTEIN

TOP LOIN Steak
68% FATS | 32% PROTEIN

TENDERLOIN Roast
40% FATS | 56% PROTEIN

TENDERLOIN Steak
27% FATS | 73% PROTEIN

SIRLOIN

TRI TIP Steak
50% FATS | 46% PROTEIN

TOP SIRLOIN Steak
62% FATS | 38% PROTEIN

TRI TIP Roast
77% FATS | 21% PROTEIN

ROUND

TOP ROUND Steak
45% FATS | 56% PROTEIN

BOTTOM ROUND Roast
57% FATS | 42% PROTEIN

BOTTOM ROUND Steak
57% FATS | 42% PROTEIN

EYE ROUND Roast
48% FATS | 51% PROTEIN

EYE ROUND Steak
45% FATS | 55% PROTEIN

ROUND TIP Roast
54% FATS | 46% PROTEIN

ROUND TIP Steak
36% FATS | 63% PROTEIN

SIRLOIN TIP CENTER Roast
33% FATS | 65% PROTEIN

SIRLOIN TIP CENTER Steak
33% FATS | 65% PROTEIN

SIRLOIN TIP SIDE Steak
28% FATS | 72% PROTEIN

BRISKET FLAT CUT
54% FATS | 46% PROTEIN

SHANK CROSS CUT
28% FATS | 72% PROTEIN

SKIRT STEAK
58% FATS | 42% PROTEIN

FLANK STEAK
36% FATS | 64% PROTEIN

CHUCK — RIB — SHORT LOIN — SIRLOIN — ROUND — BRISKET — FORE SHANK — SHORT PLATE — FLANK

NUTRITIONAL INFO (per 4 ounces)								
Pork	CALORIES	FAT	PROTEIN	CARBS	FIBER	% FAT	% PROTEIN	% CARBS
Chop	241	12	33	0	0	45%	55%	0%
Loin	265	15.5	30.8	0	0	53%	46%	0%
Hocks	285	24	17	0	0	76%	24%	0%
Leg Ham	305	20	30.4	0	0	59%	40%	0%
Rump	280	16.2	32.8	0	0	52%	47%	0%
Tenderloin	158	4	30	0	0	23%	76%	0%
Middle Ribs (Country Style)	245	16	25	0	0	59%	41%	0%
Loin Back Ribs (Baby Back Ribs)	315	27	18	0	0	77%	23%	0%
Belly	588	60	10.4	0	0	92%	7%	0%
Shoulder	285	23	19	0	0	73%	27%	0%
Butt	240	18	19	0	0	68%	32%	0%
Bacon	600	47.2	41.8	0	0	71%	28%	0%

NUTRITIONAL INFO (per 4 ounces)								
Beef	CALORIES	FAT	PROTEIN	CARBS	FIBER	% FAT	% PROTEIN	% CARBS
Rib Eye Steak	310	25	20	0	0	73%	26%	0%
Rib Roast	373	28	27	0	0	69%	30%	0%
Beef Back Ribs	310	26	19	0	0	75%	25%	0%
Porterhouse	280	22	21	0	0	70%	30%	0%
T-Bone	170	12.2	15.8	0	0	64%	36%	0%
Top Loin Steak	270	20	21	0	0	67%	31%	0%
Tenderloin Roast	180	8	25	0	0	40%	56%	0%
Tenderloin Steak	122	3	22.2	0	0	22%	73%	0%
Tri Tip Roast	340	29	18	0	0	77%	21%	0%
Tri Tip Steak	200	11	23	0	0	50%	46%	0%
Top Sirloin Steak	240	16	22	0	0	60%	37%	0%
Top Round Steak	180	9	25	0	0	45%	56%	0%
Bottom Round Roast	220	14	23	0	0	57%	42%	0%
Bottom Round Steak	220	14	23	0	0	57%	42%	0%
Eye Round Roast	253	13.4	32	0	0	48%	51%	0%
Eye Round Steak	182	9	25	0	0	45%	55%	0%
Round Tip Roast	199	12	22.9	0	0	54%	46%	0%
Round Tip Steak	150	6	23.5	0	0	36%	63%	0%
Sirloin Tip Center Roast	190	7	31	0	0	33%	65%	0%
Sirloin Tip Center Steak	190	7	31	0	0	33%	65%	0%
Sirloin Tip Side Steak	190	6	34	0	0	28%	72%	0%
Skirt Steak	255	16.5	27	0	0	58%	42%	0%
Flank Steak	200	8	32	0	0	36%	64%	0%
Shank Cross Cut	215	6.7	38.7	0	0	28%	72%	0%
Brisket Flat Cut	245	14.7	28	0	0	54%	46%	0%
Chuck 7 Bone Pot Roast	240	14	28	0	0	53%	47%	0%
Chuck Boneless Pot Roast	240	14	28	0	0	53%	47%	0%
Chuck Steak Boneless	160	8	22	0	0	45%	55%	0%
Chuck Eye Steak	250	18	21	0	0	65%	34%	0%
Shoulder Top Blade Steak	204	13	22	0	0	57%	43%	0%
Shoulder Top Blade Flat Iron	204	13	22	0	0	57%	43%	0%
Shoulder Pot Roast	185	7	30.7	0	0	34%	66%	0%
Shoulder Steak	204	12	24	0	0	53%	47%	0%
Shoulder Center Ranch Steak	152	8	24	0	0	47%	53%	0%
Shoulder Petite Tender	150	7	22	0	0	42%	59%	0%
Shoulder Petite Tender Medallions	150	7	22	0	0	42%	59%	0%
Boneless Short Ribs	440	41	16	0	0	84%	15%	0%

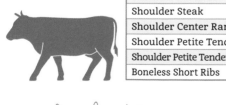

NUTRITIONAL INFO (per 4 ounces)								
Fish	CALORIES	FAT	PROTEIN	CARBS	FIBER	% FAT	% PROTEIN	% CARBS
Tuna (Yellowfin)	150	1.5	34	0	0	9%	91%	0%
Tuna (Canned)	123	0.8	27.5	1.5	0	6%	89%	5%
Salmon	206	9	31	0	0	39%	60%	0%
Anchovies	256	15.9	28	0	0	56%	44%	0%
Sardines	139	7.5	18	0	0	49%	52%	0%
Barramundi	110	2	23	0	0	16%	84%	0%
Trout	190	8.6	28	0	0	41%	59%	0%
Walleye	156	7.5	22	0	0	43%	56%	0%
Cod	113	1	26	0	0	8%	92%	0%
Sea Bass	135	3	27	0	0	20%	80%	0%
Halibut	155	3.5	30.7	0	0	20%	79%	0%
Mackerel	290	20.3	27	0	0	63%	37%	0%
Arctic Char	208	10	29	0	0	43%	56%	0%

NUTRITIONAL INFO (per 4 ounces)								
Seafood/Shellfish	CALORIES	FAT	PROTEIN	CARBS	FIBER	% FAT	% PROTEIN	% CARBS
Scallops	97	1	19	3	0	9%	78%	12%
Mussels	97	2.8	13.5	4.5	0	26%	56%	19%
Clams	82	1.1	15	3	0	12%	73%	15%
Shrimp	135	2	25.8	1.7	0	13%	76%	5%
Oysters	58	1.9	6.5	3.1	0	29%	45%	21%
Crab	107	2	22	0	0	17%	82%	0%
Lobster	116	1.8	25	0	0	14%	86%	0%
Caviar	260	12	31	8	0	41%	48%	12%

NUTRITIONAL INFO (per 4 ounces)								
Chicken and Poultry	CALORIES	FAT	PROTEIN	CARBS	FIBER	% FAT	% PROTEIN	% CARBS
Chicken Breast, Skinless	138	4	25	0	0	26%	72%	0%
Chicken Breast, Skin On	200	8.4	31	0	0	38%	62%	0%
Leg, Skinless	210	9.5	30.7	0	0	41%	58%	0%
Leg, Skin On	255	15.2	29.4	0	0	54%	46%	0%
Thigh, Skinless	165	10	19	0	0	55%	46%	0%
Thigh, Skin On	275	17.6	28.3	0	0	58%	41%	0%
Wing	320	22	30.4	0	0	62%	38%	0%
Drumstick	178	9.9	22	0	0	50%	49%	0%
Game Hen	220	16	19	0	0	65%	35%	0%
Pheasant	200	10.5	25.7	0	0	47%	51%	0%
Turkey	175	9.9	21	0	0	51%	48%	0%
Goose	340	24.9	28.5	0	0	66%	34%	0%
Duck	228	13.9	26.3	0	0	55%	46%	0%

Nuts and Seeds

Most nuts and seeds can be consumed on a keto-genic diet, but because they can take some people with metabolic syndrome out of ketosis, I do not use them in this cookbook. Cashews, chestnuts, and pistachios have too many carbohydrates and are not allowed on a ketogenic diet.

Almonds

Brazil nuts

Hazelnuts

Macadamia nuts

Pecans

Pumpkin seeds

Sesame seeds

Sunflower seeds

Walnuts

Veggies

Most people think that I'm a bit extreme when I limit not just fruit but also vegeta-ble consumption for some of my clients. Even some low-starch vegetables may keep someone with a damaged metabolism out of ketosis. Below is a list of low-starch veg-gies that will help you stay in ketosis. High-starch veggies such as sweet potatoes, carrots, potatoes, and winter squash should be avoided.

Arugula

Asparagus

Bok choy

Broccoli

Cabbage

Cauliflower

Celery

Collard greens

Cucumber

Endive

Garlic

Kale

Kelp

Lettuce: red leaf, Boston, romaine, radicchio

Mushrooms

Onions: green, yellow, white, red

Peppers: bell peppers, jalapeños, chili peppers

Seaweed

Swiss chard

Watercress

CARBS IN ONIONS
per ½ cup

Red Onion: 8.9 g

Yellow Onion: 3.5 g

White Onion: 5.8 g

Shallots: 12 g

Green Onion: 3.6 g

Herbs and Spices

For a discussion of the health benefits and high nutritional value of herbs and spices, see page 40 to 42.

Anise	Chili pepper	Galangal	Paprika
Annatto	Chives	Garlic	Parsley
Basil	Cilantro	Ginger	Peppermint
Bay leaf	Cinnamon	Lemongrass	Rosemary
Black pepper	Cloves	Licorice	Saffron
Caraway	Coriander	Mace	Spearmint
Cardamom	Cumin	Marjoram	Star anise
Cayenne pepper	Curry	Mint	Tarragon
Celery seed	Dill	Mustard seeds	Thyme
Chervil	Fenugreek	Oregano	Turmeric

Vanilla and Other Flavorings

To enhance the flavor of my foods, especially desserts, I use a variety of extracts, oils, and teas.

Vanilla

I keep a large, tightly sealed package of vanilla beans in my fridge at all times for additions to desserts and even savory dishes. (For a vegetable recipe that uses vanilla bean, visit my site, MariaMindBodyHealth.com, and type "Roasted Brussels Sprouts with Vanilla-Pecan Butter" in the search field.) To receive the full health benefits vanilla has to offer (see page 43), it's necessary to use the vanilla bean in your cooking rather than the extract. For convenience, however, I've made pure vanilla extract the first choice in the recipes in this book.

Extracts and Essential Oils

To add a certain flavor to a dish without altering its proportion of fat, protein, and carbs, I often use extracts and oils—from orange, mint, and maple to strawberry, raspberry, banana, butterscotch, and more.

Essential oils are a great way to infuse flavor into your cooking, but keep in mind that they are even more concentrated than extracts. If a recipe calls for a teaspoon of an extract, use only two or three drops of a flavored oil. Add a drop of your favorite oil to salad dressings, soups, slow cooker meals, or desserts. For example, instead of using orange extract in my Orange Cream Push Pops (page 337), you can use a few drops of orange oil. Or, if making my Herb Aioli with mint (page 114), you can use a drop of mint oil in lieu of fresh mint.

If you are using mint oil, note that the flavor of peppermint oil works best in desserts but spearmint oil works best in savory dishes.

Look for brands free of polyglycol and added coloring. My preferred brands are listed in the Resources section (page 378).

Stur

It is amazing how much we eat with our eyes; just think about how kids are drawn to brightly colored foods. One of my new favorite ways to enhance the color of foods is with Stur, a water flavor enhancer available in a variety of flavors. The sweetness isn't overwhelming and adds a perfectly balanced flavor to drinks, but I've also found this product to be very useful for adding color and additional flavor to desserts.

Fruit Teas

Fruit teas do not contain actual fruit, but the extract from the fruit allows the fantastic flavor profiles to shine through in recipes without the sugar content.

Fruits

These fruits are the lowest in sugar:

Avocados

Coconut

Cucumbers

Eggplant

Lemons

Limes

Olives

Seasonal wild berries (in moderation)

Tomatoes

Liquids
(for drinking and cooking)

Bone broth

Cream *(if not dairy-sensitive)*

Mineral water

Organic decaf Americano (espresso with water)

Teas: green tea, chai tea, fruit teas, black tea, oolong tea, white tea

Unsweetened almond milk

Unsweetened coconut milk

Unsweetened hemp milk

Water *(reverse osmosis is best)*

Baking Products

Baking powder

Baking soda

Cocoa butter

Coconut flour

Oils for flavoring *(see opposite)*

Pure vanilla extract and other extracts *(see opposite)*

Unflavored egg white protein powder *(check for added ingredients and level of carbs—they should be close to zero and below 4 grams total)*

Unflavored whey protein powder *(check for added ingredients and level of carbs—they should be close to zero and below 4 grams total)*

Unsweetened baking chocolate

Unsweetened cocoa powder

Xanthan gum and guar gum

Natural Sweeteners

Blended sweeteners such as Swerve

Erythritol

Monk fruit (luo han guo)

Stevia glycerite

Stevia with no additives

Yacón syrup

Miscellaneous Flavor Enhancers

Coconut aminos

Coconut vinegar or apple cider vinegar

Fish sauce

Sea salt

Convenience Foods

It is always better to buy fresh foods, but here are some easy keto-friendly pantry and freezer items. For brand recommendations, see Resources (pages 378 to 379) or, for a complete list of recommendations, visit my site, MariaMindBodyHealth.com, and click on "Maria's Amazon Store" under "Shop."

Banana peppers

Boxed beef broth and chicken broth

Canned salmon/tuna

Canned unsweetened coconut milk

Capers

Fermented pickles

Fermented sauerkraut

Jerky and cooked, ready-to-eat meats *(beware of added sugars)*

Marinara sauce *(look for high-quality products and check for use of low-quality oils and added sugars)*

Nori *(for wraps)*

Olives *(choose jarred over canned)*

Organic dried herbs

Pickled herring and pickled eggs

Pizza sauce *(check oils and for use of low-quality added sugars)*

Premade wraps, such as Pure Wraps*

Prepared keto-friendly noodles

Prepared Paleo baked goods, such as Mikey's Muffins

Prepared Paleo mayo

Roasted red bell peppers

Sardines

Tomato sauce and paste *(choose jarred over canned)*

Because Pure Wraps are made with coconut flour, which is high in fiber and carbohydrates, they are not a good option if you are trying to lose weight.

THE COST OF KETO INGREDIENTS

I often get questions about the cost of the ingredients I recommend. I calculated the price to make my ice cream recipe with top-notch ingredients, such as top-quality eggs and vanilla beans. Here are the results:

Homemade ice cream (pages 342 to 348) = $3.13 per pint

Ben & Jerry's = about $4.00 per pint

Cold Stone Creamery = $7.50 per pint

One way we save money is by not eating out. In a past life I loved Chipotle, but now we make a much healthier and more affordable version at home.

Tip: Make extras and wrap them in foil just like Chipotle does. You will have lunches ready for the whole week!

Chipotle Beef Barbacoa Bowl = $6 per serving

Slow Cooker Beef Barbacoa Wraps (page 210) = $2 per serving

You can also buy most of the ingredients I use in bulk and store them in a chest freezer to lower your costs even more. Eating healthy costs you a lot less in the long run due to lower medical bills, but it can also cost less now compared to buying prepackaged foods at the grocery store. It just takes a little more of your time, though this is also debatable: I would argue that the time it takes to load everyone up and drive to Dairy Queen and back is about how long it takes to make fresh ice cream at home. It also tastes so much better when you make it fresh at home!

I've created an online store where you can find specialty ingredients used in the recipes in this book, at the best prices I have found. To access it, go to my site, MariaMindBodyHealth.com, and click on "Maria's Amazon Store" under "Shop." Or go directly to the following URL:

astore.amazon.com/marisnutran05-20

Upgrade Your Pantry

TYPICAL	BETTER	BEST
Hellman's mayo	Premade Paleo mayo	Homemade mayo (page 112)
Canned tuna*	Canned salmon	Cooked fresh salmon or tuna
Store-bought BBQ sauce	Reduced-sugar, organic BBQ sauce	Homemade BBQ sauce (page 125)
Heinz ketchup	Reduced-sugar, organic ketchup	Homemade ketchup (page 127)
Store-bought salad dressing	Reduced-sugar, organic dressing made with good-quality oil	Homemade salad dressing (pages 116 to 121)
Conventional beef	Organic beef	Organic grass-fed beef
Hoy Fung Foods Sriracha	Dark Star Sriracha	Homemade Sriracha (page 124)
Morton's iodized salt		Mineralized sea salt
Store-bought seasoned salt		Homemade seasoned salt (page 109)
Store-bought spice blends		Homemade spice blends (pages 108 to 111)
Store-bought vinegar pickles	Store-bought naturally fermented pickles, such as Bubbies	Homemade pickles (page 318)
Store-bought jelly	Reduced-sugar, organic jelly	Homemade jelly (page 139)
Conventional dried herbs	Organic dried herbs	Organic fresh herbs
Conventional cinnamon		Organic cassia cinnamon
Store-bought jerky	Store-bought gluten-free jerky	Homemade jerky (page 186)
Fish sauce		Red Boat Fish Sauce**
Conventional eggs	Organic free-range eggs	Pastured eggs
Store-bought pesto made with soybean oil or canola oil	Store-bought pesto made with olive oil	Homemade pesto***
Jarred Alfredo sauce		Homemade Alfredo sauce (page 128)
Store-bought ranch dressing on store shelf	Store-bought ranch dressing in refrigerated area	Homemade ranch dressing (page 118)
Roasted conventional chicken from deli counter (has MSG)	Roasted organic chicken from market such as Whole Foods	Homemade roast chicken
Canned broth	Boxed organic broth	Homemade bone broth (page 132)
Store-bought unsweetened almond milk		Homemade almond milk (page 131)

*When buying canned tuna, opt for a brand like Vital Choice, which uses tuna that is low in mercury and is packed in BPA-free cans.

**Red Boat Fish Sauce is traditionally fermented and contains no wheat.

***There are keto recipes for pesto on my site, MariaMindBodyHealth.com, and in my book The Ketogenic Cookbook.

Kitchen
GADGETS

CHAPTER 2

I highly encourage you to invest in a few key kitchen tools and pieces of equipment. They will save you time and money in the long run. Cooking at home is so much cheaper than going out to eat. Packing lunches for my family has not only kept us keto; it has also helped us save money.

My Top Ten
KETO KITCHEN GADGETS

If it were up to my husband, we would have every kitchen gadget made, but I enjoy simplicity and do not enjoy clutter. Here are my top choices.

1.

Quality Knives (Chef's Knife and Paring Knife)

HOW OFTEN I USE IT: Daily

PRICE: $100–$300

USES: Chopping, slicing, cubing, dicing, etc.

A good-quality sharp knife makes prepping food so much more enjoyable!

2.

Cast-Iron Cookware: Large Skillet and Large Deep Skillet or Dutch Oven

HOW OFTEN I USE IT: Daily

PRICE: Under $20 (buy at a thrift store for $2)

USES: Frying eggs, Paleo mushrooms, Cheesy Fried Ravioli (page 176), Fish Sticks (page 236), Skillet Lasagna (page 266)

Cast-iron cookware is inexpensive, so I urge you to have two pieces: an all-purpose large skillet (with about 1½- to 2-inch-deep sides) and either a deep skillet with about 4-inch-deep sides or a Dutch oven. A deep skillet or Dutch oven is the best for deep frying. I once had a Fry Daddy with a good thermometer, but because of its ability to hold heat, nothing fries food as well as cast iron.

3.

Blender or Food Processor

HOW OFTEN I USE IT: Daily

PRICE: $40–$200 (regular blender or food processor); $150–$700 (high-powered blender)

USES: Pureeing; making shakes, salad dressings, dips, ice cream and Popsicle mixtures

Generally speaking, a food processor is better for grating and shredding while a blender is better for processing liquids. High-powered blenders, such as Blendtec and Vitamix brands, have better performance, durability, and speed. However, they're also more expensive.

4.

Slow Cooker, 6-Quart

HOW OFTEN I USE IT: Once a week, but I love hands-on cooking. If you don't have time, a slow cooker is a great tool that can be used daily.

PRICE: $45–$120

USES: Everything from bone broth (page 132) to Slow Cooker Beef Barbacoa Wraps (page 210), Slow Cooker BBQ Pork Wraps (page 203), Slow Cooker "Butter" Chicken with Naan (page 252), and more

5.

Spiral Slicer (aka Spiralizer)

HOW OFTEN I USE IT: Twice a week

PRICE: Under $25

PREFERRED BRAND: Veggetti Pro Table-Top Spiral Vegetable Cutter

USES: Zucchini noodles (see page 308); broccoli noodles (see page 286)

6.

Handheld Electric Mixer or Stand Mixer

HOW OFTEN I USE IT: Twice a week

PRICE: $150–$500 (for stand mixer); $60–$130 (for hand mixer)

USES: Whipping egg whites and making batters, dips, and cheesecakes

7.

Ice Cream Maker

HOW OFTEN I USE IT: Weekly

PRICE: $45–$100

USES: Homemade ice cream (pages 342 to 348)

8.

Toaster Oven, Preferably Large or Extra-Large Capacity

HOW OFTEN I USE IT: Weekly

PRICE: $100–$299. If possible, get a quality one that goes up to 400°F.

USES: Minute English Muffin (page 150), Cinnamon Roll Minute Muffins (page 152), Taco Shells or Bowls (page 271), most of the single-serving meals, and reheating just about every recipe

I love to use my toaster oven for reheating leftovers! It saves energy and doesn't heat up the whole kitchen during the summer. But I don't just use it for reheating. I cook in mine! It's amazing what you can cook in a large or extra-large capacity oven. It is awesome for someone making single servings. For the greatest flexibility, I recommend purchasing a large or extra-large capacity toaster oven.

9.

Immersion Blender

HOW OFTEN I USE IT: Once every 2 weeks

PRICE: Under $30

USES: Homemade mayo (page 112), shakes, pureed soups

10.

Cast-Iron Pizza Pan or Pizza Stone

HOW OFTEN I USE IT: Weekly

PRICE: $20–$50

USES: Upside-Down Pizza (page 264)

Homemade pizza turns out exceptionally well when you use a cast-iron pizza pan or pizza stone. Not only does a preheated pan/stone help to sear the crust and give a nice crispy edge, it also helps to hold the heat at a steady temperature during the fluctuations in temperature that tend to occur in most ovens.

TIPS FOR USING CAST-IRON PIZZA PANS AND PIZZA STONES

When using a pizza stone or cast-iron pizza pan, make sure to preheat the stone or pan (place the stone in the oven before turning the oven on). This will give you a nice crispy crust. If you have a pizza stone and notice that whenever you use it, the kitchen fills with smoke, here's why: grease from the pizza has leaked into the stone, and when you heat it, the oils start to burn in the stone, which often leads to a smoke-filled kitchen. If you are using a pizza stone, line it with a piece of unbleached parchment so the grease doesn't seep into the stone while the pizza is baking.

Bonus GADGETS

Gummy Bear Mold (50-cavity)

HOW OFTEN I USE IT: Once a month

PRICE: $10–$20

RECIPES: Gummy Bears (page 352)

Push Pop Mold (4-cavity)

HOW OFTEN I USE IT: Every other day (in the summer!)

PRICE: $5–$20

USES: Orange Cream Push Pops (page 337)

Popsicle Mold (8-cavity)

HOW OFTEN I USE IT: Every other day (in the summer!)

PRICE: $6–$20

USES: Paletas (page 336), Key Lime Lollies (page 342), Coffee Popsicles (page 343), Hibiscus Berry Popsicles (page 344), Egg-Free Creamy Popsicles (page 348), Chai Popsicles (page 345)

Truffle Mold (12-cavity, each cavity 1-ounce capacity)

HOW OFTEN I USE IT: Once a month

PRICE: $10–$20

USES: Grand Marnier Fat Bombs (page 325)

Truffle Mold (24-cavity, each cavity about 1¼ inches in diameter)

HOW OFTEN I USE IT: Once a month

PRICE: $10–$20

USES: Key Lime Fat Bombs (page 340)

Whipped Cream Canister

HOW OFTEN I USE IT: Twice a week

PRICE: $20–$99

USES: Frozen Orange Cream Bites (page 330), Frozen Snickerdoodle Cream Bites (page 332), garnish for desserts

Smoker

HOW OFTEN I USE IT: Once a week

PRICE: $100–$150

RECIPES: Smoked Brisket (page 362), Smoked Beef Long Ribs (page 364), Smoked Baby Back Ribs (page 366), Smoked Pork Shoulder (page 368), Smoked Salmon (page 370), Pan-Fried Smoked Cauliflower Steaks (page 372), Pan-Fried Smoked Eggplant (page 374)

Our smoker is my favorite cooking vessel! Using it combines two of my favorite loves: cooking and being outside. In the back of this book, I've included a bonus section on smoking for those of you who love food with a smoky flavor and want to try smoking at home. It's much easier than you might think! See page 360 for a discussion of the pros and cons of the various types of smokers available.

Dehydrator

HOW OFTEN I USE IT: Once a month

PRICE: $30–$200

USES: Teriyaki Jerky (page 186), dehydrating soaked nuts

Radio/Music

HOW OFTEN I USE IT: Daily

PRICE: $25–$$$

USES: Creating a peaceful environment is something I do whenever I cook. During the holidays you can hear holiday music throughout the house; on a warm summer day, the breeze streams through the windows with sounds of Caribbean music or Bob Marley.

Tips and Tricks

TO SIMPLIFY YOUR KETO LIFE

CHAPTER 3

I recently read a book that describes how the chicken noodle soup that we make today will never taste as good as great-grandma's. Why? Because the chickens raised today are bland, the veggies have not been grown in nutrient-rich soil that fills them with the intense flavors they once had, and the dried herbs have lost their vigor. Even celery is bland. I will never forget my first taste of my own homegrown broccoli. The color was the deepest green I have ever seen, and the flavor . . . now that is the way broccoli was meant to taste!

The lesson here is not to skimp on seasoning. Most of us do not season our food enough because we have been pressured by the mainstream media to use less salt. But salt is not the evil substance we have been taught to fear. Did you know that a fast-food milkshake contains more salt than a small order of french fries? Salt enhances flavors, even sweet ones. If you learn how to season food properly and you use quality ingredients, you will enjoy the taste of homemade food more and start to crave it.

This is just one of the many lessons I have learned on my journey to becoming keto-adapted. In this chapter, I share some of my favorite tips for cooking at home as well as eating out, if you choose to do so.

Easy Recipes
FOR BUSY COOKS

Pressed for time in the kitchen? The lists in this section are for you! Throw together delicious meals in just minutes, or let your slow cooker do the work and come home to a delicious dinner that's ready to go.

5 Fabulous Desserts in 5 Minutes

The frozen desserts are quick to prepare, but be sure to leave time for them to freeze.

 330
Frozen Orange Cream Bites

 332
Frozen Snickerdoodle Cream Bites

 336
Paletas

 337
Orange Cream Push Pops

 350
Butterscotch Mousse

5 Meals in 15 Minutes or Less

 204
Easy Tuna Salad Wraps

 220
Simple Salade Niçoise

 235
Shrimp and Grits

 264
Upside-Down Pizza

287
Pigs in a Bacon Blanket

8 Amazing Appetizers in 8 Minutes or Less

 172
Amuse-Bouche Platter

 173
BLT "Chips" and Dip

 175
Amazing Cheese Puffs

 178
Simple Relish Tray with Dill Dip

 180
Tomato Tulips

 198
Prosciutto and Arugula Roll-Ups

 199
Mini Pastrami Roll-Ups

 200
Turkey Sushi

6 Scrumptious Sauces in 6 Minutes or Less

Having homemade sauces on hand is a super fast and convenient way to increase the fat ratio of various cuts of meat or salads. I keep two of my favorite dressings and sauces in my refrigerator at all times to make dinners easier.

 112
Fat-Burning Immersion Blender Mayo

 114
Herb Aioli

 118
Dairy-Free Ranch Dressing

 120
Easy French Dressing

 121
Simple Taco Salad Dressing

 126
White BBQ Sauce

8 Slow Cooker Suppers

 207
Slow Cooker BBQ Chicken Wraps

 208
Slow Cooker Chicken Caesar Wraps

 210
Slow Cooker Beef Barbacoa Wraps

 252
Slow Cooker "Butter" Chicken with Naan

 259
Grandma Nancy's Italian Beef

 262
Slow Cooker Sweet-n-Spicy Short Ribs

 274
Slow Cooker Osso Buco

 290
Sweet-n-Sour Country-Style Ribs over Zoodles

10 Meals in 30 Minutes or Less

 232
Arctic Char with Olive Salsa

 240
King Crab Legs with Garlic Butter

 246
Chicken Alfredo

 249
Double-Fried Chicken

 263
Easy Corned Beef "Hash"

 270
Taco Bar Night

 276
Basted Rib-Eye Steak

 286
Broccoli Carbonara

 288
Brats with Simple Coleslaw

 292
Deconstructed BLT with Pork Belly

"To eat is a necessity, but to eat intelligently is an art."

—François de La Rochefoucauld

My Top 11 Tips for
KETO SUCCESS

Make Today Day 1 of 16

Imagine this: You are driving along on a smooth highway when all of a sudden your car is stripped from you, and now you are steering a horse-drawn carriage along a bumpy dirt road. That's how it can feel to suddenly change the way you eat—nothing is quite what you're used to. Existing habits are hard to break, and creating new habits can be uncomfortable. But make the choice to make today Day 1 of 16. You can do anything for 16 days! Surely you have been through worse things than changing your diet. After 16 days, that horse-drawn carriage ride will be just a memory, and before long you will be back on the highway, this time cruising along in a luxury car without any of the frustrating issues that your past diet was causing.

Remember, practice does not make perfect; it makes permanent.

Plan Ahead for Convenience

Make keto food convenient! We all like convenience. If you come home from a long day at work and are extremely hungry but have nothing prepared, you are more likely to grab takeout or something unhealthy. Here are some ways to plan ahead:

- Keep hard-boiled eggs and other keto foods handy in the fridge.

- Set aside some time on Sunday to prepare meals for the week.

- Prepare a selection of homemade ketogenic sauces and condiments to use throughout the week. See page 71 for a list of some of my fast favorites.

- Choose quick and easy recipes. Most of the recipes in this book are just that, although some are quicker and easier to prepare than others. See "Easy Recipes for Busy Cooks" on pages 70 to 71 for lists of some of the easiest recipes in this book.

- Make larger batches of the recipes that you enjoy. This way, you'll have leftovers for lunch! You can also freeze individual portions so that all you have to do is grab a container from the freezer to heat up. (This is why I love my toaster oven. It heats food fast without my having to use a microwave, which often makes leftovers dry.) I also prepare extras of meals such as keto pizzas and freeze them, so I can put them in the oven when I get home from work.

- Freeze the ingredients for slow cooker meals in gallon-sized freezer bags. Fill three to five bags so that you have multiple options in the freezer. Then all you have to do is dump the contents of the bag into the slow cooker before leaving for work.

- As someone else cleans up after dinner, prepare dinner for the next night. If I'm planning a taco bar night (page 270) for the next day, for example, I fill the slow cooker with the chicken, spices, and jar of salsa. I also cut up all the taco fixings and place them in bowls. In the morning, all I have to do is take the slow cooker insert out of the fridge and turn the slow cooker on. When I get home, I take out the taco fixings (along with big romaine lettuce leaves for me and some Pure Wraps or homemade zucchini tortillas for the rest of my family) and ta-da! Dinner is ready in 5 minutes!

Make Conscious Choices

Resolve to make good choices today. If you are wishy-washy, you are more likely to cheat. I'm a stubborn German. When I decided to change my lifestyle with eating and exercise, I stuck with it even when I didn't want to. I used my stubbornness, which is often thought of as a bad trait, as a positive trait instead.

Keep a Food Journal

If needed, record what you eat in a journal. Or, if you are a visual person like me, take pictures of your food with your phone. Better yet, find a keto buddy who can help keep you accountable and send that person photos of the food you eat.

Bonus points if you write down what you plan to eat the next day and prepare that food ahead of time!

Let Cooking Be Your Therapy After Stressful Days

Cooking is very therapeutic. Turn on some relaxing music and let simple tasks like chopping and measuring ease your mind. It also can be a great time to bond with children and other family members. Families used to gather around the kitchen to cook.

Eat Before Social Events

I often didn't even remember what I ate as I chatted away at social events. Instead, eat beforehand so that you can focus on having quality conversations and avoid the buffet table. You won't be as hungry, so you won't be as tempted by the unhealthy choices that are offered.

I also keep a dessert in my freezer at all times. That way, I know that I can enjoy a tasty keto dessert at home, which helps me not reach for sugary treats while I'm out.

Bring a Dish to Pass

Don't assume that there will be keto-friendly options at social events like barbecues and potlucks. Bring something healthy that you can eat and others may enjoy, too. As a host, I always appreciate it when people bring food.

Limit the Options on Your Plate

If you have a lot of different flavors on your plate, it is easy to overeat. Your neural sensory system experiences something called habituation, in which your sensory neurons become less receptive with constant exposure to a stimulus. You experience habituation to the smell and taste of food as you eat it. This is why it is easy to overeat at a potluck or buffet . . . so many choices to keep stimulating the senses! But if you have just one food on your plate, your brain will get bored and signal you to stop eating.

Go Dairy- and Nut-Free for Two Weeks

If healing and weight loss aren't happening as fast as you desire, try cutting out dairy and nuts for 14 days. Look for recipes marked with the dairy-free and nut-free symbols, or find them in the index (pages 385 to 387).

SLEEP!

I know this sounds simple, but it isn't. With work, family, and activities, sleep is often the first thing to go. How does sleep interfere with ketosis? Sleep deprivation often triggers sugar and carbohydrate cravings, which tempt you to stray from the ketogenic way of eating. Not to mention being so tired that the last thing you want to do is cook! The graphic below shows how sleep deprivation can lead to obesity.

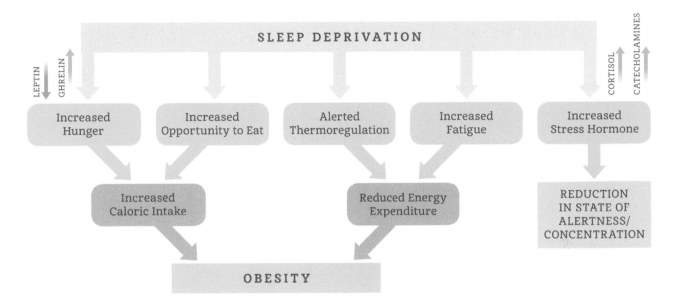

Lower Stress to Aid Digestion

Do you notice that you get indigestion or diarrhea after a stressful eating situation? When you are under stress, your heart rate goes up, your blood pressure rises, and blood is forced away from your digestive system and moved to your legs, arms, and head for quick thinking. Less blood flow to your digestive system (as much as four times less!) means that your body can't burn those calories as effectively, resulting in a sluggish metabolism.

The issue with eating while under stress is that you could be eating the most nutritious food in the world, but you won't be able to digest and absorb those nutrients properly because of the dramatically decreased enzymatic output in your intestines. You're more susceptible to indigestion, acid reflux, and heartburn.

My suggestions: Enjoy a peaceful little break for lunch rather than scheduling a lunch meeting. Try dining alfresco, which helps lower stress and encourages you to chew your food adequately (which you can't do if you are busy chatting away during a lunch meeting). Also, try not to eat right after an argument; instead, do some yoga for exercise—the blood flow is going to your extremities anyway!

"Food can be the most powerful form of medicine or the slowest form of poison."

—Ann Wigmore

EATING KETO AT RESTAURANTS

Top Tips for

Craig and I used to enjoy going out to dinner on date nights, but now we prefer to cook at home. Restaurant food never tastes as good as what we can whip up together in our own kitchen. We prefer to spend the money on quality food that we can cook ourselves, and we end up saving money by not going out to eat.

Eating out while trying to maintain a keto lifestyle is not impossible, though. If you do choose to eat out, here are my top menu picks.

Omelet

Many restaurants serve omelets not just for breakfast but also for lunch, which I adore. Just look out for non-ketogenic fillings, such as beans. Choose keto fillings like mushrooms, onions, cheeses, and meats. My favorite omelet to order at a restaurant is ham and Emmentaler cheese with a side of house-made hollandaise for dipping (and to increase the keto level).

Be aware, however, that some restaurants add non-ketogenic ingredients to the eggs used to make omelets. Some large breakfast chains such as IHOP add pancake batter to their omelets. That's right—they add sugar, carbs, and wheat to the omelet base for "fluffiness" . . . yuck! A spinach and mushroom omelet at IHOP contains 24 grams of carbs and 7 grams of sugar. That just isn't right.

Ask your server to have the chef cook your omelet in butter instead of vegetable oil, which most restaurants use.

Poached Eggs Benedict

I often order eggs Benedict, skip the English muffin, and request extra hollandaise. My eggs Benedict is often served with two slices of ham, two poached eggs, a large side of hollandaise, and a side salad. That way I don't worry about the oils in which the eggs are fried.

Make sure that the hollandaise is house-made and not made from a mix.

Hamburger on a Side Salad

Skip the bun. Order a hamburger with a large side salad with a house salad dressing made without sugar (ranch, blue cheese, and Italian are usually good options). Bonus points if you bring your own dressing.

Beware of hidden sugars, such as in BBQ sauce–basted burgers or caramelized onions made with soda. Yes, you read that right: some restaurants caramelize onions in Coke.

Sandwich on a Side Salad

Ask for no bread or fries and sub in a large salad. I have even ordered a Reuben over a large salad. Beware of hidden sugars in sandwich condiments or dressings such as Thousand Island.

Salmon with Broccoli

Skip the rice or potatoes and ask for a nonstarchy vegetable side, such as broccoli. Smother the salmon in extra butter.

Steak and Mushrooms

Again, skip the starchy potatoes and ask for a ketogenic vegetable, such as sautéed mushrooms. Bonus points if you choose a ketogenic cut of steak. (For helpful charts on the best cuts, see pages 53 and 54.) Skip the steak sauce, which is filled with sugar.

Chicken Alfredo and Other Pasta Dishes

Ask the chef to omit the pasta and put the sauce over sautéed broccoli instead. Even at popular chain Italian restaurants, I have enjoyed chicken Alfredo and shrimp scampi over broccoli instead of pasta. Make sure that the Alfredo sauce is not thickened with a roux, which includes wheat flour.

Ramen and Pho

I love getting pho at a Vietnamese restaurant in Minneapolis. I ask them not to put any noodles in the soup; instead, they use extra cabbage sliced very thin, which reminds me of noodles. Beware of the soy sauce the restaurant uses. Is it true fermented soy sauce or an Americanized sauce that has gluten added to it? Bonus points if you bring your own coconut aminos and skip the soy sauce entirely.

Thai Food

I adore going to Thai restaurants. Sure, it can take a while to get your food, but that's because they are making everything so fresh. I often get Thai food and swap out the noodles for sautéed cabbage noodles. Tom kha gai (coconut chicken soup) is one of my favorite dishes.

Beware of added sugars, which are common at some Thai restaurants. Ask the chef not to add any sugar to your dish.

Nacho Toppings on Lettuce

I love nachos. One local restaurant called San Pedro makes awesome nachos. Instead of serving the toppings on chips, they serve them over bite-sized crispy romaine lettuce. I have asked for this preparation at a number of restaurants, and all of them have been very open to my request.

Sushi

Sushi can be a great choice if you skip the rice and get sashimi style. Again, beware of the soy sauce the restaurant uses. Is it true fermented soy sauce or an Americanized sauce that has gluten added to it? Bonus points if you bring your own coconut aminos and skip the soy sauce entirely.

If you need another reason to skip the rice, here's an anecdote: Craig likes to go out and get "healthified" sushi (sashimi, no rice) with Micah. Once, at a restaurant, Craig overheard the sushi chef tell the waiter to try the sushi rice because someone else had made it the day before and it didn't taste right. He said that he adds over 3 quarts of sugar to each batch of rice, which comes out to 34 grams of added sugar per cup! We never eat rice, but that sure is another good reason to avoid it at restaurants.

Crab, Lobster, or Shrimp with Butter

Once we went to a local crab restaurant, and when the crab arrived, it was served with oil. I asked for real butter. The young waiter scurried to the kitchen, and when he came back he stated proudly, "We don't have any butter, but we do have this vegetable oil blend" . . . as if butter was going to kill us.

Huh?!? A restaurant with no butter? We took our crab to go and picked up some butter at a nearby market so we could enjoy a picnic outside instead. Crab without butter just isn't right!

Shellfish is always a tasty choice as long as the butter it's served with is really butter and not a vegetable oil mixture. Ask for a salad or sautéed keto vegetable, such as broccoli, on the side.

Sausages and/or Brats with a Side of Sauerkraut

But beware of Bavarian-style sauerkraut, which contains added sugar.

Fast Food

Chipotle is the only fast food option I would recommend. I suggest ordering lettuce layered with your choice of meat, topped with sautéed bell peppers, salsa, and guacamole (as well as sour cream and cheese if you're not dairy-sensitive).

These are just a few ideas of what to order at restaurants. There is no place you can't go and modify the menu to make it keto. One final tip is to look at the menu online and plan your order before you get there. Stick to your plan and do not allow your friends or your server to tempt you into ordering unhealthy options. Steer clear of food pushers!

Quick & Easy

KETOGENIC MEAL PLANS

CHAPTER 4

In this chapter you will find two seven-day meal plans complete with shopping lists. The first is a weight loss and healing meal plan, designed to get you losing weight and healing fast. The second is a maintenance and healing meal plan to use if you want to heal, but not lose or even gain weight. I've included shopping lists with these two plans to make it easy for you to pick up what you need and get started.

In addition, I have provided four 30-day meal plans: two for weight loss and two for maintenance. Each type has one plan that is dairy-free and one that isn't. Many of my clients see better, quicker results by going dairy-free for the first few weeks or month, so it is a good idea to start out dairy-free. After a month of being dairy-free, you can either switch to the 30-day weight loss plan that includes dairy (see below about testing dairy tolerance) or repeat the dairy-free 30-day weight loss plan to keep the weight loss and healing moving quickly.

Although the seven-day meal plans are not dairy-free, many of the recipes in those two plans have a dairy-free option. If you would like to replace a recipe in a seven-day plan that has dairy, such as the Orange Cream Shake (page 142), you may substitute one of the recipes included in the corresponding thirty-day dairy-free plan.

Dairy Tolerance

At any time, you can test your dairy tolerance. First, weigh yourself in the morning in a fasted state. Then consume dairy during the day and weigh yourself the next morning in a fasted state. If you retained water (gained weight), then eliminate dairy for a few more weeks. You process dairy at the ends of the villi in your intestinal tract. Eating grains or a higher-carb diet damages the villi, which makes it harder to tolerate and process dairy. But after eliminating grains and excess carbs, your villi will heal over time, and you should be able to tolerate dairy much better.

Practical Tips

Each meal plan is designed for one person. Since most of the recipes included in the meal plans will serve a family of four or six, they provide plenty of leftovers. Please scale the recipes up or down to suit your needs, remembering to increase or decrease the quantities of the ingredients in the shopping lists accordingly. If you have food allergies or intolerances, see the individual recipes for possible ingredient substitutions. Read through the recipes before going shopping to determine if special equipment is required; for example, you may need a spiral slicer to make vegetable noodles.

In the shopping lists for the seven-day plans, I have included both the smallest and/or most typical size or quantity in which the ingredient can be purchased (which may be more than is used in the recipes for the week) and, in parentheses, the exact amount used in the recipes. For example:

Fresh dill, 1 small bunch (2 tablespoons chopped)

Use the information in parentheses (the exact amount needed to make the recipes for the week) to determine whether you have enough of an ingredient on hand before heading out to the grocery store to purchase it.

INTERMITTENT FASTING

Breakfast isn't the most important meal of the day. "Breaking your fast" (or "breakfast") is!

Fasting really isn't as drastic as it sounds. When you sleep, you are starting to fast a little. During the first ten hours after eating, your body is digesting and absorbing nutrients. It isn't until after not eating for ten hours that you actually get into a fasted state. If you restrict your window of eating to only seven hours a day (six hours is better), then, after ten to twelve hours of not eating, you get into a fasted state where you can burn fat more efficiently.

When I first heard about intermittent fasting (IF), I thought, "No, no, no. This is not good for anyone who wants to maintain their muscle." But a ketogenic diet spares protein from being oxidized, which preserves muscle. This is why you do not go into "starvation mode."

As I started putting IF into practice, not only did I experience physical benefits, but the mental benefits were outstanding! Now I work and write in a fasted state for about three hours in the morning, and my mind has never been clearer.

Remember that fasting is not a diet; it is a pattern of eating. You can eat very poorly while practicing intermittent fasting, but that decision would cause you to reap fewer benefits than if you were to eat a well-formulated keto-adapted diet.

Benefits of Intermittent Fasting

Saves time: Intermittent fasting saves you time, as you aren't thinking about food and what you are going to eat all day. You generally eat less at each meal, and usually eat two meals instead of three, so meal planning and preparation are reduced. Also, as your cravings and appetite decline, you spend less time thinking about food.

Conveys health benefits: Intermittent fasting, as well as longer-term multiple-day fasting, is not only natural for our bodies when in a ketogenic state but also has many health benefits. IF can:

- Improve mitochondria health and increase mitochondrial energy efficiency
- Help you live longer and slow aging
- Reduce the risk of cancer and cardiovascular disease
- Reduce inflammation and lower triglyceride levels
- Help increase ketones, which improves focus and memory and further suppresses appetite

Accelerates weight loss: Practicing intermittent fasting in combination with a ketogenic lifestyle speeds weight loss. That is why I suggest you practice IF when following the 7-Day or 30-Day Weight Loss and Healing Meal Plan. A ketogenic lifestyle greatly reduces your appetite, which makes IF much easier to do. In fact, many times my clients have to remind themselves to eat. I have found that implementing an IF routine helps most clients get past a stall or plateau in weight loss.

Guidelines

When implementing an IF routine, you want to follow a couple of simple guidelines. All food needs to be eaten within a six- to eight-hour window. This eating window can be in the morning (break your fast in the morning) or later in the day (skip breakfast and break your fast at noon), as shown in the charts below. Just make sure to eat all your food for the day during this window of time. Outside the window, consume only water and other low-calorie liquids (like tea). The general rule is that anything over 50 calories will break your fast, so no bulletproof coffee!

Also, make sure to end your eating window at least three hours before going to bed. Eating too close to bedtime can inhibit human growth hormone production while you sleep and slow weight loss.

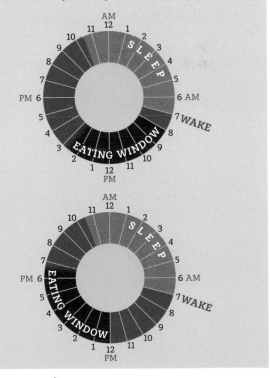

WEIGHT LOSS AND HEALING MEAL PLAN

Day 1

BEGIN EATING WINDOW

Orange Cream Shake — 142

TOTAL SERVINGS 4

NUTRITIONAL INFO (per serving)

calories	fat	protein	carbs	fiber
215	20.6g	4.6g	2.1g	0g
	87%	9%	4%	

SIDE

Wedge Salad — 225

TOTAL SERVINGS 4

NUTRITIONAL INFO (per serving)

calories	fat	protein	carbs	fiber
204	18.4g	6.3g	4.2g	1g
	81%	12%	8%	

SNACK/DESSERT

Strawberry Cheesecake in Jars — 334

TOTAL SERVINGS 6

NUTRITIONAL INFO (per serving)

calories	fat	protein	carbs	fiber
220	21.3g	3.4g	5.4g	1.7g
	86%	5%	9%	

END EATING WINDOW

South of the Border Salad** — 223

TOTAL SERVINGS 4

NUTRITIONAL INFO (per serving)

calories	fat	protein	carbs	fiber
471	35g	32.5g	5.7g	1.7g
	67%	28%	5%	

DAY 1 TOTAL

calories	fat	protein	carbs	fiber
1110	95.3g	46.8g	17.4g	4.4g
	79%	17%	5%	

Day 2

BEGIN EATING WINDOW

Eggs in Purgatory — 148

TOTAL SERVINGS 2

NUTRITIONAL INFO (per serving)

calories	fat	protein	carbs	fiber
488	38.7g	27.5g	7g	1.7g
	72%	23%	5%	

SIDE

Creamy Cilantro-Lime Pasta — 303

TOTAL SERVINGS 4

NUTRITIONAL INFO (per serving)

calories	fat	protein	carbs	fiber
338	35g	1.6g	5.7g	1.6g
	93%	2%	5%	

SNACK/DESSERT

French Silk Mousse — 351

TOTAL SERVINGS 12

NUTRITIONAL INFO (per serving)

calories	fat	protein	carbs	fiber
218	21.5g	3.4g	2.8g	0.8g
	89%	6%	5%	

END EATING WINDOW

Chicken Alfredo — 246

TOTAL SERVINGS 4

NUTRITIONAL INFO (per serving)

calories	fat	protein	carbs	fiber
468	42.4g	21.3g	1.1g	0g
	81%	18%	1%	

DAY 2 TOTAL

calories	fat	protein	carbs	fiber
1512	137.6g	53.8g	16.6g	4.1g
	82%	14%	4%	

Day 3

BEGIN EATING WINDOW

Cream of No-Wheat Cereal* — 157

TOTAL SERVINGS 1

NUTRITIONAL INFO (per serving)

calories	fat	protein	carbs	fiber
691	69.8g	14.4g	5g	1.8g
	90%	7.5%	2.5%	

SIDE

Curry Braised Cucumbers — 311

TOTAL SERVINGS 4

NUTRITIONAL INFO (per serving)

calories	fat	protein	carbs	fiber
78	7g	0.6g	3.5g	0.6g
	80%	3%	17%	

SNACK/DESSERT

Crispy Mocha Fat Bombs — 326

TOTAL SERVINGS 4

NUTRITIONAL INFO (per serving)

calories	fat	protein	carbs	fiber
89	10.8g	0g	0g	0g
	100%	0%	0%	

END EATING WINDOW

Slow Cooker Chicken Caesar Wraps — 208

TOTAL SERVINGS 6

NUTRITIONAL INFO (per serving)

calories	fat	protein	carbs	fiber
517	35.7g	43g	3g	0.6g
	63%	34%	3%	

DAY 3 TOTAL

calories	fat	protein	carbs	fiber
1375	119g	58g	11.5g	3g
	80%	17%	3%	

Day 4

BEGIN EATING WINDOW

Chocolate Breakfast Custard — 158

TOTAL SERVINGS 4

NUTRITIONAL INFO (per serving)

calories	fat	protein	carbs	fiber
474	50.3g	3.7g	4.3g	0g
	94%	3%	3%	

SIDE

Eggs Gribiche — 193

TOTAL SERVINGS 4

NUTRITIONAL INFO (per serving)

calories	fat	protein	carbs	fiber
229	20.7g	8.5g	0.9g	0g
	82%	16%	2%	

SNACK/DESSERT

Crispy Maple Bacon Fat Bombs — 328

TOTAL SERVINGS 4

NUTRITIONAL INFO (per serving)

calories	fat	protein	carbs	fiber
137	14.1g	2.5g	0g	0g
	93%	7%	0%	

END EATING WINDOW

Arctic Char with Olive Salsa — 232

TOTAL SERVINGS 2

NUTRITIONAL INFO (per serving)

calories	fat	protein	carbs	fiber
439	33.6g	32.5g	1.1g	0g
	69%	30%	1%	

DAY 4 TOTAL

calories	fat	protein	carbs	fiber
1279	118.7g	47.2g	6.3g	0g
	84%	15%	2%	

Day 5

BEGIN EATING WINDOW

Green Eggs and Ham
168

TOTAL SERVINGS 1

NUTRITIONAL INFO (per serving)

calories	fat	protein	carbs	fiber
278	22.7g	15.8g	2.2g	0g
	74%	23%	3%	

SIDE

Cheesy Grits
302

TOTAL SERVINGS 4

NUTRITIONAL INFO (per serving)

calories	fat	protein	carbs	fiber
408	37.8g	16.9g	1.1g	0g
	83%	16%	1%	

SNACK/DESSERT

Butterscotch Mousse
350

TOTAL SERVINGS 4

NUTRITIONAL INFO (per serving)

calories	fat	protein	carbs	fiber
129	12.9g	1.9g	0.9g	0g
	90%	7%	3%	

END EATING WINDOW

Grilled Lamb Chops with Mint Aioli
282

TOTAL SERVINGS 4

NUTRITIONAL INFO (per serving)

calories	fat	protein	carbs	fiber
862	76g	38.2g	0.4g	0g
	80%	19%	1%	

DAY 5 TOTAL

calories	fat	protein	carbs	fiber
1167	149.4g	72.8g	4.6g	0g
	74%	25%	1%	

Day 6

BEGIN EATING WINDOW

Taco Breakfast Bake
164

TOTAL SERVINGS 6

NUTRITIONAL INFO (per serving)

calories	fat	protein	carbs	fiber
301	22.4g	21.8g	2.5g	0g
	68%	29%	3%	

SIDE

Creamy Cilantro-Lime Pasta
LEFTOVER

TOTAL SERVINGS 4

NUTRITIONAL INFO (per serving)

calories	fat	protein	carbs	fiber
338	35g	1.6g	5.7g	1.6g
	93%	2%	5%	

SNACK/DESSERT

Grand Marnier Fat Bombs
325

TOTAL SERVINGS 12

NUTRITIONAL INFO (per serving)

calories	fat	protein	carbs	fiber
275	31g	0g	0g	0g
	100%	0%	0%	

END EATING WINDOW

Cheesy Fried Ravioli
176

TOTAL SERVINGS 6

NUTRITIONAL INFO (per serving)

calories	fat	protein	carbs	fiber
315	25.5g	22.5g	1.2g	0g
	72%	27%	1%	

DAY 6 TOTAL

calories	fat	protein	carbs	fiber
1299	113.9g	45.9g	9.4g	1.6g
	82%	16%	3%	

Day 7

BEGIN EATING WINDOW

Dairy-Free Milk Chocolate Protein Bars
154

TOTAL SERVINGS 8

NUTRITIONAL INFO (per serving)

calories	fat	protein	carbs	fiber
238	23g	4g	2.5g	1.5g
	89%	7%	4%	

SIDE

Cheesy Grits
LEFTOVER

TOTAL SERVINGS 4

NUTRITIONAL INFO (per serving)

calories	fat	protein	carbs	fiber
408	37.8g	16.9g	1.1g	0g
	83%	16%	1%	

SNACK/DESSERT

Grand Marnier Fat Bombs
LEFTOVER

NUTRITIONAL INFO (per serving)

calories	fat	protein	carbs	fiber
275	31g	0g	0g	0g
	100%	0%	0%	

END EATING WINDOW

Slow Cooker Laotian Chicken and Herbs (Larb)
250

TOTAL SERVINGS 6

NUTRITIONAL INFO (per serving)

calories	fat	protein	carbs	fiber
438	28.3g	39.5g	3.6g	0.8g
	59%	36%	4%	

DAY 7 TOTAL

calories	fat	protein	carbs	fiber
1359	120.1g	60.4g	7.2g	2.3g
	80%	18%	2%	

---

*The nutritional information listed here is for Cream of No-Wheat Cereal made with coconut milk. When made with heavy cream, the nutritional information is slightly different (see page 157).

**If you're inclined to try smoking your own foods at home, you can replace the South of the Border Salad with Smoked Beef Long Ribs (page 364).

Shopping List for 7-Day Weight Loss and Healing Meal Plan

Produce

Basil, 1 small bunch (1 teaspoon chopped)

Chives, 1 small bunch (2 tablespoons chopped)

Cilantro, 1 medium bunch (½ cup chopped)

Cucumbers, 2 (4-inch)

Flat-leaf parsley, 1 medium bunch (¼ cup chopped)

Garlic, 1 head (if using roasted garlic, increase to 4 heads)

Ginger, 1 (2-inch-long) piece (2 tablespoons grated)

Green onions, 1 medium bunch

Iceberg lettuce, 1 head

Lime, 1 small (1 teaspoon juice) (or 1 [14.4-ounce] bottle lime juice)

Mint, 1 bunch (3 tablespoons chopped)

Onion, 1 large

Radicchio, 2 heads

Red chili peppers, 2 small

Romaine lettuce, 1 head

Rosemary, 1 sprig

Spring salad mix, 1 large bag (4 cups)

Tarragon, 1 small bunch (1 teaspoon chopped)

Thai basil, 1 small bunch (2 tablespoons chopped) (substitute Italian basil if unavailable)

Tomatoes, 2 small + 1 medium

Zucchini, 4 medium (no longer than 12 inches) (or 4 [7-ounce] packages Miracle Noodles)

Protein

Arctic char, 2 (5-ounce) fillets, about ¾ inch thick

Bacon, 4 slices

Chicken thighs, boneless, skinless, 3½ pounds

Chicken thighs, bone-in, skin-on, 2 pounds

Chorizo or Italian sausage, links or bulk ground, ¼ pound

Ground beef, 80% lean, 1½ pounds

Ham, no sugar added, 2 slices

Lamb loin chops, 8 chops, 1¼ inches thick

Prosciutto, thinly sliced, ½ pound

Dairy, Dairy Subs, and Eggs

Almond milk, unsweetened, 3¼ cups (about ¾ quart)

Butter, unsalted, 2 sticks (1 cup) + 2 tablespoons

Cheddar cheese, sharp, 2 ounces

Coconut milk, full-fat, 2 (13½-ounce) cans (2⅓ cups or 19 ounces) (or heavy cream if not dairy-sensitive)

Cream cheese, 2 (8-ounce) packages (12 ounces)

Eggs, large, preferably organic, 3 dozen

Heavy cream, 4 ounces (½ cup)

Mascarpone cheese or cream cheese, 1 (8-ounce) package

Monterey Jack or sharp cheddar cheese, 3 ounces

Parmesan cheese, 4 ounces

Provolone cheese (from the deli counter), 4 round slices (for Taco Bowls for South of the Border Salad; omit for dairy-free)

Oils

Cocoa butter, 2 ounces (¼ cup)

Coconut oil, 34 ounces (4¼ cups)

MCT oil, 4.25 ounces (½ cup + 1 tablespoon)

Condiments, Sauces & Spice Blends

Caesar dressing, unsweetened, with no soybean oil, 1 bottle (½ cup) (or homemade, page 116)

Cilantro Lime Sauce (page 115), 1½ cups

Dairy-Free Ranch Dressing (page 118), ½ cup

Herb Aioli made with mint (page 114), ½ cup

Olive Salsa (page 135), ½ scant cup

Simple Chimichurri Sauce (page 130), 2 tablespoons

Taco Salad Dressing (page 121), ½ cup

Taco Seasoning (page 110), ¼ cup + 2 teaspoons

Other Pantry Items

Baking chocolate, unsweetened, 3 ounces

Beef bone broth, 6 ounces (¾ cup) (or homemade, page 132)

Butterscotch extract, 1 teaspoon

Chicken bone broth, 18.5 ounces (2⅓ cups) (or homemade, page 132)

Chocolate-flavored egg white protein, 0.7 ounce (¼ cup) (or whey protein if not dairy-sensitive)

Cocoa powder, unsweetened, 1 cup + 1 tablespoon

Coconut aminos or wheat-free tamari, 1 tablespoon

Coconut vinegar or apple cider vinegar, 4 ounces (½ cup)

Cornichons, 3 (1 tablespoon chopped)

Espresso powder, 1 teaspoon

Fish sauce, 2 ounces (¼ cup)

Grass-fed gelatin, powdered, 1½ tablespoons

Maple extract, 1 tablespoon + 1 teaspoon

Orange extract, 1 tablespoon

Smoked paprika, 2 tablespoons

Strawberry extract, 1 teaspoon

Strawberry or hibiscus tea, 1 bag (¼ cup brewed)

Swerve natural sweetener or equivalent liquid or powdered sweetener, 2 (16-ounce) packages (3 cups + 2 tablespoons) (see page 37 for equivalents)

Swerve natural sweetener or equivalent powdered erythritol or monk fruit, 1 (16-ounce) package (2 cups) (see page 37 for equivalents)

Turmeric powder, 2 teaspoons

Vanilla extract, 1 tablespoon + 2 teaspoons (or 5 vanilla beans, about 6 inches long)

Whole-grain mustard, 1 teaspoon

Canned/Jarred Goods

Capers, 1 (8-ounce) jar (1 tablespoon)

Salsa, 1 (8-ounce) jar (½ cup)

Sliced black olives, 1 (2.25-ounce) can (½ cup)

Tomato paste, jarred, 1 tablespoon

Tomato sauce, jarred, 2 ounces (¼ cup)

Optional Add-Ins

Grass-fed gelatin, powdered, 1 tablespoon (for Orange Cream Shake)

L-glutamine powder, 1 tablespoon (for Orange Cream Shake)

Pure aloe vera juice, 1 tablespoon (for Orange Cream Shake)

Stur orange-mango-flavored liquid water enhancer, 1 teaspoon (for Grand Marnier Fat Bombs)

Yacón syrup, 1 tablespoon (for Dairy-Free Milk Chocolate Protein Bars)

*Looking for organic keto spices? Maria's signature spice blends are available for purchase here:
http://keto-adapted.com/keto-spices/

WEIGHT LOSS AND HEALING MEAL PLAN

	BEGIN EATING WINDOW	SNACK/DESSERT	SIDE	END EATING WINDOW
1 SUNDAY	2 eggs any way, 2 strips bacon	Frozen Orange Cream Bites — 330	Refrigerator Pickles — 318	Slow Cooker Pork Ragu over Paleo Polenta — 291
2 MONDAY	Dairy-Free Chocolate Shake — 145	Orange Cream Push Pops — 337	Cheesy Grits — 302	Upside-Down Pizza — 264
3 TUESDAY	Cinnamon Roll Minute Muffins — 152	Frozen Orange Cream Bites — LEFTOVER	Wedge Salad* — 225	Schwein-shaxen — 294
4 WEDNESDAY	Dairy-Free Chocolate Shake — LEFTOVER	Orange Cream Push Pops — LEFTOVER	Refrigerator Pickles — LEFTOVER	Slow Cooker Pork Ragu over Paleo Polenta — LEFTOVER
5 THURSDAY	Cinnamon Roll Minute Muffins — LEFTOVER	Egg-Free Ice Cream — 348	Pizza Sticks — 304	Goat Cheese Panna Cotta with Crispy Prosciutto and Fried Basil — 296
6 FRIDAY	Dairy-Free Chocolate Shake — LEFTOVER	Frozen Orange Cream Bites — 330	Wedge Salad* — LEFTOVER	Masala Mussels — 238
7 SATURDAY	Cinnamon Roll Minute Muffins — LEFTOVER	Orange Cream Push Pops — LEFTOVER	Refrigerator Pickles — LEFTOVER	Upside-Down Pizza — LEFTOVER
8 SUNDAY	Dairy-Free Chocolate Shake — LEFTOVER	Crispy Raspberry Fat Bombs — 326	Wedge Salad* — LEFTOVER	Broccoli "Noodle" Cheese Soup — 216
9 MONDAY	Cinnamon Roll Minute Muffins — LEFTOVER	Frozen Orange Cream Bites — LEFTOVER	Easy Kimchi — 316	Easy as Portobello Pizza Pie — 306
10 TUESDAY	2 eggs any way, 2 strips bacon	Crispy Raspberry Fat Bombs — LEFTOVER	Wedge Salad* — LEFTOVER	Upside-Down Pizza — LEFTOVER

If you're inclined to try smoking your own foods at home, you can replace the Wedge Salad with Pan-Fried Smoked Cauliflower Steaks (page 372).

	BEGIN EATING WINDOW	SNACK/DESSERT	SIDE	END EATING WINDOW
11 WEDNESDAY	Cinnamon Roll Minute Muffins — LEFTOVER	Frozen Orange Cream Bites — LEFTOVER	Pizza Sticks — 304	Skillet Lasagna — 266
12 THURSDAY	Pizza Muffins — 162	Orange Cream Push Pops — LEFTOVER	Easy Kimchi — 316	Open-Faced Hamburgers on "Buns" — 268
13 FRIDAY	Cream of No-Wheat Cereal — 157	Crispy Raspberry Fat Bombs — LEFTOVER	Curry Braised Cucumbers — 311	Skillet Lasagna — LEFTOVER
14 SATURDAY	Pizza Muffins — LEFTOVER	Egg-Free Ice Cream — 348	Easy Kimchi — LEFTOVER	King Crab Legs with Garlic Butter — 240
15 SUNDAY	Pizza Muffins — LEFTOVER	Crispy Raspberry Fat Bombs — LEFTOVER	Easy Kimchi — LEFTOVER	Easy Tomato Soup with Grilled Cheese — 218
16 MONDAY	2 eggs any way, 2 strips bacon	Gummy Bears — 352	Cucumber Salad — 224	Skillet Lasagna — LEFTOVER
17 TUESDAY	Breakfast Burritos — 169	Egg-Free Ice Cream — LEFTOVER	Caramelized Endive — 313	Sardine Salad Wraps — 206
18 WEDNESDAY	Eggs in Purgatory — 148	Gummy Bears — LEFTOVER	Pizza Sticks — LEFTOVER	Open-Faced Hamburgers on "Buns" — LEFTOVER
19 THURSDAY	Breakfast Burritos — LEFTOVER	Egg-Free Ice Cream — LEFTOVER	Cucumber Salad — LEFTOVER	Skillet Lasagna — LEFTOVER
20 FRIDAY	Eggs in Purgatory — LEFTOVER	Gummy Bears — LEFTOVER	Caramelized Endive — LEFTOVER	Open-Faced Hamburgers on "Buns" — LEFTOVER

	BEGIN EATING WINDOW	SNACK/DESSERT	SIDE	END EATING WINDOW
21 SATURDAY	Breakfast Burritos LEFTOVER	Flourless Fudgy Brownies 354	Curry Braised Cucumbers 311	Sardine Salad Wraps LEFTOVER
22 SUNDAY	Taco Breakfast Bake 164	Savory Pizza Gelato 347	Caramelized Endive LEFTOVER	Fish Sticks 236
23 MONDAY	Breakfast Burritos LEFTOVER	Flourless Fudgy Brownies LEFTOVER	Paleo Polenta 320	Grilled Chicken with White BBQ Sauce 248
24 TUESDAY	2 eggs any way, 2 strips bacon	Savory Pizza Gelato LEFTOVER	Caramelized Endive LEFTOVER	Fish Tacos 230
25 WEDNESDAY	Strawberry Cheesecake Protein Bars 156	Deconstructed Crème Brûlée 324	Pizza Sticks 304	Grilled Chicken with White BBQ Sauce LEFTOVER
26 THURSDAY	Taco Breakfast Bake LEFTOVER	Flourless Fudgy Brownies LEFTOVER	Paleo Polenta LEFTOVER	Fish Tacos LEFTOVER
27 FRIDAY	Strawberry Cheesecake Protein Bars LEFTOVER	Deconstructed Crème Brûlée 324	Eggs Gribiche 193	Grilled Chicken with White BBQ Sauce LEFTOVER
28 SATURDAY	Taco Breakfast Bake LEFTOVER	Savory Pizza Gelato LEFTOVER	Bordelaise Mushrooms 310	Fish Tacos LEFTOVER
29 SUNDAY	Strawberry Cheesecake Protein Bars LEFTOVER	Deconstructed Crème Brûlée 324	Paleo Polenta LEFTOVER	Grilled Chicken with White BBQ Sauce LEFTOVER
30 MONDAY	2 eggs any way, 2 strips bacon	Flourless Fudgy Brownies	Eggs Gribiche LEFTOVER	Fish Tacos LEFTOVER

30-Day Dairy-Free
WEIGHT LOSS AND HEALING MEAL PLAN

	BEGIN EATING WINDOW	SNACK/DESSERT	SIDE	END EATING WINDOW
1 SUNDAY	2 eggs any way, 2 strips bacon	Grand Marnier Fat Bombs — 325	Refrigerator Pickles — 318	Slow Cooker Pork Ragu over Paleo Polenta — 291
2 MONDAY	Dairy-Free Chocolate Shake — 145	Coffee Ice Cream — 343	Mushroom Ragu — 300	20-Minute Ground Lamb Casserole — 280
3 TUESDAY	Cinnamon Roll Minute Muffins — 152	Grand Marnier Fat Bombs — LEFTOVER	Wedge Salad — 225	Schwein-shaxen — 294
4 WEDNESDAY	Dairy-Free Chocolate Shake — LEFTOVER	Coffee Ice Cream — LEFTOVER	Refrigerator Pickles — LEFTOVER	Slow Cooker Pork Ragu over Paleo Polenta — LEFTOVER
5 THURSDAY	Cinnamon Roll Minute Muffins — LEFTOVER	French Silk Mousse — 351	Mushroom Ragu — LEFTOVER	Sweet-n-Sour Country-Style Ribs over Zoodles — 290
6 FRIDAY	Dairy-Free Chocolate Shake — LEFTOVER	Grand Marnier Fat Bombs — LEFTOVER	Wedge Salad — LEFTOVER	Masala Mussels — 238
7 SATURDAY	Cinnamon Roll Minute Muffins — LEFTOVER	Coffee Ice Cream — LEFTOVER	Refrigerator Pickles — LEFTOVER	20-Minute Ground Lamb Casserole — LEFTOVER
8 SUNDAY	Dairy-Free Chocolate Shake — LEFTOVER	Crispy Raspberry Fat Bombs — 326	Wedge Salad — LEFTOVER	Brats with Simple Coleslaw — 288
9 MONDAY	Cinnamon Roll Minute Muffins — LEFTOVER	Grand Marnier Fat Bombs — LEFTOVER	Easy Kimchi — 316	Sweet-n-Sour Country-Style Ribs over Zoodles — LEFTOVER
10 TUESDAY	2 eggs any way, 2 strips bacon	Crispy Raspberry Fat Bombs — LEFTOVER	Wedge Salad — LEFTOVER	20-Minute Ground Lamb Casserole — LEFTOVER

	BEGIN EATING WINDOW	SNACK/DESSERT	SIDE	END EATING WINDOW
11 **WEDNESDAY**	Cinnamon Roll Minute Muffins — LEFTOVER	French Silk Mousse — LEFTOVER	Bordelaise Mushrooms — 310	Sweet-n-Sour Country-Style Ribs over Zoodles — LEFTOVER
12 **THURSDAY**	Spring Popovers — 146	Coffee Ice Cream — LEFTOVER	Easy Kimchi — LEFTOVER	Open-Faced Hamburgers on "Buns" — 268
13 **FRIDAY**	Minute English Muffin made with coconut oil — 150	Crispy Raspberry Fat Bombs — LEFTOVER	Curry Braised Cucumbers — 311	20-Minute Ground Lamb Casserole — LEFTOVER
14 **SATURDAY**	Spring Popovers — LEFTOVER	Chai Ice Cream — 345	Easy Kimchi — LEFTOVER	King Crab Legs with Garlic Butter — 240
15 **SUNDAY**	Spring Popovers — LEFTOVER	Crispy Raspberry Fat Bombs — LEFTOVER	Easy Kimchi — LEFTOVER	Sweet-n-Sour Country-Style Ribs over Zoodles — LEFTOVER
16 **MONDAY**	2 eggs any way, 2 strips bacon	Gummy Bears — 352	Cucumber Salad — 224	Slow Cooker BBQ Chicken Wraps — 207
17 **TUESDAY**	Spring Popovers — LEFTOVER	Chai Ice Cream — LEFTOVER	Caramelized Endive — 313	Deconstructed BLT with Pork Belly — 292
18 **WEDNESDAY**	Eggs in Purgatory — 148	Gummy Bears — LEFTOVER	Bordelaise Mushrooms — LEFTOVER	Slow Cooker BBQ Chicken Wraps — LEFTOVER
19 **THURSDAY**	Dairy-Free Milk Chocolate Protein Bars — 154	Chai Ice Cream — LEFTOVER	Cucumber Salad — LEFTOVER	Open-Faced Hamburgers on "Buns" — LEFTOVER
20 **FRIDAY**	Eggs in Purgatory — LEFTOVER	Gummy Bears — LEFTOVER	Caramelized Endive — LEFTOVER	Slow Cooker BBQ Chicken Wraps — LEFTOVER

If you're inclined to try smoking your own foods at home, you can replace the Wedge Salad with Pan-Fried Smoked Cauliflower Steaks (page 372).

DAIRY-FREE

	BEGIN EATING WINDOW	SNACK/DESSERT	SIDE	END EATING WINDOW
21 SATURDAY	Spring Popovers *LEFTOVER*	Flourless Fudgy Brownies **354**	Curry Braised Cucumbers **311**	Deconstructed BLT with Pork Belly *LEFTOVER*
22 SUNDAY	Dairy-Free Milk Chocolate Protein Bars *LEFTOVER*	Savory Pizza Gelato **347**	Caramelized Endive *LEFTOVER*	Arctic Char with Olive Salsa **232**
23 MONDAY	Spring Popovers *LEFTOVER*	Flourless Fudgy Brownies *LEFTOVER*	Eggs Gribiche **193**	Grilled Chicken with White BBQ Sauce **248**
24 TUESDAY	2 eggs any way, 2 strips bacon	Savory Pizza Gelato *LEFTOVER*	Caramelized Endive *LEFTOVER*	Fish Tacos **230**
25 WEDNESDAY	Dairy-Free Chocolate Shake **145**	Chai Ice Cream *LEFTOVER*	Bordelaise Mushrooms **310**	Grilled Chicken with White BBQ Sauce *LEFTOVER*
26 THURSDAY	Dairy-Free Milk Chocolate Protein Bars *LEFTOVER*	Flourless Fudgy Brownies *LEFTOVER*	Eggs Gribiche *LEFTOVER*	Fish Tacos *LEFTOVER*
27 FRIDAY	Dairy-Free Chocolate Shake *LEFTOVER*	Chai Ice Cream *LEFTOVER*	Wedge Salad* **225**	Grilled Chicken with White BBQ Sauce *LEFTOVER*
28 SATURDAY	Dairy-Free Milk Chocolate Protein Bars *LEFTOVER*	Savory Pizza Gelato *LEFTOVER*	Bordelaise Mushrooms *LEFTOVER*	Fish Tacos *LEFTOVER*
29 SUNDAY	Dairy-Free Chocolate Shake *LEFTOVER*	Chai Ice Cream *LEFTOVER*	Eggs Gribiche *LEFTOVER*	Grilled Chicken with White BBQ Sauce *LEFTOVER*
30 MONDAY	2 eggs any way, 2 strips bacon	Flourless Fudgy Brownies *LEFTOVER*	Wedge Salad* *LEFTOVER*	Fish Tacos *LEFTOVER*

7-Day
MAINTENANCE AND HEALING MEAL PLAN

Day 1	Day 2	Day 3	Day 4

BREAKFAST

Day 1	Day 2	Day 3	Day 4
Orange Cream Shake TOTAL SERVINGS 4 **142**	Eggs in Purgatory TOTAL SERVINGS 2 **148**	Cream of No-Wheat Cereal* TOTAL SERVINGS 1 **157**	Chocolate Breakfast Custard TOTAL SERVINGS 4 **158**

NUTRITIONAL INFO (per serving)

calories	fat	protein	carbs	fiber	calories	fat	protein	carbs	fiber	calories	fat	protein	carbs	fiber	calories	fat	protein	carbs	fiber
215	20.6g	4.6g	2.1g	0g	488	38.7g	27.5g	7g	1.7g	691	69.8g	14.4g	5g	1.8g	474	50.3g	3.7g	4.3g	0g
	87%	9%	4%			72%	23%	5%			90%	7.5%	2.5%			94%	3%	3%	

LUNCH

Day 1	Day 2	Day 3	Day 4
Easy Corned Beef "Hash" TOTAL SERVINGS 8 **263**	Chicken Alfredo TOTAL SERVINGS 4 **246**	Slow Cooker Chicken Caesar Wraps TOTAL SERVINGS 6 **208**	Slow Cooker "Butter" Chicken with Naan** TOTAL SERVINGS 8 **252**

NUTRITIONAL INFO (per serving)

calories	fat	protein	carbs	fiber	calories	fat	protein	carbs	fiber	calories	fat	protein	carbs	fiber	calories	fat	protein	carbs	fiber
532	46.3g	22.8g	4.1g	2.8g	468	42.4g	21.3g	1.1g	0g	517	35.7g	43g	3g	0.6g	536	37g	42.6g	6.4g	1.4g
	79%	18%	3%			81%	18%	1%			63%	34%	3%			64%	32.5%	5%	

DINNER

Day 1	Day 2	Day 3	Day 4
South of the Border Salad*** TOTAL SERVINGS 4 **223**	20-Minute Ground Lamb Casserole TOTAL SERVINGS 4 **280**	Sweet-n-Sour Country-Style Ribs over Zoodles TOTAL SERVINGS 6-8 **290**	Arctic Char with Olive Salsa TOTAL SERVINGS 2 **232**

NUTRITIONAL INFO (per serving)

calories	fat	protein	carbs	fiber	calories	fat	protein	carbs	fiber	calories	fat	protein	carbs	fiber	calories	fat	protein	carbs	fiber
471	35g	32.5g	5.7g	1.7g	256	17.1g	14.6g	11g	3g	476	28.1g	45.5g	7.3g	1.4g	439	33.6g	32.5g	1.1g	0g
	67%	28%	5%			60%	23%	17%			54%	39%	7%			69%	30%	1%	

SIDE

Day 1	Day 2	Day 3	Day 4
Wedge Salad TOTAL SERVINGS 4 **225**	Creamy Cilantro-Lime Pasta TOTAL SERVINGS 4 **303**	Curry Braised Cucumbers TOTAL SERVINGS 4 **311**	Eggs Gribiche TOTAL SERVINGS 4 **193**

NUTRITIONAL INFO (per serving)

calories	fat	protein	carbs	fiber	calories	fat	protein	carbs	fiber	calories	fat	protein	carbs	fiber	calories	fat	protein	carbs	fiber
204	18.4g	6.3g	4.2g	1g	338	35g	1.6g	5.7g	1.6g	78	7g	0.6g	3.5g	0.6g	229	20.7g	8.5g	0.9g	0g
	81%	12%	8%			93%	2%	5%			80%	3%	17%			82%	16%	2%	

SNACK/DESSERT

Day 1	Day 2	Day 3	Day 4
Strawberry Cheesecake in Jars TOTAL SERVINGS 6 **334**	French Silk Mousse TOTAL SERVINGS 12 **351**	Crispy Mocha Fat Bombs TOTAL SERVINGS 4 **326**	Crispy Maple Bacon Fat Bombs TOTAL SERVINGS 4 **328**

NUTRITIONAL INFO (per serving)

calories	fat	protein	carbs	fiber	calories	fat	protein	carbs	fiber	calories	fat	protein	carbs	fiber	calories	fat	protein	carbs	fiber
220	21.3g	3.4g	5.4g	1.7g	218	21.5g	3.4g	2.8g	0.8g	89	10.8g	0g	0g	0g	137	14.1g	2.5g	0g	0g
	86%	5%	9%			89%	6%	5%			100%	0%	0%			93%	7%	0%	

DAY TOTALS

	DAY 1 TOTAL					DAY 2 TOTAL					DAY 3 TOTAL					DAY 4 TOTAL			
calories	fat	protein	carbs	fiber	calories	fat	protein	carbs	fiber	calories	fat	protein	carbs	fiber	calories	fat	protein	carbs	fiber
1642	141.6g	69.6g	7.2g	5.3g	1768	154.7g	68.4g	27.6g	7.1g	1851	147.1g	103.5g	18.8g	4.4g	1815	155.7g	89.8g	12.7g	1.4g
	79%	17%	4%			79%	15%	6%			73%	23%	4%			78%	19%	3%	

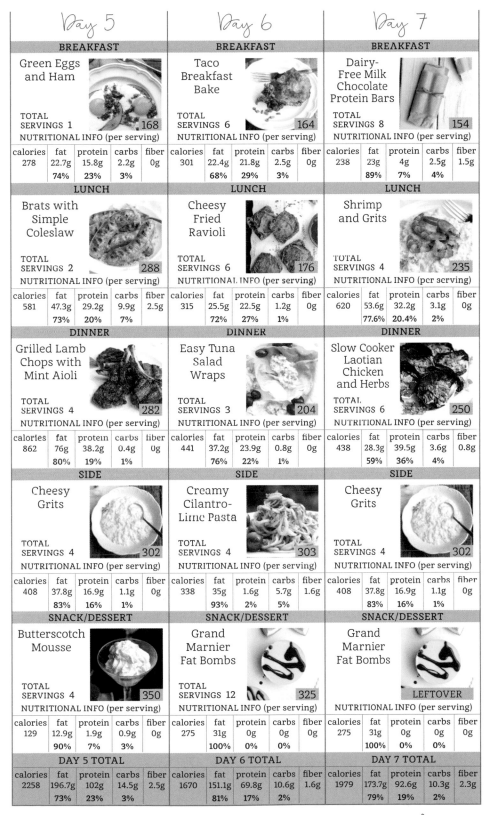

Day 5

BREAKFAST
Green Eggs and Ham
TOTAL SERVINGS 1 — 168
NUTRITIONAL INFO (per serving)

calories	fat	protein	carbs	fiber
278	22.7g	15.8g	2.2g	0g
	74%	23%	3%	

LUNCH
Brats with Simple Coleslaw
TOTAL SERVINGS 2 — 288
NUTRITIONAL INFO (per serving)

calories	fat	protein	carbs	fiber
581	47.3g	29.2g	9.9g	2.5g
	73%	20%	7%	

DINNER
Grilled Lamb Chops with Mint Aioli
TOTAL SERVINGS 4 — 282
NUTRITIONAL INFO (per serving)

calories	fat	protein	carbs	fiber
862	76g	38.2g	0.4g	0g
	80%	19%	1%	

SIDE
Cheesy Grits
TOTAL SERVINGS 4 — 302
NUTRITIONAL INFO (per serving)

calories	fat	protein	carbs	fiber
408	37.8g	16.9g	1.1g	0g
	83%	16%	1%	

SNACK/DESSERT
Butterscotch Mousse
TOTAL SERVINGS 4 — 350
NUTRITIONAL INFO (per serving)

calories	fat	protein	carbs	fiber
129	12.9g	1.9g	0.9g	0g
	90%	7%	3%	

DAY 5 TOTAL

calories	fat	protein	carbs	fiber
2258	196.7g	102g	14.5g	2.5g
	73%	23%	3%	

Day 6

BREAKFAST
Taco Breakfast Bake
TOTAL SERVINGS 6 — 164
NUTRITIONAL INFO (per serving)

calories	fat	protein	carbs	fiber
301	22.4g	21.8g	2.5g	0g
	68%	29%	3%	

LUNCH
Cheesy Fried Ravioli
TOTAL SERVINGS 6 — 176
NUTRITIONAL INFO (per serving)

calories	fat	protein	carbs	fiber
315	25.5g	22.5g	1.2g	0g
	72%	27%	1%	

DINNER
Easy Tuna Salad Wraps
TOTAL SERVINGS 3 — 204
NUTRITIONAL INFO (per serving)

calories	fat	protein	carbs	fiber
441	37.2g	23.9g	0.8g	0g
	76%	22%	1%	

SIDE
Creamy Cilantro-Lime Pasta
TOTAL SERVINGS 4 — 303
NUTRITIONAL INFO (per serving)

calories	fat	protein	carbs	fiber
338	35g	1.6g	5.7g	1.6g
	93%	2%	5%	

SNACK/DESSERT
Grand Marnier Fat Bombs
TOTAL SERVINGS 12 — 325
NUTRITIONAL INFO (per serving)

calories	fat	protein	carbs	fiber
275	31g	0g	0g	0g
	100%	0%	0%	

DAY 6 TOTAL

calories	fat	protein	carbs	fiber
1670	151.1g	69.8g	10.6g	1.6g
	81%	17%	2%	

Day 7

BREAKFAST
Dairy-Free Milk Chocolate Protein Bars
TOTAL SERVINGS 8 — 154
NUTRITIONAL INFO (per serving)

calories	fat	protein	carbs	fiber
238	23g	4g	2.5g	1.5g
	89%	7%	4%	

LUNCH
Shrimp and Grits
TOTAL SERVINGS 4 — 235
NUTRITIONAL INFO (per serving)

calories	fat	protein	carbs	fiber
620	53.6g	32.2g	3.1g	0g
	77.6%	20.4%	2%	

DINNER
Slow Cooker Laotian Chicken and Herbs
TOTAL SERVINGS 6 — 250
NUTRITIONAL INFO (per serving)

calories	fat	protein	carbs	fiber
438	28.3g	39.5g	3.6g	0.8g
	59%	36%	4%	

SIDE
Cheesy Grits
TOTAL SERVINGS 4 — 302
NUTRITIONAL INFO (per serving)

calories	fat	protein	carbs	fiber
408	37.8g	16.9g	1.1g	0g
	83%	16%	1%	

SNACK/DESSERT
Grand Marnier Fat Bombs
LEFTOVER
NUTRITIONAL INFO (per serving)

calories	fat	protein	carbs	fiber
275	31g	0g	0g	0g
	100%	0%	0%	

DAY 7 TOTAL

calories	fat	protein	carbs	fiber
1979	173.7g	92.6g	10.3g	2.3g
	79%	19%	2%	

*The nutritional information listed is for Cream of No-Wheat Cereal made with coconut milk. When it is made with heavy cream, the nutritional information is slightly different (see page 157).

**The nutritional information listed for Slow Cooker "Butter" Chicken with Naan is the totaled information for the chicken and naan. For separate nutritional information for the chicken and the naan, see page 252.

***If you're inclined to try smoking your own foods at home, you can replace the South of the Border Salad with Smoked Beef Long Ribs (page 364).

Shopping List for 7-Day Maintenance and Healing Meal Plan

Produce

Avocado, 1

Basil, 1 small bunch (1 teaspoon chopped)

Boston lettuce, 1 head (6 large leaves)

Cabbage, ½ head

Chives, 1 small bunch (2 tablespoons chopped)

Cilantro, 1 medium bunch (½ cup chopped)

Cucumbers, 2 (4-inch)

Flat-leaf parsley, 1 medium bunch (½ cup chopped)

Garlic, 2 heads (if using roasted garlic, increase to 5 heads)

Ginger, 1 (4-inch-long) piece (3 tablespoons grated)

Green cabbage, 1 medium head (about 2 pounds)

Green onions, 1 medium bunch

Iceberg lettuce, 1 head

Lemon, 1 small (1½ teaspoons juice)

Lime, 1 small (1 teaspoon juice) (or 1 [14.4-ounce] bottle lime juice)

Mint, 1 bunch (3 tablespoons chopped)

Onions, 1 medium + 2 large

Radicchio, 2 heads

Red chili peppers, 2 small

Romaine lettuce, 1 head

Rosemary, 1 sprig

Spring salad mix, 1 large bag (4 cups)

Tarragon, 1 small bunch (1 teaspoon chopped)

Thai basil, 1 small bunch (2 tablespoons chopped) (substitute Italian basil if unavailable)

Tomatoes, 1 small + 2 medium

Zucchini, 10 medium (no longer than 12 inches) (or 9 [7-ounce] packages Miracle Noodles)

Protein

Arctic char, 2 (5-ounce) fillets, about ¾ inch thick

Bacon, 8 slices

Boneless, skinless chicken thighs, 8 pounds

Brats, 4 (4-ounce)

Chicken thighs, boneless, skin-on, 2½ pounds

Chicken thighs, boneless, skinless, 3½ pounds

Chicken thighs, bone-in, skin-on, 2 pounds

Chorizo or Italian sausage, links or bulk ground, ¼ pound

Corned beef brisket, premade, 1½ pounds

Country-style pork spareribs, 3 pounds

Ground beef, 80% lean, 1½ pounds

Ground lamb, 1 pound

Ham, no sugar added, 2 slices

Lamb loin chops, 8 chops, 1¼ inches thick

Prosciutto, thinly sliced, ½ pound

Shrimp, precooked, preferably with tails on, 12 large

Tuna, 2 (3¾-ounce) cans

Dairy, Dairy Subs, and Eggs

Almond milk, unsweetened, 3¼ cups (or homemade, page 131)

Butter, unsalted, 3 sticks (1½ cups) + 2 tablespoons

Cheddar cheese, sharp, 4 ounces

Coconut milk, full-fat, 2 (13½-ounce) cans (3⅓ cups) (or heavy cream if not dairy-sensitive)

Cream cheese, 3 (8-ounce) packages (23 ounces)

Eggs, large, preferably organic, 4 dozen

Heavy cream, 1 pint (2 scant cups)

Mascarpone cheese or cream cheese, 1 (8-ounce) package

Monterey Jack or more sharp cheddar cheese, 3 ounces

Parmesan cheese, 4 ounces

Provolone cheese (from the deli counter), 4 round slices (for Taco Bowls for South of the Border Salad; omit for dairy-free)

Oils

Cocoa butter, 2 ounces (¼ cup)

Coconut oil, 38 ounces (4½ cups + 3 tablespoons)

MCT oil, 7 ounces (¾ cup + 2 tablespoons)

Other Pantry Items

Baking chocolate, unsweetened, 3 ounces

Beef bone broth, ¾ cup (or homemade, page 132)

Butterscotch extract, 1 teaspoon

Chicken bone broth, 2⅓ cups (or homemade, page 132)

Chicken or beef bone broth, 2 cups (or homemade, page 132)

Chili powder, 1 teaspoon

Chocolate-flavored whey protein, 0.7 ounce (¼ cup) (or egg white protein if not egg-sensitive)

Cocoa powder, unsweetened, 3 ounces (1 cup + 1 tablespoon)

Coconut aminos or wheat-free tamari, 4½ ounces (½ cup + 1 tablespoon)

Coconut vinegar or apple cider vinegar, 6.5 ounces (¾ cup + 1 tablespoon)

Cornichons, 3 (1 tablespoon chopped)

Cream of tartar, ½ teaspoon

Dried onion flakes, ⅛ teaspoon

Egg white protein, unflavored, 3 ounces (¼ cup) (or whey protein if not dairy-sensitive)

Espresso powder, 1 teaspoon

Fenugreek powder, 1 teaspoon

Fish sauce, 2 ounces (¼ cup)

Grass-fed gelatin, powdered, 1½ tablespoons

Ground cardamom, ½ teaspoon

Ground coriander, ½ teaspoon

Maple extract, 1 tablespoon + 1 teaspoon

Orange extract, 1 tablespoon

Smoked paprika, 2 tablespoons

Strawberry extract, 1 teaspoon

Strawberry or hibiscus tea, 1 bag (¼ cup brewed)

Swerve natural sweetener or equivalent liquid or powdered sweetener, 2 (16-ounce) packages (3½ cups) (see page 37 for equivalents)

Swerve natural sweetener or equivalent powdered erythritol or monk fruit, 1 (16-ounce) package (2 cups) (see page 37 for equivalents)

Turmeric powder, 1 tablespoon + 1 teaspoon

Vanilla extract, 1 tablespoon + 2 teaspoons (or 5 vanilla beans, about 6 inches long)

Whole-grain mustard, 3½ tablespoons

Condiments, Sauces & Spice Blends

Caesar dressing, unsweetened, with no soybean oil, 1 bottle (½ cup) (or homemade, page 116)

Cilantro Lime Sauce (page 115), 3 cups

Dairy-Free Ranch Dressing (page 118), ¾ cup

Herb Aioli made with mint (page 114), ½ cup

Mayonnaise, ¼ cup + 2 tablespoons (or homemade, page 112)

Olive Salsa (page 135), ½ scant cup

Simple Chimichurri Sauce (page 130), 2 tablespoons

Taco Salad Dressing (page 121), ½ cup

Taco Seasoning (page 110), ¼ cup + 2 teaspoons

Canned/Jarred Goods

Capers, 1 (8-ounce) jar (1 tablespoon)

Diced tomatoes, 1 (14½-ounce) can

Salsa, 1 (8-ounce) jar (½ cup)

Sliced black olives, 1 (2.25-ounce) can (½ cup)

Tomato paste, 2 (6-ounce) jars (1 [6-ounce] jar + 3 tablespoons)

Tomato sauce, 1 (20-ounce) jar (2¼ cups)

Tuna, 2 (3.75-ounce) cans

Optional Add-Ins

Grass-fed gelatin, powdered, 1 tablespoon (for Orange Cream Shake)

L-glutamine powder, 1 tablespoon (for Orange Cream Shake)

Pure aloe vera juice, 1 tablespoon (for Orange Cream Shake)

Stur orange-mango-flavored liquid water enhancer, 1 teaspoon (for Grand Marnier Fat Bombs)

Yacón syrup, 1 tablespoon (for Dairy-Free Milk Chocolate Protein Bars)

Looking for organic keto spices? Maria's signature spice blends are available for purchase here: http://keto-adapted.com/keto-spices/

30-Day
MAINTENANCE AND HEALING MEAL PLAN

	BREAKFAST	SNACK/DESSERT	SIDE	LUNCH	DINNER
1 SUNDAY	2 eggs any way, 2 strips bacon	Frozen Orange Cream Bites — 330	Refrigerator Pickles — 318	South of the Border Salad* — 223	Slow Cooker Pork Ragu over Paleo Polenta — 291
2 MONDAY	Dairy-Free Chocolate Shake — 145	Orange Cream Push Pops — 337	Cheesy Grits — 302	Slow Cooker Beef Barbacoa Wraps — 210	Upside-Down Pizza — 264
3 TUESDAY	Cinnamon Roll Minute Muffins — 152	Frozen Orange Cream Bites — LEFTOVER	Wedge Salad* — 225	Broccoli Carbonara — 286	Schwein-shaxen — 294
4 WEDNESDAY	Dairy-Free Chocolate Shake — LEFTOVER	Orange Cream Push Pops — LEFTOVER	Refrigerator Pickles — LEFTOVER	Slow Cooker Beef Barbacoa Wraps — LEFTOVER	Slow Cooker Pork Ragu over Paleo Polenta — LEFTOVER
5 THURSDAY	Cinnamon Roll Minute Muffins — LEFTOVER	Egg-Free Ice Cream — 348	Pizza Sticks — 304	Broccoli Carbonara — LEFTOVER	Goat Cheese Panna Cotta with Crispy Prosciutto and Fried Basil — 296
6 FRIDAY	Dairy-Free Chocolate Shake — LEFTOVER	Frozen Orange Cream Bites — LEFTOVER	Wedge Salad* — LEFTOVER	South of the Border Salad* — LEFTOVER	Masala Mussels — 238
7 SATURDAY	Cinnamon Roll Minute Muffins — LEFTOVER	Orange Cream Push Pops — LEFTOVER	Refrigerator Pickles — LEFTOVER	Slow Cooker Beef Barbacoa Wraps — LEFTOVER	Upside-Down Pizza — LEFTOVER
8 SUNDAY	Dairy-Free Chocolate Shake — LEFTOVER	Crispy Raspberry Fat Bombs — 326	Wedge Salad* — LEFTOVER	Slow Cooker Beef Barbacoa Wraps — LEFTOVER	Broccoli "Noodle" Cheese Soup — 216
9 MONDAY	Cinnamon Roll Minute Muffins — LEFTOVER	Crispy Orange Fat Bombs — 326	Easy Kimchi — 316	South of the Border Salad* — LEFTOVER	Easy as Portobello Pizza Pie — 306
10 TUESDAY	2 eggs any way, 2 strips bacon	Crispy Raspberry Fat Bombs — LEFTOVER	Wedge Salad* — LEFTOVER	Double-Fried Chicken — 249	Upside-Down Pizza — LEFTOVER

*If you're inclined to try smoking your own foods at home, you can replace the
South of the Border Salad with Smoked Baby Back Ribs (page 366) and the Wedge
Salad with Pan-Fried Smoked Cauliflower Steaks (page 372).*

	BREAKFAST	SNACK/DESSERT	SIDE	LUNCH	DINNER
11 WEDNESDAY	Cinnamon Roll Minute Muffins LEFTOVER	Crispy Orange Fat Bombs LEFTOVER	Pizza Sticks LEFTOVER	Mexican Meatloaf Cupcakes 278	Skillet Lasagna 266
12 THURSDAY	Pizza Muffins 162	Orange Cream Push Pops LEFTOVER	Easy Kimchi LEFTOVER	South of the Border Salad* LEFTOVER	Open-Faced Hamburgers on "Buns" 268
13 FRIDAY	Cream of No-Wheat Cereal 157	Crispy Raspberry Fat Bombs LEFTOVER	Curry Braised Cucumbers 311	Mexican Meatloaf Cupcakes LEFTOVER	Skillet Lasagna LEFTOVER
14 SATURDAY	Pizza Muffins LEFTOVER	Egg-Free Ice Cream 348	Easy Kimchi LEFTOVER	Double-Fried Chicken LEFTOVER	King Crab Legs with Garlic Butter 240
15 SUNDAY	Pizza Muffins LEFTOVER	Crispy Raspberry Fat Bombs LEFTOVER	Easy Kimchi LEFTOVER	Chicken Alfredo 246	Easy Tomato Soup with Grilled Cheese 218
16 MONDAY	2 eggs any way, 2 strips bacon	Gummy Bears 352	Cucumber Salad 224	Cheesy Fried Ravioli 176	Skillet Lasagna LEFTOVER
17 TUESDAY	Breakfast Burritos 169	Egg-Free Ice Cream LEFTOVER	Caramelized Endive 313	Double-Fried Chicken LEFTOVER	Sardine Salad Wraps 206
18 WEDNESDAY	Eggs in Purgatory 148	Gummy Bears LEFTOVER	Pizza Sticks LEFTOVER	Chicken Alfredo LEFTOVER	Open-Faced Hamburgers on "Buns" LEFTOVER
19 THURSDAY	Breakfast Burritos LEFTOVER	Egg-Free Ice Cream LEFTOVER	Cucumber Salad LEFTOVER	Cheesy Fried Ravioli LEFTOVER	Skillet Lasagna LEFTOVER
20 FRIDAY	Eggs in Purgatory LEFTOVER	Gummy Bears LEFTOVER	Caramelized Endive LEFTOVER	Chicken Alfredo LEFTOVER	Open-Faced Hamburgers on "Buns" LEFTOVER

	BREAKFAST	SNACK/DESSERT	SIDE	LUNCH	DINNER
21 SATURDAY	Breakfast Burritos LEFTOVER	Flourless Fudgy Brownies 354	Curry Braised Cucumbers 311	Cheesy Fried Ravioli LEFTOVER	Sardine Salad Wraps LEFTOVER
22 SUNDAY	Taco Breakfast Bake 164	Savory Pizza Gelato 347	Caramelized Endive LEFTOVER	Chicken Alfredo LEFTOVER	Fish Sticks 236
23 MONDAY	Breakfast Burritos LEFTOVER	Flourless Fudgy Brownies LEFTOVER	Paleo Polenta 320	Cheesy Fried Ravioli LEFTOVER	Grilled Chicken with White BBQ Sauce 248
24 TUESDAY	2 eggs any way, 2 strips bacon	Savory Pizza Gelato LEFTOVER	Caramelized Endive LEFTOVER	Grilled Lamb Chops with Mint Aioli 282	Fish Tacos 230
25 WEDNESDAY	Strawberry Cheesecake Protein Bars 156	Deconstructed Crème Brûlée 324	Pizza Sticks 304	Easy Corned Beef "Hash" 263	Grilled Chicken with White BBQ Sauce LEFTOVER
26 THURSDAY	Taco Breakfast Bake LEFTOVER	Flourless Fudgy Brownies LEFTOVER	Paleo Polenta LEFTOVER	Grilled Lamb Chops with Mint Aioli LEFTOVER	Fish Tacos LEFTOVER
27 FRIDAY	Strawberry Cheesecake Protein Bars LEFTOVER	Deconstructed Crème Brûlée LEFTOVER	Eggs Gribiche 193	Easy Corned Beef "Hash" LEFTOVER	Grilled Chicken with White BBQ Sauce LEFTOVER
28 SATURDAY	Taco Breakfast Bake LEFTOVER	Savory Pizza Gelato LEFTOVER	Bordelaise Mushrooms 310	Slow Cooker Chicken Fajitas 244	Fish Tacos LEFTOVER
29 SUNDAY	Strawberry Cheesecake Protein Bars LEFTOVER	Deconstructed Crème Brûlée LEFTOVER	Paleo Polenta LEFTOVER	Easy Corned Beef "Hash" LEFTOVER	Grilled Chicken with White BBQ Sauce LEFTOVER
30 MONDAY	2 eggs any way, 2 strips bacon	Flourless Fudgy Brownies	Eggs Gribiche LEFTOVER	Slow Cooker Chicken Fajitas LEFTOVER	Fish Tacos LEFTOVER

30-Day Dairy-Free
MAINTENANCE AND HEALING MEAL PLAN

DAIRY-FREE

	BREAKFAST	SNACK/DESSERT	SIDE	LUNCH	DINNER
1 SUNDAY	2 eggs any way, 2 strips bacon	Grand Marnier Fat Bombs — 325	Refrigerator Pickles — 318	Taco Bar Night — 270	Slow Cooker Pork Ragu over Paleo Polenta — 291
2 MONDAY	Dairy-Free Chocolate Shake — 145	Coffee Ice Cream — 343	Mushroom Ragu — 300	Slow Cooker Laotian Chicken and Herbs — 250	20-Minute Ground Lamb Casserole — 280
3 TUESDAY	Cinnamon Roll Minute Muffins — 152	Grand Marnier Fat Bombs — LEFTOVER	Wedge Salad* — 225	Taco Bar Night — LEFTOVER	Schwein-shaxen — 294
4 WEDNESDAY	Dairy-Free Chocolate Shake — LEFTOVER	Coffee Ice Cream — LEFTOVER	Refrigerator Pickles — LEFTOVER	Slow Cooker Laotian Chicken and Herbs — LEFTOVER	Slow Cooker Pork Ragu over Paleo Polenta — LEFTOVER
5 THURSDAY	Cinnamon Roll Minute Muffins — LEFTOVER	French Silk Mousse — 351	Mushroom Ragu — LEFTOVER	Taco Bar Night — LEFTOVER	Sweet-n-Sour Country-Style Ribs over Zoodles — 290
6 FRIDAY	Dairy-Free Chocolate Shake — LEFTOVER	Grand Marnier Fat Bombs — LEFTOVER	Wedge Salad^ — LEFTOVER	South of the Border Salad* — 223	Masala Mussels — 238
7 SATURDAY	Cinnamon Roll Minute Muffins — LEFTOVER	Coffee Ice Cream — LEFTOVER	Refrigerator Pickles — LEFTOVER	Taco Bar Night — LEFTOVER	20-Minute Ground Lamb Casserole — LEFTOVER
8 SUNDAY	Dairy-Free Chocolate Shake — LEFTOVER	Crispy Raspberry Fat Bombs — 326	Wedge Salad* — LEFTOVER	South of the Border Salad* — LEFTOVER	Brats with Simple Coleslaw — 288
9 MONDAY	Cinnamon Roll Minute Muffins — LEFTOVER	Grand Marnier Fat Bombs — LEFTOVER	Easy Kimchi — 316	Crab-Stuffed Avocado with Lime — 234	Sweet-n-Sour Country-Style Ribs over Zoodles — LEFTOVER
10 TUESDAY	2 eggs any way, 2 strips bacon	Crispy Raspberry Fat Bombs — LEFTOVER	Wedge Salad* — LEFTOVER	Deconstructed BLT with Pork Belly — 292	20-Minute Ground Lamb Casserole — LEFTOVER

quick & easy *quick & easy* KETOGENIC COOKING **101**

If you're inclined to try smoking your own foods at home, you can replace the South of the Border Salad with Smoked Baby Back Ribs (page 366) and the Wedge Salad with Pan-Fried Smoked Cauliflower Steaks (page 372).

	BREAKFAST	SNACK/DESSERT	SIDE	LUNCH	DINNER
WEDNESDAY 11	Cinnamon Roll Minute Muffins LEFTOVER	French Silk Mousse 351	Curry Braised Cucumbers 311	Crab-Stuffed Avocado with Lime LEFTOVER	Sweet-n-Sour Country-Style Ribs over Zoodles LEFTOVER
THURSDAY 12	Spring Popovers 146	Coffee Ice Cream LEFTOVER	Easy Kimchi LEFTOVER	South of the Border Salad* LEFTOVER	Open-Faced Hamburgers on "Buns" 268
FRIDAY 13	Minute English Muffin made with coconut oil 150	Crispy Raspberry Fat Bombs LEFTOVER	Curry Braised Cucumbers LEFTOVER	Simple Salade Niçoise 220	20-Minute Ground Lamb Casserole LEFTOVER
SATURDAY 14	Spring Popovers LEFTOVER	Chai Ice Cream 345	Easy Kimchi LEFTOVER	Double-Fried Chicken 249	King Crab Legs with Garlic Butter 240
SUNDAY 15	Spring Popovers LEFTOVER	Crispy Raspberry Fat Bombs LEFTOVER	Easy Kimchi LEFTOVER	Slow Cooker Laotian Chicken and Herbs LEFTOVER	Sweet-n-Sour Country-Style Ribs over Zoodles LEFTOVER
MONDAY 16	2 eggs any way, 2 strips bacon	Gummy Bears 352	Cucumber Salad 224	Simple Salade Niçoise LEFTOVER	Slow Cooker BBQ Chicken Wraps 207
TUESDAY 17	Spring Popovers LEFTOVER	Chai Ice Cream LEFTOVER	Caramelized Endive 313	Slow Cooker Laotian Chicken and Herbs LEFTOVER	Deconstructed BLT with Pork Belly 292
WEDNESDAY 18	Eggs in Purgatory 148	Gummy Bears LEFTOVER	Bordelaise Mushrooms 310	Simple Salade Niçoise LEFTOVER	Slow Cooker BBQ Chicken Wraps LEFTOVER
THURSDAY 19	Dairy-Free Milk Chocolate Protein Bars 154	Chai Ice Cream LEFTOVER	Cucumber Salad LEFTOVER	Double-Fried Chicken 249	Open-Faced Hamburgers on "Buns" LEFTOVER
FRIDAY 20	Eggs in Purgatory LEFTOVER	Gummy Bears LEFTOVER	Caramelized Endive LEFTOVER	Chicken "Noodle" Soup 222	Slow Cooker BBQ Chicken Wraps LEFTOVER

DAIRY-FREE

	BREAKFAST	SNACK/DESSERT	SIDE	LUNCH	DINNER
21 SATURDAY	Spring Popovers LEFTOVER	Flourless Fudgy Brownies 354	Curry Braised Cucumbers 311	Simple Salade Niçoise LEFTOVER	Deconstructed BLT with Pork Belly LEFTOVER
22 SUNDAY	Dairy-Free Milk Chocolate Protein Bars LEFTOVER	Savory Pizza Gelato 347	Caramelized Endive LEFTOVER	Chicken "Noodle" Soup 222	Arctic Char with Olive Salsa 232
23 MONDAY	Spring Popovers LEFTOVER	Flourless Fudgy Brownies 354	Eggs Gribiche 193	Chicken "Noodle" Soup LEFTOVER	Grilled Chicken with White BBQ Sauce 248
24 TUESDAY	2 eggs any way, 2 strips bacon	Savory Pizza Gelato 347	Caramelized Endive LEFTOVER	Chicken "Noodle" Soup LEFTOVER	Fish Tacos 230
25 WEDNESDAY	Dairy-Free Chocolate Shake 145	Chai Ice Cream LEFTOVER	Bordelaise Mushrooms LEFTOVER	Crab-Stuffed Avocado with Lime 234	Grilled Chicken with White BBQ Sauce LEFTOVER
26 THURSDAY	Dairy-Free Milk Chocolate Protein Bars LEFTOVER	Flourless Fudgy Brownies 354	Eggs Gribiche 193	Crab-Stuffed Avocado with Lime LEFTOVER	Fish Tacos LEFTOVER
27 FRIDAY	Dairy-Free Chocolate Shake 145	Chai Ice Cream LEFTOVER	Wedge Salad* 225	Slow Cooker "Butter" Chicken with Naan 252	Grilled Chicken with White BBQ Sauce LEFTOVER
28 SATURDAY	Dairy-Free Milk Chocolate Protein Bars LEFTOVER	Savory Pizza Gelato 347	Bordelaise Mushrooms LEFTOVER	Slow Cooker "Butter" Chicken with Naan LEFTOVER	Fish Tacos LEFTOVER
29 SUNDAY	Dairy-Free Chocolate Shake LEFTOVER	Chai Ice Cream LEFTOVER	Eggs Gribiche LEFTOVER	Brats with Simple Coleslaw 288	Grilled Chicken with White BBQ Sauce LEFTOVER
30 MONDAY	2 eggs any way, 2 strips bacon	Flourless Fudgy Brownies 354	Wedge Salad* 225	Slow Cooker "Butter" Chicken with Naan LEFTOVER	Fish Tacos LEFTOVER

PART 2

Easy
Ketogenic
Recipes

Basics

SAUCES, DIPS, DRESSINGS, AND MORE

I've always adored sauces on my foods. A simple sauce can take a dish to another level. I love the creamy mouthfeel and flavors a sauce can give to even a boring piece of chicken. Sauces rich in fat also kick up the level of keto for all foods. Something that is too low in fat can be made ketogenic with the right sauce.

CHAPTER 5

Rib RUB

EGG-FREE NUT-FREE DAIRY-FREE VEGE-TARIAN

Prep Time: 4 minutes

Yield: ¾ cup (1½ tablespoons per serving)

¼ cup paprika

1 tablespoon Swerve confectioners'-style sweetener or equivalent amount of powdered erythritol or monk fruit (see page 37)

1 tablespoon fine sea salt

1 tablespoon fresh ground black pepper

1 tablespoon onion powder

1½ teaspoons celery salt

1½ teaspoons cayenne pepper

1½ teaspoons garlic powder

1½ teaspoons dry mustard

½ teaspoon ground cumin

Use to season ribs or other meat.

Place all the ingredients in a jar and shake until well combined. Store in an airtight container in the pantry for up to 2 months.

L — M — H
KETO

NUTRITIONAL INFO (per serving)				
calories	fat	protein	carbs	fiber
20	0.7g	0.9g	3g	1.4g
	20%	30%	50%	

Seasoned SALT

EGG-FREE · NUT-FREE · DAIRY-FREE · VEGETARIAN

Prep Time: 3 minutes

Yield: ¼ cup plus 2 tablespoons (¾ teaspoon per serving)

¼ cup fine sea salt

1 tablespoon plus 1 teaspoon Swerve confectioners'-style sweetener or equivalent amount of powdered erythritol or monk fruit (see page 37)

1 teaspoon paprika

1 teaspoon chili powder

½ teaspoon turmeric powder

½ teaspoon onion powder

½ teaspoon garlic powder

I love going to spice shops to gather organic dried spices to make my own mixes at home. Of all the blends I make, this is the one I use most frequently. If you like this seasoned salt, I suggest making a quadruple batch to keep in your pantry for easy additions to your favorite recipes.

Place all the ingredients in a jar and shake until well combined. Store in an airtight container in the pantry for up to 3 months.

KETO (L M H)

NUTRITIONAL INFO (per serving)				
calories	fat	protein	carbs	fiber
1	0g	(trace)	0.15g	0g
	0%	15%	85%	

Taco SEASONING

EGG-FREE NUT-FREE DAIRY-FREE VEGE-TARIAN

Prep Time: 4 minutes

Yield: ⅔ cup (1¼ heaping teaspoons per serving)

¼ cup chili powder

1½ tablespoons ground cumin

1 tablespoon fine sea salt

1 tablespoon fresh ground black pepper

1 tablespoon Swerve confectioners'-style sweetener or equivalent amount of powdered erythritol or monk fruit (see page 37) (optional)2 teaspoons paprika

1 teaspoon red pepper flakes

1 teaspoon garlic powder

1 teaspoon onion powder

1 teaspoon dried ground oregano

1 teaspoon ground coriander

Many store-bought taco seasonings contain sugar, artificial sweeteners (such as maltodextrin), or both. If you'd like to mimic the slightly sweet profile of store-bought mixes, add the optional sweetener.

Place all the ingredients in a jar and shake until well combined. Store in an airtight container in the pantry for up to 2 months.

TIP:

This spice mix is used in several recipes in this book. I recommend that you make a triple batch to keep in the pantry for easy additions to meals.

KETO

NUTRITIONAL INFO (per serving)				
calories	fat	protein	carbs	fiber
8	0.3g	0.3g	1.3g	0.7g
	18%	18%	64%	

SPICE MIX

EGG-FREE NUT-FREE DAIRY-FREE (OPTION) VEGE-TARIAN

Prep Time: 3 minutes

Yield: ½ cup (2 tablespoons per serving)

¼ cup grated Parmesan cheese (about 1 ounce) (omit for dairy-free; see Note)

3 tablespoons garlic powder

1 tablespoon onion powder

1 tablespoon dried oregano leaves

This is one of my favorite spice mixes. It reminds me of the Pizza Hut breadsticks I ate as a kid. I use it whenever I want a hit of classic pizza flavor, such as in scrambled eggs, Pizza Muffins (page 162), or sautéed chicken thighs.

Place all the ingredients in a jar and shake until well combined. Store in an airtight jar in the fridge for up to 2 weeks.

NOTE:

If you do not tolerate dairy, replace the Parmesan cheese with 2 teaspoons fine sea salt and 2 teaspoons nutritional yeast. This substitution will change the yield to ¼ cup plus 2 tablespoons. Store the spice mix in the pantry in an airtight jar for up to 1 month.

M
L H
KETO

NUTRITIONAL INFO (per serving)				
calories	fat	protein	carbs	fiber
60	2.4g	4.4g	6.7g	1.2g
	33%	26%	41%	

Fat-Burning
IMMERSION BLENDER MAYO

NUT-FREE   DAIRY-FREE   VEGE-TARIAN

Prep Time: *5 minutes*

Yield: *1½ cups (about 1 tablespoon per serving)*

2 large egg yolks

2 teaspoons lemon juice

1 cup MCT oil or other neutral-flavored oil, such as macadamia nut or avocado oil

1 tablespoon Dijon mustard

½ teaspoon fine sea salt

Special Equipment:
Immersion blender

Homemade mayonnaise has a milder and more neutral flavor than store-bought mayo—plus, it's so much healthier! You can personalize this basic mayo to your taste by adding finely chopped or roasted garlic or your favorite herb.

Place the ingredients in the order listed in a wide-mouth, pint-sized mason jar. Place the immersion blender at the bottom of the jar. Turn the blender on and very slowly move the blender to the top. Be patient! It should take you about a minute to reach the top. Moving the blender slowly is key to getting the mayonnaise to emulsify. Voilà! Simple mayo! Store in the fridge for up to 5 days.

VARIATION: COPYCAT BACONNAISE.

Replace the MCT oil with melted, but not hot, bacon fat. Taste and add salt if needed (it may be salty enough from the bacon fat).

KETO (L M H)

NUTRITIONAL INFO (per serving)				
calories	fat	protein	carbs	fiber
92	10g	0.3g	0.1g	0g
	98%	1.5%	0.4%	

Spicy
MAYO

		OPTION
NUT-FREE	DAIRY-FREE	VEGE-TARIAN

Prep Time: 4 minutes

Yield: ¾ cup (1½ tablespoons per serving)

½ cup mayonnaise, store-bought or homemade (page 112)

2 tablespoons Sriracha, store-bought or homemade (page 124)

1 tablespoon chicken or beef bone broth, store-bought or homemade (page 132) (or vegetable broth for vegetarian)

One of our favorite ways to make an easy meal is to go to the local fish shop and purchase the freshest sushi-grade tuna brought in that day and serve it with this spicy mayo.

Place the mayo, Sriracha, and broth in a small bowl and stir well to combine. Store in an airtight container in the fridge for up to 2 weeks.

KETO

NUTRITIONAL INFO (per serving)				
calories	fat	protein	carbs	fiber
103	11.2g	0.2g	0.3g	0g
	98%	1%	1%	

Herb
AIOLI

NUT-FREE DAIRY-FREE VEGE-TARIAN

Prep Time: 5 minutes

Yield: 1½ cups (2 tablespoons per serving)

1 cup mayonnaise, store-bought or homemade (page 112)

2 tablespoons finely chopped fresh herb(s) of choice

1 tablespoon coconut vinegar or apple cider vinegar

1 teaspoon finely chopped garlic, or cloves from ½ head roasted garlic (page 134)

½ teaspoon fine sea salt

This sauce is so amazing and flexible. Serving it with chicken? Use fresh parsley or tarragon. Having it with lamb chops? Use mint. Or, if you are like me and do not like mint with any type of meat, use your favorite herb.

In a small bowl, combine all the ingredients. Stir until well combined. Store in an airtight container in the fridge for up to 4 days.

TIP:

This aioli can be made up to 4 days ahead.

L M H
KETO

NUTRITIONAL INFO (per serving)				
calories	fat	protein	carbs	fiber
121	13.3g	0g	0.2g	0g
	99%	0%	1%	

Cilantro Lime
SAUCE

OPTION

EGG-FREE · NUT-FREE · DAIRY-FREE · VEGE-TARIAN

Prep Time: 8 minutes

Yield: 1½ cups (about 2 tablespoons per serving)

1 jalapeño, seeded and coarsely chopped

1 cup mayonnaise, store-bought or homemade (page 112) (or sour cream for egg-free, if not dairy-sensitive)

¼ cup finely chopped fresh cilantro

¼ cup lime juice

2 tablespoons grated fresh ginger

2 tablespoons chopped fresh chives

1 teaspoon finely chopped garlic

½ teaspoon fine sea salt

Place all the ingredients in a food processor and puree until very smooth. Store in an airtight container in the refrigerator for up to 1 week. Shake well before using.

KETO

NUTRITIONAL INFO (per serving)				
calories	fat	protein	carbs	fiber
124	13.4g	0.1g	0.8g	0g
	97%	1%	3%	

Caesar DRESSING

NUT-FREE   DAIRY-FREE   OPTION VEGE-TARIAN

Prep Time: 8 minutes

Yield: ¾ cup (about 2 tablespoons per serving)

1 tablespoon Dijon mustard

1 tablespoon coconut vinegar or apple cider vinegar

1 teaspoon finely chopped garlic, or cloves from ½ head roasted garlic (page 134)

¼ teaspoon fine sea salt, plus more if needed

¼ teaspoon fresh ground black pepper, plus more if needed

½ cup MCT oil or extra-virgin olive oil

2 tablespoons mayonnaise, store-bought or homemade (page 112)

1 teaspoon lemon juice

1 (2-ounce) can anchovies, finely chopped (optional; omit for vegetarian)

1. Place the mustard, vinegar, garlic, salt, and pepper in a blender and combine until smooth and thick. With the blender running on low speed, slowly add the MCT oil and mayo. Scrape the sides as needed. Add the lemon juice and combine well.

2. If desired, add the anchovies and puree until smooth. Adding anchovies will create a richer and saltier dressing. Taste and add up to ¾ teaspoon more salt and pepper, if needed, adding them ¼ teaspoon at a time and blending after each addition.

3. Store in an airtight container in the fridge for up to 4 days.

KETO

NUTRITIONAL INFO (per serving)				
calories	fat	protein	carbs	fiber
222	22.8g	2.3g	0.4g	0g
	94%	4%	1%	

Green Goddess
DRESSING

Prep Time: 8 minutes

Yield: 2 cups (2 tablespoons per serving)

1½ cups mayonnaise, store-bought or homemade (page 112)

2 tablespoons coconut vinegar, apple cider vinegar, or tarragon vinegar

2 tablespoons finely chopped fresh chives and/or scallions

1 tablespoon lemon juice

2 teaspoons anchovy paste (about 1 anchovy) or 1 teaspoon coarse sea salt

⅛ teaspoon fresh ground black pepper

1 small clove garlic, smashed with the side of a knife and finely chopped

2 to 4 tablespoons chicken bone broth, store-bought or homemade (page 132) (or vegetable broth for vegetarian), to thin the dressing

This is a fantastic dressing to use on greens as well as on Grilled Radicchio with Sweet-and-Sour Hot Bacon Dressing (page 312) (it goes great with the bacon dressing) and Primal Sliders (page 191).

Place all the ingredients except the broth in a blender or large bowl and combine until smooth. Add just enough broth to thin to the desired consistency. Store in an airtight container in the refrigerator for up to 1 week. Shake well before using.

KETO

NUTRITIONAL INFO (per serving)				
calories	fat	protein	carbs	fiber
145	21.4g	0.1g	0.1g	0g
	99%	0.5%	0.5%	

Dairy-Free Ranch
DRESSING

Prep Time: 3 minutes, plus 2 hours to chill

Yield: 1¾ cups (2½ scant tablespoons per serving)

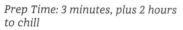

1 cup mayonnaise, store-bought or homemade (page 112)

¾ cup chicken or beef bone broth, store-bought or homemade (page 132) (or vegetable broth for vegetarian)

½ teaspoon dried chives

½ teaspoon dried parsley

½ teaspoon dried dill weed

¼ teaspoon garlic powder

¼ teaspoon onion powder

⅛ teaspoon fine sea salt

⅛ teaspoon fresh ground black pepper

Place all the ingredients a 16-ounce (or larger) jar and shake vigorously until well combined. Cover and refrigerate for 2 hours before serving (it will thicken up as it rests). Store in the fridge for up to 5 days.

KETO

NUTRITIONAL INFO (per serving)				
calories	fat	protein	carbs	fiber
123	13.4g	0.3g	0.2g	0g
	98%	1%	1%	

Blue Cheese DRESSING

EGG-FREE NUT-FREE VEGE-TARIAN (OPTION)

Prep Time: 2 minutes, plus 2 hours to chill

Yield: 2¼ cups (3 tablespoons per serving)

1 (8-ounce) package cream cheese, softened

¾ cup chicken or beef bone broth, store-bought or homemade (page 132) (or vegetable broth for vegetarian)

½ cup crumbled blue cheese (about 3 ounces)

¼ teaspoon garlic powder

¼ teaspoon onion powder

⅛ teaspoon fine sea salt

⅛ teaspoon fresh ground black pepper

I love to use this dressing as a dip for BLT "Chips" (page 173).

1. Place the cream cheese and broth in a medium bowl and combine until smooth. Stir in the blue cheese, garlic powder, onion powder, salt, and pepper.

2. Cover and refrigerate for 2 hours before serving (it will thicken up as it rests). Store in the fridge for up to 5 days.

KETO — L M H

NUTRITIONAL INFO (per serving)				
calories	fat	protein	carbs	fiber
90	8.4g	3.2g	0.7g	0g
	84%	14%	2%	

Easy French DRESSING

EGG-FREE NUT-FREE DAIRY-FREE

Prep Time: 5 minutes, plus 2 hours to chill

Yield: 3 cups (4 tablespoons per serving)

1 cup MCT oil or other neutral-flavored oil, such as macadamia nut or avocado oil

1 cup tomato sauce

½ cup Swerve confectioners'-style sweetener or equivalent amount of liquid or powdered sweetener (see page 37)

¼ cup coconut vinegar or apple cider vinegar

¼ cup chicken or beef bone broth, store-bought or homemade (page 132)

1 teaspoon fish sauce

1 teaspoon garlic powder

1 teaspoon fresh ground black pepper

¼ teaspoon fine sea salt

Place all the ingredients in a 24-ounce (or larger) jar and shake vigorously until well combined. Cover and refrigerate for 2 hours before serving to allow the flavors to meld. Store in the refrigerator for up to 5 days.

KETO

NUTRITIONAL INFO (per serving)				
calories	fat	protein	carbs	fiber
187	19.4g	0.5g	1.3g	0g
	94%	2%	3%	

Simple Taco
SALAD DRESSING

NUT-FREE DAIRY-FREE OPTION VEGE-TARIAN

Prep Time: 5 minutes

Yield: 2¼ cups (3 tablespoons per serving)

1 cup mayonnaise, store-bought or homemade (page 112)

1 cup chicken or beef bone broth, store-bought or homemade (page 132) (or vegetable broth for vegetarian)

2 tablespoons Taco Seasoning (page 110)

1 tablespoon chopped fresh chives

Place the mayonnaise in a 20-ounce (or larger) jar. Add the broth, taco seasoning, and chives and shake vigorously until well combined. Store in an airtight container in the refrigerator for up to 2 weeks.

NOTE:

If you prefer a thicker dressing, add more mayo; if you prefer a thinner dressing, add more broth.

KETO

NUTRITIONAL INFO (per serving)				
calories	fat	protein	carbs	fiber
123	13.3g	0.8g	0.1g	0g
	97%	3%	0%	

Creamy Tarragon
KETO SAUCE

Prep Time: 5 minutes

Yield: 1 cup (1½ scant tablespoons per serving)

¾ cup mayonnaise, store-bought or homemade (page 112)

2 tablespoons coconut vinegar or apple cider vinegar

1 tablespoon lemon juice

1 tablespoon finely chopped fresh tarragon

¼ teaspoon fine sea salt

⅛ teaspoon cayenne pepper

Use this sauce on meat, chicken, or fish, or use it to dress shredded cabbage for a tasty coleslaw that goes great with fish sticks (page 236).

Combine all the ingredients in a bowl and mix until smooth. Store in an airtight container in the refrigerator for up to 2 weeks.

KETO

NUTRITIONAL INFO (per serving)				
calories	fat	protein	carbs	fiber
94	10.3g	0.1g	0.2g	0g
	98%	1%	1%	

Keto
FRY SAUCE

NUT-FREE · DAIRY-FREE · VEGE-TARIAN

Prep Time: 5 minutes

Yield: ¼ cup plus 2 tablespoons (about 1 tablespoon per serving)

¼ cup mayonnaise, store-bought or homemade (page 112)

2 tablespoons Swerve confectioners'-style sweetener or equivalent amount of liquid or powdered sweetener (see page 37)

½ tablespoon tomato paste

1 teaspoon coconut vinegar or apple cider vinegar

½ teaspoon fresh ground black pepper

½ teaspoon Seasoned Salt (page 109)

Fry sauce is a regional dipping sauce typically composed of equal parts mayonnaise and ketchup. This keto recipe for fry sauce is sure to become a family favorite! We use it for dipping mushroom "fries" and chicken fingers and on grilled meats and veggies.

Combine all the ingredients in an 8-ounce (or larger) jar. Cover and shake vigorously. Store in an airtight container in the refrigerator for up to 2 weeks.

KETO

NUTRITIONAL INFO (per serving)				
calories	fat	protein	carbs	fiber
62	6.7g	0.1g	0.4g	0g
	97%	1%	2%	

Homemade
SRIRACHA

EGG-FREE · NUT-FREE · DAIRY-FREE · VEGE-TARIAN

Prep Time: 5 minutes, plus 8 hours to soak

Yield: 2¾ cups (1 teaspoon per serving)

½ pound red Fresno chiles or jalapeños, finely chopped

1 cup coconut vinegar or apple cider vinegar

¼ cup MCT oil or other neutral-flavored oil, such as macadamia nut or avocado oil

2 tablespoons Swerve confectioners'-style sweetener or equivalent amount of liquid or powdered sweetener (see page 37)

2 teaspoons finely chopped garlic, or cloves from 1 head roasted garlic (page 134)

1 teaspoon fine sea salt

I am a typical German girl who is not a fan of anything hot, but my sons spent their first few years in Ethiopia, so a taste for spicy food is ingrained in them. I have learned to embrace their love for hot food and keep this tasty and nutrient-dense sauce in my fridge to kick up my mild German recipes!

1. Combine all the ingredients in a large glass or stainless-steel bowl. Cover and let sit in the refrigerator overnight to soften the heat of the peppers.

2. Place the chile mixture in a blender and puree for 5 minutes, until you have a smooth, orange-red sauce. Run through a fine-mesh strainer and press out as much juice from the peppers as you can.

3. Discard the peppers and pour the strained liquid into a 24-ounce (or larger) jar. Store in the refrigerator for up to 2 weeks or in the freezer for up to one month.

KETO

NUTRITIONAL INFO (per serving)				
calories	fat	protein	carbs	fiber
5	0.5g	(trace)	0.1g	0g
	87%	3%	10%	

BBQ
SAUCE

EGG-FREE   NUT-FREE   DAIRY-FREE   OPTION VEGE-TARIAN

Prep Time: 4 minutes

Cook Time: 2 minutes

Yield: 2¾ cups (3½ tablespoons per serving)

6 ounces tomato paste

1½ cups chicken or beef bone broth, store-bought or homemade (page 132) (or vegetable broth for vegetarian)

⅓ cup Swerve confectioners'-style sweetener or equivalent amount of liquid or powdered sweetener (see page 37)

¼ cup coconut vinegar or apple cider vinegar

1 tablespoon yacón syrup

2 teaspoons lemon juice

¾ teaspoon liquid smoke

½ teaspoon fine sea salt

½ teaspoon garlic powder

⅛ teaspoon ground cumin

¼ teaspoon guar gum (optional)

Boxed broth will work for this recipe, but true bone broth will create a thicker sauce. Yacón syrup is an amazing keto sweetener that reminds me of a milder molasses, without the carbs.

1. Place all the ingredients except the optional guar gum in a microwave-safe bowl and combine well. Microwave for 2 minutes, stirring every 30 seconds.

2. If you prefer a thicker sauce, sift in the guar gum once the sauce is hot; it will thicken in a few minutes. Pour into a 24-ounce jar and refrigerate until ready to use. Store in the fridge for up to 5 days.

NOTE:

If you prefer to not use a microwave, place the sauce mixture in a small saucepan and bring to a boil over medium-high heat, then reduce the heat to low, sift in the guar gum, if desired, and simmer for 5 minutes. Remove from the heat and pour into a glass jar.

M
L   H
KETO

NUTRITIONAL INFO (per serving)				
calories	fat	protein	carbs	fiber
19	0.2g	1.2g	3.3g	0.6g
	8%	22%	70%	

quick & easy **KETOGENIC COOKING** 125

White BBQ SAUCE

NUT-FREE · DAIRY-FREE · VEGE-TARIAN OPTION

Prep Time: 5 minutes

Yield: 1⅓ cups (1¾ tablespoons per serving)

1 cup baconnaise or mayonnaise, store-bought or homemade (page 112)

¼ cup coconut vinegar or apple cider vinegar

1 tablespoon prepared yellow mustard

1 teaspoon fresh ground black pepper, plus more as needed

¼ teaspoon fine sea salt

⅛ teaspoon liquid smoke

Use this sauce on fried chicken, chicken wings, grilled meats, and veggies.

Combine all the ingredients in a bowl and mix until smooth. Taste the sauce and add more pepper if needed. Store in an airtight container in the fridge for up to 2 weeks.

KETO (L M H)

NUTRITIONAL INFO (per serving)				
calories	fat	protein	carbs	fiber
149	14g	0.5g	1g	0g
	93%	3%	4%	

Easy
KETCHUP

EGG-FREE · NUT-FREE · DAIRY-FREE · OPTION VEGE-TARIAN

Prep Time: 4 minutes

Yield: 2½ cups (2 tablespoons per serving)

2 scant cups tomato sauce

½ cup chicken or beef bone broth, store-bought or homemade (page 132) (or vegetable broth for vegetarian)

2 tablespoons Swerve confectioners'-style sweetener or equivalent amount of liquid or powdered sweetener (see page 37)

1 teaspoon onion powder

Place all the ingredients in a 24-ounce (or larger) jar and shake vigorously until well combined. Store in an airtight container in the refrigerator for up to 1 week.

KETO

NUTRITIONAL INFO (per serving)				
calories	fat	protein	carbs	fiber
24	1.3g	0.9g	2.1g	0g
	49%	15%	35%	

Alfredo SAUCE

EGG-FREE   NUT-FREE   OPTION VEGE-TARIAN

Prep Time: 5 minutes

Cook Time: 20 minutes

Yield: 1½ cups (about 6 tablespoons per serving)

½ cup (1 stick) unsalted butter

1 teaspoon finely chopped garlic, or cloves from 1 head roasted garlic (page 134)

½ cup grated Parmesan cheese (about 2 ounces)

2 ounces (¼ cup) cream cheese

⅓ cup chicken or beef bone broth, store-bought or homemade (page 132) (or vegetable broth for vegetarian)

Serve this sauce over zucchini noodles (page 308) or your choice of seafood.

1. Place the butter and garlic in a saucepan and cook until the butter is a light golden brown, stirring constantly to prevent the butter from burning.

2. Reduce the heat to low. If using roasted garlic, smash up the cloves in the butter. Stir in the Parmesan, cream cheese, and broth and simmer for at least 15 minutes (the flavors open up if it simmers longer).

3. Store in an airtight container in the fridge for up to 4 days.

M
L   H
KETO

NUTRITIONAL INFO (per serving)				
calories	fat	protein	carbs	fiber
302	31g	7.4g	0.6g	0g
	91%	8%	1%	

Minute
HOLLANDAISE

NUT-FREE · DAIRY-FREE OPTION · VEGE-TARIAN · VIDEO

Prep Time: 5 minutes

Cook Time: 1 minute

Yield: about ¾ cup (about 3 tablespoons per serving)

½ cup (1 stick) unsalted butter (or duck fat or lard for dairy-free)

2 large egg yolks

2 teaspoons lemon juice

⅛ teaspoon cayenne pepper

⅛ teaspoon fine sea salt

Pinch of fresh ground black pepper

VARIATION: BROWN BUTTER HOLLANDAISE

Follow the recipe as written, but in Step 1, heat the butter in the microwave until it froths and brown flecks appear, about 2 minutes. (Note: This variation does not have a dairy-free option. If using duck fat or lard, you will not get the "browned fat" effect that you can get with butter.)

I made this hollandaise while on vacation and in a hurry, and I accidentally browned the butter in the microwave. But it was a fortunate accident! You can make this with just heated butter or take it a step further and make brown butter for a Brown Butter Hollandaise (see Variation below). If you make a dairy-free version with duck fat or lard, you will not achieve the "browned fat" effect, with brown specks, that you can get with butter. Either way, though, it's delicious.

If you're a visual learner like me and would like to see how easy it is to make brown butter, check out the video on my site, MariaMindBodyHealth.com (type the word *video* in the search field).

1. Place the butter in a microwave-safe dish, cover with a paper towel, and microwave on high for 1 minute. You want the butter to be very hot.

2. Meanwhile, place the egg yolks and lemon juice in a heat-safe bowl and whisk until smooth. Once the butter is hot, very slowly whisk the hot butter into the yolks, drop by drop, until the mixture has thickened. Whisk constantly or the yolks will cook.

3. Season with the cayenne, salt, and pepper. Ta-da! Easy! Store in the fridge for up to 5 days.

KETO

NUTRITIONAL INFO (per serving)				
calories	fat	protein	carbs	fiber
231	25.3g	1.6g	0.6g	0g
	97%	2%	1%	

Simple
CHIMICHURRI SAUCE

EGG-FREE · NUT-FREE · DAIRY-FREE · VEGE-TARIAN

Prep Time: 5 minutes

Yield: 2 cups (about 1½ tablespoons per serving)

1 packed cup fresh flat-leaf parsley leaves

½ cup MCT oil or other neutral-flavored oil, such as macadamia nut or avocado oil

⅓ cup coconut vinegar or apple cider vinegar

¼ packed cup fresh cilantro leaves

1 tablespoon finely chopped garlic, or cloves from 1 large head roasted garlic (page 134)

¾ teaspoon crushed red pepper

¾ teaspoon fine sea salt

I like to serve this sauce with grilled meats and over baked Zoodles (page 308).

Place all the ingredients in a blender or food processor and puree until smooth. Store in an airtight container in the refrigerator for up to 2 weeks.

KETO (L M H)

NUTRITIONAL INFO (per serving)				
calories	fat	protein	carbs	fiber
51	5.3g	0.1g	0.3g	0g
	95%	1%	3%	

Homemade
ALMOND MILK

EGG-FREE   DAIRY-FREE   VEGE-TARIAN

Prep Time: 2 minutes, plus 8 hours to soak

Yield: 4 cups (½ cup per serving)

1½ cups raw almonds, soaked in water overnight

4 cups reverse-osmosis or filtered water

TIP:

Save the pulp after making almond milk to make homemade almond flour. Place the pulp on a rimmed baking sheet and dehydrate on your oven's lowest heat setting until the pulp is completely dry. Then place the dehydrated pulp in a high-powered blender and puree until you have a very fine powder. Use this powder as almond flour if you can tolerate nut flours.

This delicious, creamy milk is free of harmful ingredients and sweeteners.

1. Drain the soaked nuts, then place them in a food processor with the 4 cups of water. Puree until it has a smooth, somewhat thick texture, about the consistency of a smoothie.

2. Strain in a colander lined with cheesecloth or in a fine-mesh strainer to remove the almond pulp. Discard the pulp. Store the milk in an airtight container in the refrigerator for up to 1 week.

VARIATION: VANILLA-FLAVORED ALMOND MILK.

In Step 1, add 1 teaspoon vanilla extract or the seeds scraped from 1 vanilla bean (about 6 inches long) to the blender with the nuts and water. Then proceed with the recipe as written.

KETO

NUTRITIONAL INFO (per serving)				
calories	fat	protein	carbs	fiber
55	5g	1.2g	1.6g	1g
	81%	9%	10%	

Simple Slow Cooker
BONE BROTH

EGG-FREE · NUT-FREE · DAIRY-FREE · SLOW COOKER

Prep Time: 6 minutes

Cook Time: 1 to 3 days

Yield: 4 quarts (1 cup per serving)

4 quarts cold water (reverse-osmosis or filtered water is best)

4 large beef bones (about 4 pounds), leftover bones and skin from 1 pastured chicken (ideally the chicken feet, too), or 4 pounds fish bones and heads

1 medium onion, chopped

2 stalks celery, cut into ¼-inch slices

2 tablespoons coconut vinegar or apple cider vinegar

2 tablespoons fresh rosemary leaves or other herb of choice

2 teaspoons finely chopped garlic, or cloves from 1 head roasted garlic (page 134)

2 teaspoons fine sea salt

1 teaspoon fresh or dried thyme leaves

In a pinch, it's not unheard-of to find me opening up a box of Trader Joe's organic beef broth instead of making my own broth. But when I'm not overwhelmed with work, I slow down and prepare a lot of things that I know I should be making from scratch, like bone broth. There is something so special about homemade broth.

When my boys were babies, you could find slow cooker bone broth simmering away in my kitchen just about every day. They drank this broth as one of their first foods.

The longer you cook this broth, the thicker it will get. If you roast the beef bones before making the broth, they will create a darker and more flavorful broth (see Note below).

1. Place all the ingredients in a 6-quart slow cooker, cover, and set the heat to high. After 1 hour, turn the heat to low. Simmer for a minimum of 1 day or up to 3 days. The longer it cooks, the more nutrients and minerals will be extracted from the bones.

2. When the broth is done, pour it through a strainer and discard the solids.

3. The broth will keep in the fridge for about 5 days or in the freezer for several months.

TIP:

Make a double batch in two slow cookers and freeze in large freezer-safe mason jars to have on hand as needed.

NOTE:

Roast large beef bones on a rimmed sheet pan at 375°F for 50 to 60 minutes, and smaller bones for 30 to 40 minutes.

KETO

NUTRITIONAL INFO (per serving)				
calories	fat	protein	carbs	fiber
20	4g	1.5g	1.7g	0g
	60%	19%	21%	

ROASTED GARLIC

Slow Cooker

EGG-
FREE | NUT-
FREE | DAIRY-
FREE | VEGE-
TARIAN | SLOW
COOKER

Prep Time: 5 minutes

Cook Time: 4 to 5 hours

Yield: 10 heads (about 1 clove per serving)

10 heads garlic

2 tablespoons MCT oil, melted lard, or melted coconut oil

TIP:

For easy additions to recipes, I always make extra heads of roasted garlic and store them in an airtight container in my freezer, where they'll keep for up to 2 months. When I want to use some, I defrost a head and squeeze the garlic from the bulb as needed.

1. Slice ⅛ inch off the top of each head of garlic to expose the cloves.

2. Place each garlic bulb in a 4-inch square piece of foil lined with unbleached parchment paper. Drizzle the MCT oil into the bulbs and wrap up tightly. Place each wrapped bulb in a 2-quart slow cooker, cover, and cook on low for 4 to 5 hours.

3. Unwrap one of the bulbs to test for doneness. Squeeze the bulb. If garlic squirts out and is soft to the touch, it's done; if not, wrap it back up and cook the bulbs for another hour.

4. Store whole heads of roasted garlic in an airtight container in the fridge for up to 5 days or in the freezer for up to 2 months (see Tip).

L M H
KETO

NUTRITIONAL INFO (per serving)				
calories	fat	protein	carbs	fiber
30	1.9g	0.6g	3.3g	(trace)
	53%	6%	41%	

Olive SALSA

EGG-FREE · NUT-FREE · DAIRY-FREE · VEGE-TARIAN

Prep Time: 5 minutes

Yield: 6 cups (½ cup per serving)

2 cups pitted green olives, chopped

2 cups pitted purple or black Greek olives, chopped

1 large tomato, chopped

½ cup diced red onions

½ cup capers, rinsed

2 cloves garlic, finely chopped

¼ cup MCT oil or extra-virgin olive oil

2 tablespoons coconut vinegar or apple cider vinegar

1 teaspoon finely chopped fresh basil, or ¼ teaspoon dried basil

½ teaspoon dried oregano leaves

⅛ teaspoon dried rosemary leaves

This salsa tastes great on grilled fish and chicken!

Place the olives, tomato, onions, capers, and garlic in a medium-sized bowl. Add the oil, vinegar, and herbs to the bowl and stir with a spoon until well combined. Store in an airtight container in the refrigerator for up to 1 week.

TIP:

To save time, make sure to purchase pitted olives.

KETO

NUTRITIONAL INFO (per serving)				
calories	fat	protein	carbs	fiber
116	11.1g	0.5g	3.8g	1g
	86%	2%	13%	

GUACAMOLE

EGG-FREE NUT-FREE DAIRY-FREE VEGE-TARIAN

Prep Time: 4 minutes

Yield: about 3 cups (½ cup per serving)

3 avocados, peeled, halved, and pitted

½ cup diced onions

2 cloves garlic, crushed to a paste, or cloves from ½ head roasted garlic (page 134), smashed to a paste

2 plum tomatoes, diced

3 tablespoons lime juice, plus 1 tablespoon more if desired

3 tablespoons chopped fresh cilantro leaves

1 teaspoon fine sea salt

½ teaspoon ground cumin

Guacamole is one of my favorite foods. I love to serve it with Zucchini Chips (page 194), or as a topping or flavorful side dish for any number of foods. But I have to admit that it becomes unappealing when it turns brown. There is a solution, though! You simply need to use the pit and keep the guacamole sealed as airtight as possible. Place the pit in the middle of your bowl of guacamole, then cover the guacamole with large chunks of onion. The onion releases gases to inhibit the oxidation of polyphenol, which is what causes the fruit to turn brown. Cover tightly with plastic wrap, pressing the wrap directly onto the surface of the onions, and refrigerate until ready to serve. Just before serving, remove the chunks of onion.

You can use this same technique with unused avocado. If you use only half of an avocado, keep the pit in the other half and place it in a resealable bag. Slice an onion into chunks and place the onion in the bag with the avocado half. Then get as much air out of the bag as possible, seal it, and place it in the fridge.

1. Place the avocados in a large bowl and mash to the desired consistency.

2. Add the onions, garlic, tomatoes, lime juice, cilantro, salt, and cumin. Stir until well combined. Taste and add up to 1 tablespoon more lime juice if you like.

3. Cover tightly and refrigerate for 1 hour for the best flavor, or serve immediately.

M
L   H
KETO

NUTRITIONAL INFO (per serving)				
calories	fat	protein	carbs	fiber
220	20g	2.6g	11g	7.4g
	78%	4%	18%	

Dairy-Free Minute
"CREAM CHEESE" SPREAD

NUT-FREE • DAIRY-FREE • VEGE-TARIAN (OPTION)

Prep Time: 5 minutes, plus 3 hours to set

Cook Time: 1 minute

Yield: about ¾ cup (about 3 tablespoons per serving)

½ cup duck fat or lard (or ghee or butter if not dairy-sensitive and for vegetarian)

2 large egg yolks

2 teaspoons lemon juice

1 tablespoon nutritional yeast

⅛ teaspoon fine sea salt

Pinch of fresh ground black pepper

This homemade dairy-free cream cheese is a great option to use in place of regular cream cheese, but only in recipes that don't require cooking. I use it to make dairy-free Mini Pastrami Roll-Ups (page 199) and spread it on keto-friendly bagels. (There's a recipe for Keto Bagels and Lox in my previous book, *The Ketogenic Cookbook*.)

1. Heat the fat in a microwave-safe dish in the microwave on high for 1 minute, or until almost boiling.

2. Meanwhile, place the egg yolks and lemon juice in a heatproof bowl and whisk together until smooth.

3. Once the fat is hot, very slowly whisk it into the yolks, drop by drop, until the mixture has thickened. Whisk constantly or the yolks will cook.

4. Season with the nutritional yeast, salt, and pepper. Place in the refrigerator to cool until set, at least 3 hours or overnight. Store in the fridge for up to 5 days.

L — M — H
KETO

NUTRITIONAL INFO (per serving)				
calories	fat	protein	carbs	fiber
268	28.1g	2.5g	1.5g	0.7g
	94%	4%	2%	

Orange MARMALADE

EGG-FREE NUT-FREE DAIRY-FREE

Prep Time: 2 minutes, plus 2 hours to cool and set

Cook Time: 3 minutes

Yield: 1½ cups (2 tablespoons per serving)

1 orange tea bag

2 teaspoons grass-fed powdered gelatin

⅓ cup Swerve confectioners'-style sweetener or equivalent amount of liquid or powdered sweetener (see page 37)

2 teaspoons orange extract

⅛ teaspoon citric acid (for natural preservation and sour taste)

1 teaspoon Stur orange-mango flavored liquid water enhancer (see page 58) (optional, for color and taste)

NOTE:

If the marmalade is too thick or too thin, you can adjust the consistency with water or gelatin. First, reheat it until it liquefies. If it's too thick, add some water; if it's too thin, add a touch more gelatin.

KETO

NUTRITIONAL INFO (per serving)				
calories	fat	protein	carbs	fiber
4	0g	1g	0g	0g
	0%	100%	0%	

I enjoy this marmalade on slices of my keto bread that I've fried in coconut oil to give the bread a nice crusty and golden exterior. (You can find my recipe for keto bread on my site, MariaMindBodyHealth.com—search for "keto bread"—or in my previous cookbook, *The Ketogenic Cookbook*.) You can also use this recipe to make other fruit-flavored marmalades. Simply swap out the orange tea bag with another fruit-flavored tea of your choice and use a corresponding fruit-flavored extract.

1. Bring 1 cup of water to a boil in a tea kettle. Place the tea bag in a cup and pour the hot water into the cup. Let steep for a few minutes, then remove the tea bag.

2. Place 2 tablespoons of cool water in a bowl. Sift the gelatin over the water and allow it to soften for a few minutes. Add the brewed tea to the softened gelatin.

3. Add the sweetener (adding more or less to desired sweetness) and stir to combine.

4. Add the extract, citric acid, and Stur, if using, and stir to combine. Let sit on the counter to cool for at least 2 hours before using. Store in the fridge for up to 5 days.

Breakfast

CHAPTER 6

Orange Cream
SHAKE

EGG-FREE   NUT-FREE (OPTION)   VEGE-TARIAN

Prep Time: 5 minutes
Yield: 4 servings

1 (8-ounce) package cream cheese

1¼ cups unsweetened (unflavored or vanilla) almond milk, store-bought or homemade (page 131) (or unsweetened [unflavored or vanilla] hemp milk for nut-free)

¼ cup Swerve confectioners'-style sweetener or equivalent amount of liquid or powdered sweetener (see page 37)

1 teaspoon vanilla extract, or seeds scraped from 1 vanilla bean (about 6 inches long)

1 teaspoon orange extract

1 cup crushed ice

HEALTHY ADD-INS (OPTIONAL):

1 tablespoon pure aloe vera juice

1 tablespoon l-glutamine powder

1 tablespoon grass-fed powdered gelatin (omit for vegetarian)

This is my go-to quick breakfast. To make an already simple breakfast recipe even simpler, I do most of the work the night before (see Tip below).

This keto-friendly smoothie inspired by Orange Julius is also a great way to sneak in some immune-boosting and gut-healing nutrients, such as aloe vera and l-glutamine, which help heal the intestinal lining. I also add l-glutamine to my drink after a hard workout to help repair my muscles faster. Adding gelatin helps with hair and nail growth, joint pain, or other ailments you may be suffering from, especially when you don't want to drink a glass of homemade bone broth (page 132).

Place all the ingredients in a blender and blend until smooth.

TIP:

I make this drink while I'm cleaning up the kitchen after dinner but leave out the crushed ice. I store it in the blender jar in the fridge overnight, and when I'm ready to serve it the next morning, I add the crushed ice and pulse until smooth.

KETO

NUTRITIONAL INFO (per serving)				
calories	fat	protein	carbs	fiber
215	20.6g	4.6g	2.1g	0g
	87%	9%	4%	

Crème de Menthe
SHAKE

Prep Time: 5 minutes

Yield: 2 servings

1 cup unsweetened vanilla-flavored almond milk, store-bought or homemade (page 131) (or unsweetened vanilla-flavored hemp milk for nut-free)

4 ounces (½ cup) cream cheese (or ½ cup coconut cream for dairy-free)

½ cup fresh mint leaves

2 tablespoons Swerve confectioners'-style sweetener or equivalent amount of liquid or powdered sweetener (see page 37), or to desired sweetness

1 teaspoon mint extract

1 cup crushed ice

HEALTHY ADD-INS (OPTIONAL):

1 tablespoon aloe vera

1 tablespoon l-glutamine powder

1 tablespoon grass-fed powdered gelatin (omit for vegetarian)

To maximize weight loss and counter leptin resistance, I always recommend that clients "chew their calories." But if you are looking for a tasty keto shake for your kids or you're trying to maintain or gain weight, this recipe is fantastic! You can also make convenient single-serving portions for busy mornings (see Tip below).

Place all the ingredients in a blender and blend until smooth.

TIP:

Make on-the-go servings for one or more! Prepare one or more double batches and store the extra in the freezer in single-serving to-go cups. Grab one on your way to work or school, and by the time you're hungry, the drink will be thawed.

NUTRITIONAL INFO (per serving)				
calories	fat	protein	carbs	fiber
238	21.2g	8.5g	3.9g	2g
	80%	14%	6%	

CHOCOLATE SHAKE

OPTION

⊗ EGG-FREE   ⊗ NUT-FREE   ⊗ DAIRY-FREE   ⊗ VEGE-TARIAN

Prep Time: 5 minutes

Yield: 4 servings

¾ cup plus 2 tablespoons coconut oil (or unsalted butter if not dairy-sensitive)

¼ cup MCT oil, avocado oil, or macadamia nut oil

2 cups water or unsweetened (unflavored or vanilla) hemp milk (or unsweetened [unflavored or vanilla] almond milk, store-bought or homemade, page 131, if not nut-sensitive)

4 whole large eggs plus 4 large egg yolks (or 4 ounces/½ cup cream cheese if not dairy-sensitive)

¼ cup unsweetened cocoa powder

1 teaspoon vanilla extract, or seeds scraped from 1 vanilla bean (about 6 inches long)

¼ cup Swerve confectioners'-style sweetener or equivalent amount of liquid or powdered sweetener (see page 37), or to desired sweetness

¼ teaspoon fine sea salt

2 to 4 cups crushed ice, for serving

It's easy to use this basic recipe to create different flavored shakes. Simply omit the cocoa powder and replace the vanilla extract with another extract, like mint, banana, or strawberry. You can also make convenient single-serving portions for busy mornings (see Tip below).

Place all the ingredients, except the ice, in a blender and blend until smooth. Store in the fridge until ready to consume (it will thicken when stored overnight). Add ½ to 1 cup crushed ice to each glass just before serving.

TIP:

Make on-the-go servings for one or more! Prepare one or more double batches and store the extra in the freezer in single-serving to-go cups. Grab one on your way to work or school, and by the time you're hungry, the drink will be thawed.

L — M — H
KETO

NUTRITIONAL INFO (per serving)				
calories	fat	protein	carbs	fiber
664	70.6g	8.2g	1.2g	0g
	94%	5%	1%	

Spring POPOVERS

OPTION — NUT-FREE OPTION — DAIRY-FREE VEGETARIAN

Prep Time: 8 minutes

Cook Time: 27 minutes

Yield: 12 popovers (1 per serving)

1 cup unflavored whey protein (or ½ cup unflavored egg white protein for dairy-free)

1 teaspoon baking powder

½ cup melted butter, divided, plus more for greasing (or coconut oil for dairy-free)

2 cups unsweetened, unflavored almond milk, store-bought or homemade (page 131) (or unsweetened, unflavored hemp milk for nut-free)

4 large eggs

2 tablespoons chopped fresh chives

2 tablespoons chopped fresh dill

½ teaspoon fine sea salt

I call these "spring popovers" because I adore them when chives and dill start to come up out of the ground in the spring, but they taste great any time of the year! I like to serve them warm with Minute Hollandaise (page 129) and gravlax.

1. Preheat the oven to 425°F. Because these are best served warm, plan to bake just the number you will be eating. If baking the full amount, grease two 6-cup popover pans or a 12-cup muffin pan (or twelve 6-ounce ramekins) with butter or coconut oil. Place the pan(s) or ramekins in the hot oven for about 8 minutes. If baking less than the full amount, follow the guidance in the Single Serving Option below for storing and baking unused batter.

2. Meanwhile, in a blender, food processor, or medium-sized mixing bowl with a hand mixer, blend together the whey protein and baking powder until smooth.

3. Add ¼ cup of the melted butter, the almond milk, eggs, chives, dill, and salt and blend until evenly combined.

4. Carefully remove the hot pan(s) or ramekins from the oven. Pour 1 teaspoon of melted butter into each hot cup, then pour the batter into the cups, filling each cup two-thirds full.

5. Bake for 15 minutes, then reduce the heat to 325°F and bake for an additional 10 to 12 minutes, until puffed and golden brown. Allow to cool in the pan(s) or ramekins for 5 minutes. Transfer to a serving plate and enjoy warm.

SINGLE SERVING OPTION *Prepare the popover batter and store in the fridge for up to 3 days. Bake in individual greased ramekins.*

KETO

NUTRITIONAL INFO (per serving)				
calories	fat	protein	carbs	fiber
110	9.7g	5.3g	0.8g	0g
	79%	19%	2%	

Eggs in PURGATORY

NUT-FREE   DAIRY-FREE   ONE POT/ BOWL

Prep Time: 5 minutes

Cook Time: 12 minutes

Yield: 2 servings

1 tablespoon coconut oil or other keto-friendly fat, for frying

¼ pound chorizo or Italian sausage, removed from casings

¼ cup diced onions

1 teaspoon finely chopped garlic, or cloves from ½ head roasted garlic (page 134)

1 cup diced tomatoes with juices, jarred or fresh

1 tablespoon tomato paste

2 tablespoons smoked paprika

1 teaspoon fine sea salt

4 large eggs

Chopped fresh herbs of choice, for garnish (optional)

1. Heat the coconut oil in a large cast-iron skillet over medium heat. Add the sausage, onions, and garlic and cook until the sausage is cooked through, about 5 minutes, stirring to break up the sausage.

2. Add the tomatoes with juices, tomato paste, paprika, and salt and stir until well combined.

3. Crack the eggs over the tomato mixture, cover, and cook for 7 minutes, or until the eggs are cooked to your liking. Garnish with fresh herbs, if desired.

KETO

NUTRITIONAL INFO (per serving)				
calories	fat	protein	carbs	fiber
488	38.7g	27.5g	7g	1.7g
	72%	23%	5%	

Tex-Mex
BREAKFAST GRAVY

EGG-FREE NUT-FREE

Prep Time: 3 minutes

Cook Time: 10 minutes

Yield: 12 servings (about ¼ cup per serving)

10 ounces ground pork or 80% lean ground beef

1 (8-ounce) package cream cheese

1 cup chicken or beef bone broth, store-bought or homemade (page 132)

2 teaspoons Taco Seasoning (page 110)

Fine sea salt and fresh ground black pepper

I made this recipe for Easter brunch with a group of friends. I usually make it with ground pork, but one of the guests didn't eat pork, so I made it with ground beef instead. It was a real crowd-pleaser! You can also omit the taco seasoning and prepare this recipe using traditionally seasoned bulk breakfast sausage. Serve over fried eggs or keto biscuits. (To try my recipe for keto biscuits, search for *biscuits* on my site, MariaMindBodyHealth.com.)

1. Cook the meat in a large skillet over medium heat for 5 to 6 minutes, until thoroughly cooked and browned, stirring frequently.

2. Gradually add the cream cheese, broth, and taco seasoning, stirring constantly. Cook until the mixture comes to a gentle simmer and thickens.

3. Reduce the heat to medium-low and simmer for 2 minutes, stirring constantly. Season to taste with salt and pepper. Store in an airtight container in the fridge for up to 5 days. Freezing is not recommended.

KETO

NUTRITIONAL INFO (per serving)				
calories	fat	protein	carbs	fiber
131	11.8g	5.6g	0.6g	0g
	81%	17%	2%	

Minute
ENGLISH MUFFIN

NUT-FREE | DAIRY-FREE OPTION | VEGE-TARIAN

Prep Time: 2 minutes

Cook Time: 1 to 12 minutes, depending on method

Yield: 1 English muffin (1 serving)

1 teaspoon unsalted butter, softened (or coconut oil for dairy-free), for greasing

1 large egg

2 teaspoons coconut flour

Pinch of baking soda

Pinch of fine sea salt

1 tablespoon grated Parmesan cheese (optional; omit for dairy-free)

2 teaspoons coconut oil, for frying (optional)

This muffin is an easy substitute for a bagel or toast. Cut in half, it's the perfect vehicle for your favorite spread or toppings—I like it with gravlax, my Dairy-Free Minute "Cream Cheese" Spread (page 138), red onion, capers, and a squeeze of lime, as shown. Or try it with Orange Marmalade (page 139)! You can make the muffin in either a microwave or a toaster oven. I love using my toaster oven for small jobs like this because it takes less time to preheat, plus it doesn't heat up the kitchen on hot summer days.

1. Grease a 4-ounce dessert ramekin with the butter. If using a toaster oven, preheat the toaster oven to 400°F.

2. In a small mixing bowl, mix together the egg and coconut flour with a fork until well combined, then add the rest of the ingredients and stir to combine.

3. Place the dough in the greased ramekin. If using a microwave, cook on high for 1 minute, or until a toothpick inserted in the middle comes out clean. If using a toaster oven, bake for 12 minutes, or until a toothpick inserted in the middle comes out clean.

4. Allow to cool in the ramekin for 5 minutes. Remove the muffin from the ramekin and allow to cool completely. Slice in half.

5. If you like your muffin with crispy edges, melt the coconut oil in a medium skillet over medium-heat heat. When the oil is hot, place the muffin halves in the hot oil, cut side down, and fry until the edges are crispy.

KETO

NUTRITIONAL INFO (per serving)				
calories	fat	protein	carbs	fiber
188	16.7g	6.7g	3.3g	2g
	79%	14%	7%	

Cinnamon Roll
MINUTE MUFFINS

OPTION

NUT-FREE   DAIRY-FREE   VEGE-TARIAN

Prep Time: 3 minutes

Cook Time: 1½ to 12 minutes, depending on method

Yield: 5 muffins (1 per serving)

---

5 teaspoons coconut oil, for greasing

½ cup coconut flour

¼ cup Swerve confectioners'-style sweetener or equivalent amount of liquid or powdered sweetener (see page 37)

1 teaspoon ground cinnamon, plus extra for dusting (optional)

1 teaspoon baking soda

Pinch of fine sea salt

4 large eggs

¼ cup coconut oil, melted, not hot

½ cup unsweetened, unflavored almond milk, store-bought or homemade (page 131) (or unsweetened, unflavored hemp milk or full-fat coconut milk for nut-free)

1 teaspoon vanilla extract, or seeds scraped from 1 vanilla bean (about 6 inches long)

GLAZE (OPTIONAL):

3 tablespoons coconut oil

3 tablespoons Swerve confectioners'-style sweetener or equivalent amount of powdered erythritol or monk fruit (see page 37)

¾ teaspoon maple extract or 1 drop of maple oil

L   M   H
KETO

NUTRITIONAL INFO (per serving)				
calories	fat	protein	carbs	fiber
311	28.1g	7.7g	8.4g	5.3g
	81%	9%	10%	

This small job is perfect for a toaster oven, but you can also use a microwave or an oven. Ketosis isn't all about weight loss, but if you are using it as a weight-loss tool, I recommend avoiding coconut flour–based baked goods like these muffins.

1. If using the oven or toaster oven, preheat to 350°F.

2. Because these are best served warm, plan to bake just the number you will be eating. If baking the full amount, grease five 4-ounce microwave-safe cups or ramekins with the coconut oil. (Use ramekins if baking the muffins in the oven.) If baking less than the full amount, follow the guidance in the Single Serving Option below.

3. In a medium bowl, whisk together the coconut flour, sweetener, cinnamon, baking soda, and salt. Then stir in the eggs, coconut oil, almond milk, and vanilla extract.

4. Divide the batter among the greased cups or ramekins, filling each about three-quarters full. Dust additional cinnamon over the filled cups, if desired.

5. If using a microwave, cook each cup or ramekin, one at a time, on high for about 1 minute 30 seconds, until a toothpick inserted in the middle comes out clean.

6. If using a toaster oven, bake one at a time for 8 to 12 minutes, until a toothpick inserted in the middle comes out clean.

7. If using the oven, place all of the ramekins in the oven and bake for 15 minutes, or until a toothpick inserted in the middle comes out clean.

8. Meanwhile, stir together the ingredients for the glaze, if using.

9. Remove the muffins from the microwave or toaster oven and top each with 1 tablespoon of the glaze, if desired. Eat warm right out of the cup or ramekin.

SINGLE SERVING OPTION

Fill the cups or ramekins with the batter, cover with plastic wrap, and store in the refrigerator to be cooked as needed for easy breakfasts on the go. The batter will keep in the fridge for 3 days.

Dairy-Free Milk Chocolate
PROTEIN BARS

EGG-FREE · NUT-FREE · DAIRY-FREE · VEGE-TARIAN

Prep Time: 5 minutes, plus 30 minutes to chill

Cook Time: 2 minutes

Yield: 8 bars (1 per serving)

½ cup coconut oil (or unsalted butter if not dairy-sensitive)

¼ cup cocoa butter

¼ cup finely chopped unsweetened baking chocolate

¼ cup chocolate-flavored whey protein (or chocolate-flavored egg white protein if not egg-sensitive)

¼ cup Swerve confectioners'-style sweetener or equivalent amount of liquid or powdered sweetener (see page 37) (or to desired sweetness)

1 teaspoon vanilla extract, or seeds scraped from 1 vanilla bean (about 6 inches long)

1 tablespoon yacón syrup (optional, for a chewier bar)

If you're looking for a great bar to pack on a hiking trip or when traveling, this is it; it needs no refrigeration if made with coconut oil! Besides being convenient, this protein bar is customized for your keto lifestyle, which isn't the case with store-bought options.

Many of my clients grab low-carb protein bars, such as Quest, for easy breakfasts or snacks. Here are a few issues I have with those bars:

- One bar has too much protein for people with damaged metabolisms to stay in ketosis.

- They are made with whey protein, which is dairy. And for people who do not digest dairy well, they simply are not an option.

These homemade bars are much better for ketosis and are completely dairy-free.

1. Line an 8-inch square glass dish or storage container with parchment paper.

2. Place the coconut oil and cocoa butter in a microwave-safe bowl and heat on high in 1-minute increments, stirring after each increment, until the cocoa butter is totally melted, about 2 minutes total. Add the baking chocolate and stir until melted.

3. Place the melted cocoa butter mixture along with the rest of the ingredients in a blender and puree until smooth. Alternatively, stir the protein powder, sweetener, vanilla extract, and yacón syrup (if using) into the melted cocoa butter mixture by hand until smooth.

4. Pour the mixture into the lined dish or container. Place in the fridge to chill, uncovered, for about 30 minutes. Cut into eight 2-by-4-inch bars.

5. Store in an airtight container at room temperature for up to 2 weeks (if you used butter instead of coconut oil, store the bars in the fridge). The bars can be stacked.

KETO

NUTRITIONAL INFO (per serving)				
calories	fat	protein	carbs	fiber
238	23g	4g	2.5g	1.5g
	89%	7%	4%	

Strawberry Cheesecake PROTEIN BARS

EGG-FREE NUT-FREE VEGE-TARIAN

Prep Time: 5 minutes, plus 30 minutes to chill

Cook Time: 2 minutes

Yield: 8 bars (1 per serving)

½ cup (1 stick) unsalted butter or coconut oil

½ cup cocoa butter

4 ounces (½ cup) cream cheese

¼ cup strawberry-flavored whey protein (or strawberry-flavored egg white protein if not egg-sensitive)

¼ cup Swerve confectioners'-style sweetener or equivalent amount of liquid or powdered sweetener (see page 37) (or to desired sweetness)

1 teaspoon strawberry extract

1 tablespoon yacón syrup (optional, for a chewier bar)

I often have a variety of people test my recipes to make sure that even a novice cook or baker can tackle them, as well as to make sure that people enjoy the taste. One of my favorite recipe testers is a client named Stacey. She is very honest with her feedback, and she has two young kids who also eat keto. After she tested these protein bars, she immediately wrote to me: "The nonrefrigerated batter was so good that I immediately made another batch. My keto kid just loves this recipe, and my girl, who is very hard to impress, also loved it, even though she does not like store-bought protein bars. The best part is that these have no nuts, so my son can bring them to school in his bento box."

1. Line an 8-inch square glass dish or storage container with parchment paper.

2. Place the butter and cocoa butter in a microwave-safe bowl and heat on high in 1-minute increments, stirring after each increment, until the cocoa butter is totally melted, about 2 minutes total.

3. Place the melted cocoa butter mixture along with the rest of the ingredients in a blender and puree until smooth. Alternatively, stir the cream cheese, whey protein, sweetener, strawberry extract, and yacón syrup (if using) into the melted cocoa butter mixture by hand until smooth.

4. Pour the mixture into the lined dish or container. Place in the fridge to chill, uncovered, for about 30 minutes. Cut into eight 2-by-4-inch bars.

5. Store in an airtight container in the fridge for up to 2 weeks. The bars can be stacked.

NOTE:

If you need a dairy-free bar, try the Dairy-Free Milk Chocolate Protein Bars (page 154).

KETO

NUTRITIONAL INFO (per serving)				
calories	fat	protein	carbs	fiber
280	30.6g	2.7g	0.7g	0g
	97%	3%	1%	

Cream of No-Wheat
CEREAL

NUT-FREE · DAIRY-FREE · VEGE-TARIAN

Prep Time: 2 minutes

Cook Time: 4 minutes

Yield: 1 serving

2 large eggs

⅓ cup full-fat coconut milk (or heavy cream if not dairy-sensitive)

2 tablespoons Swerve confectioners'-style sweetener or equivalent amount of liquid or powdered sweetener (see page 37)

1 teaspoon maple extract

⅛ teaspoon fine sea salt

1 tablespoon coconut oil (or unsalted butter if not dairy-sensitive)

SAUCE:

2 tablespoons coconut oil (or unsalted butter if not dairy-sensitive)

2 tablespoons Swerve confectioners'-style sweetener or equivalent amount of liquid or powdered sweetener (see page 37)

1 teaspoon maple extract

⅛ teaspoon fine sea salt

1. In a small bowl, whisk together the eggs, coconut milk, sweetener, maple extract, and salt.

2. In a medium saucepan, melt the 1 tablespoon of coconut oil over medium heat. Add the egg mixture to the pan and cook until the mixture thickens and small curds form, all the while scraping the bottom of the pan and stirring to keep large curds from forming. (A whisk works well for this task.) This will take about 4 minutes. Transfer the thickened eggs to a serving bowl.

3. Place the ingredients for the sauce in a microwave-safe bowl and microwave for 20 seconds, or until the coconut oil is melted.

4. Pour the sauce over the eggs just before serving.

KETO · *using heavy cream*

NUTRITIONAL INFO (per serving)				
calories	fat	protein	carbs	fiber
645	65.5g	13.4g	2.4g	0g
	91%	8%	1%	

KETO · *using coconut milk*

NUTRITIONAL INFO (per serving)				
calories	fat	protein	carbs	fiber
691	69.8g	14.4g	5g	1.8g
	90%	7.5%	2.5%	

Chocolate
BREAKFAST CUSTARD

EGG-
FREE

OPTION
NUT-
FREE

DAIRY-
FREE

Prep Time: 4 minutes, plus 1 hour to set

Cook Time: 1 to 3 minutes, depending on method

Yield: 4 servings

2 cups full-fat coconut milk (or heavy cream if not dairy-sensitive), divided

1 tablespoon grass-fed powdered gelatin

1 cup unsweetened (unflavored or vanilla) almond milk, store-bought or homemade (page 131) (or unsweetened [unflavored or vanilla] hemp milk if nut-free)

½ cup Swerve confectioners'-style sweetener or equivalent amount of liquid or powdered sweetener (see page 37)

½ cup unsweetened cocoa powder

1 teaspoon vanilla extract, or seeds scraped from 1 vanilla bean (about 6 inches long)

⅛ teaspoon fine sea salt

I suggest preparing this custard the night before so you have an easy breakfast on the go!

1. Pour ¼ cup of the coconut milk into a medium bowl. Sift the gelatin over the milk and let it soften while you prepare the rest of the ingredients.

2. Heat the almond milk and remaining 1¾ cups of coconut milk in a saucepan over medium heat for a few minutes, until hot. Alternatively, heat the almond and coconut milk in a microwave-safe container in the microwave for 1 minute.

3. Whisk the sweetener and cocoa powder into the cool coconut milk–gelatin mixture. Stir until well combined.

4. Pour the hot coconut milk into the gelatin mixture while stirring constantly. Add the vanilla extract and salt. Pour the custard into four 4-ounce serving cups.

5. Place in the refrigerator for 1 hour, or until the custard is set but not chilled. It is best served at room temperature but can be served cold. Store extras in an airtight container or covered with plastic wrap in the fridge for up to 4 days or in the freezer for up to a month. If frozen, thaw at room temperature before serving.

L M H
KETO

NUTRITIONAL INFO (per serving)				
calories	fat	protein	carbs	fiber
237	21g	5g	6g	2g
	80%	9%	11%	

Chorizo
BREAKFAST PATTIES

EGG-FREE NUT-FREE DAIRY-FREE

Prep Time: 8 minutes

Cook Time: 10 minutes per batch

Yield: 12 patties (1 per serving)

2½ pounds bulk ground chorizo or chorizo sausage links, removed from casings (see Notes)

½ pound ground pork fat (see Notes)

2 teaspoons fine sea salt

2 teaspoons fresh ground black pepper

½ teaspoon ground cumin

Lard or coconut oil, for the pan

Keto dipping sauce of choice (pages 122 to 127) (optional)

1. Place the ground chorizo, ground pork fat, salt, pepper, and cumin in a large bowl. Mix well to evenly combine the ingredients. Using your hands, form the mixture into twelve 3-inch patties.

2. Heat 1 tablespoon of lard or coconut oil in a large pan over medium heat. Sauté the patties in batches for 3 to 5 minutes per side, until cooked through. Add additional fat for the pan as needed.

3. Serve with the keto dipping sauce of your choice, if desired.

NOTES:

If using chorizo in casings, after removing the sausage from the casings, pulse the meat in batches in a food processor just until finely ground; do not puree.

Ask your butcher to grind the pork fat for you. Or, if you are grinding it at home, first cut it into cubes and freeze it on a rimmed baking sheet for an hour. Then pulse it in batches in a food processor until finely ground.

TIP:

Make a double batch of this recipe and store the cooked patties in the fridge or freezer for easy breakfasts on the go. Cooked patties will keep in the fridge for 5 days or in the freezer for 6 months.

SINGLE SERVING OPTION
Form the patties and store them in the fridge for up to 3 days, cooking the desired number of patties when needed.

M
L H
KETO

NUTRITIONAL INFO (per serving)				
calories	fat	protein	carbs	fiber
602	55.1g	22.8g	2g	0g
	83%	15%	1%	

Pizza MUFFINS

NUT-FREE VEGE-TARIAN (OPTION)

Prep Time: 15 minutes

Cook Time: 15 minutes

Yield: 12 regular-size or 24 mini muffins (1 regular-size/2 mini muffins per serving)

7 large eggs

1 cup sour cream

1 tablespoon dried oregano leaves

½ teaspoon baking powder

½ teaspoon fine sea salt

6 ounces mozzarella cheese, shredded

3 tablespoons grated Parmesan cheese

¼ cup chopped onions

¼ teaspoon finely chopped garlic

ADD-INS (OPTIONAL):

¼ to ½ cup sliced olives

¼ cup diced green peppers

¼ cup sliced mushrooms

½ cup chopped or crumbled precooked Italian sausage (omit for vegetarian)

Pizza Spice Mix (page 111), for garnish (optional)

Marinara sauce, warmed, for serving (optional)

I love making these muffins because my kids can choose which pizza toppings they prefer to add to their muffins. Fun and individualized!

1. Preheat the oven to 350°F. Grease a 24-well mini muffin pan or a 12-well muffin pan.

2. Beat the eggs in a large mixing bowl. In another bowl, combine the sour cream, oregano, baking powder, and salt, then add the sour cream mixture to the bowl with the eggs. Blend with a hand mixer until well combined.

3. Add the mozzarella, Parmesan, onions, garlic, and pizza add-ins of your choice. Stir with a spoon until well combined.

4. Pour the batter into the greased muffin cups, filling each about two-thirds full. Sprinkle with Pizza Spice Mix, if desired.

5. Bake until puffy and lightly browned, 10 to 12 minutes for mini muffins, 12 to 15 minutes for regular-sized muffins. The muffins are done when a knife inserted in the center comes out clean. Allow to cool slightly in the pan, then transfer to a serving platter.

6. Serve with marinara sauce either spooned on top or on the side for dipping, if desired. Store extras in an airtight container in the fridge for up to 3 days. Reheat leftovers in a 350°F oven for 3 minutes or in the microwave for 30 seconds, or until heated through.

TIP:

Prepare the batter the night before (or up to 3 days before baking) and store in the fridge. The next morning, fill the greased muffin cups as described above and pop the pan in the oven. The baked muffins also taste great as leftovers. Who doesn't love leftover pizza for breakfast?

VEGE-TARIAN OPTION

These muffins are a great option for a vegetarian meal! Simply replace the sausage with another vegetarian add-in of your choice.

KETO

NUTRITIONAL INFO (per serving)				
calories	fat	protein	carbs	fiber
256	19.3g	17.4g	4.4g	0g
	67%	27%	7%	

Taco
BREAKFAST BAKE

NUT-
FREE

Prep Time: 8 minutes

Cook Time: 37 minutes

Yield: 6 servings

2 tablespoons unsalted butter

½ pound 80% lean ground beef

½ cup chopped onions

2 tablespoons Taco Seasoning (page 110)

¼ cup tomato sauce

8 large eggs, beaten

¼ cup beef bone broth, store-bought or homemade (page 132)

¾ cup shredded Monterey Jack or sharp cheddar cheese (about 3 ounces)

1 ounce (2 tablespoons) cream cheese

1 teaspoon finely chopped garlic, or cloves from ½ head roasted garlic (page 134)

½ cup chopped fresh cilantro

1 teaspoon fine sea salt

½ teaspoon fresh ground black pepper

Sliced fresh chives and/or chopped fresh cilantro, for garnish (optional)

Marinara sauce, warmed, for serving (optional)

1. Preheat the oven to 350°F.

2. In large oven-safe skillet, heat the butter over medium heat. Add the ground beef, onions, and taco seasoning and cook until the beef is cooked all the way through and the onions are translucent, about 7 minutes. Add the tomato sauce and stir well to combine.

3. In large bowl, mix together the eggs, broth, cheeses, garlic, cilantro, salt, and pepper.

4. Add the egg mixture to the beef mixture and stir to combine. Cook over medium heat for 3 minutes, until the eggs are just slightly set, stirring continuously.

5. Place the skillet in the oven and bake for 27 minutes, or until the eggs are cooked through in the center. Remove from the oven and let rest for 3 minutes, then slice and serve. If desired, garnish with fresh chives and/or cilantro and serve with marinara sauce. Store leftovers in an airtight container in the fridge for up to 3 days. Reheat in a 350°F oven for 3 minutes or in the microwave for 30 seconds, or until heated through.

VARIATION: TACO BREAKFAST MUFFINS.

To shorten the cooking time, bake as individual muffins. Grease a 12-well muffin pan and follow the recipe as written through Step 4. Then transfer the mixture to the greased muffin cups, filling each about two-thirds full. Bake for 10 to 13 minutes, until golden and puffed. Allow to cool slightly in the pan, then transfer the muffins to a serving platter and serve warm. Makes 12 muffins (2 per serving).

TIP:

I brown the ground beef, combine the ingredients, and place them in the skillet the night before. In the morning, all I have to do is pop the skillet in the oven for an easy breakfast or brunch. This dish makes great leftovers, too!

M

L H

KETO

NUTRITIONAL INFO (per serving)				
calories	fat	protein	carbs	fiber
301	22.4g	21.8g	2.5g	0g
	68%	29%	3%	

Healthy
HASH BROWNS

NUT-FREE   DAIRY-FREE   VEGE-TARIAN

Prep Time: 4 minutes

Cook Time: 10 minutes per batch

Yield: 4 hash browns (1 per serving)

4 cups shredded cabbage

4 large eggs

½ cup chopped leeks or green onions

1 teaspoon fine sea salt

½ teaspoon fresh ground black pepper

Additional spices and/or chopped fresh herbs to taste, such as cayenne, cilantro, or basil (optional)

1 tablespoon coconut oil or unsalted butter, plus more as needed, for frying

These are so tasty, your family will never miss potato hash browns again! I love to serve them with guacamole (page 136). This is an easy breakfast to make for one person. I often make it for myself because I always have cabbage, eggs, and leeks or green onions in the fridge.

1. In a medium bowl, combine the cabbage, eggs, leeks, salt, pepper, and additional spices or herbs of your choice (if using).

2. Heat the oil in a large skillet over medium-low heat.

3. Using a ½-cup measuring cup, scoop up a heaping portion of the cabbage mixture, place it in the hot skillet, and form into a 3-inch circle with a spatula. If your skillet is large enough, add a second hash brown to the skillet, but do not overcrowd the pan.

4. Cook until golden brown and the cabbage is fork-tender, about 5 minutes. When firm, flip and cook for another 3 to 5 minutes, until golden brown. Repeat with the remaining hash brown mixture, adding more oil to the skillet as needed. Remove from the heat and serve. These are best eaten hot out of the skillet.

TIP:

The hash brown mixture can be made up to 4 days ahead. Make a single or double batch of the mixture, depending on the size of your family, then fry the hash browns as needed for quick breakfasts throughout the week.

SINGLE SERVING OPTION

To make a single serving, use 1 cup shredded cabbage, 1 large egg, 2 tablespoons chopped leeks or green onions, ¼ teaspoon fine sea salt, and ⅛ teaspoon fresh ground black pepper and form into one hash brown.

KETO

NUTRITIONAL INFO (per serving)				
calories	fat	protein	carbs	fiber
204	18.5g	6.7g	5.3g	2.1g
	80%	11%	9%	

Green Eggs
AND HAM

NUT-FREE DAIRY-FREE

Prep Time: 4 minutes

Cook Time: 4 minutes

Yield: 1 serving

1 teaspoon coconut oil (or unsalted butter if not dairy-sensitive), for frying

2 large eggs

2 slices ham

2 tablespoons Simple Chimichurri Sauce (page 130)

I adore Dr. Seuss. I once worked at a camp where we put on a play of Dr. Seuss's book *The Lorax* to teach the children about trees and to respect Mother Nature. Every March 2, Dr. Seuss Day, I make a breakfast of green eggs and ham.

1. Heat the oil in a large cast-iron skillet over medium heat. Once hot, crack the eggs into the skillet and cover with a lid. Fry the eggs sunny side up until the whites are cooked through and the yolks are still runny, about 4 minutes.

2. When the eggs are nearly done, place the ham in the skillet to heat through.

3. Remove the ham from the skillet, place on a serving plate, top with the fried eggs, and spoon the chimichurri sauce on top.

KETO
L M H

NUTRITIONAL INFO (per serving)				
calories	fat	protein	carbs	fiber
278	22.7g	15.8g	2.2g	0g
	74%	23%	3%	

Breakfast
BURRITOS

NUT-FREE

Prep Time: 10 minutes

Cook Time: 18 minutes

Yield: 8 burritos (2 per serving)

2 tablespoons coconut oil or unsalted butter

½ pound chorizo, removed from casings, or bulk ground chorizo sausage

½ cup diced onions

5 large eggs, beaten

½ teaspoon fine sea salt

½ cup salsa

8 large slices roast chicken breast (from the deli counter)

1½ cups shredded Monterey Jack cheese (about 12 ounces)

ADDITIONAL FILLINGS (OPTIONAL):

Diced avocado

Sliced jalapeños, fresh or jarred

Sriracha, store-bought or homemade (page 124)

Salsa or diced tomatoes

Sour cream, for serving (optional)

Fresh cilantro leaves, for garnish (optional)

KETO

NUTRITIONAL INFO (per serving)				
calories	fat	protein	carbs	fiber
596	47.7g	37.7g	3.4g	0g
	72%	25%	2%	

1. Preheat the oven to 350°F.

2. Heat the oil in a large skillet over medium heat. Add the chorizo and diced onions and cook until the sausage is no longer pink, about 5 minutes, breaking it into pieces as you fry it. Set aside on a plate to cool, leaving the grease in the pan.

3. Reduce the heat to low. Add the eggs and salt to the pan and scramble until cooked through.

4. Meanwhile, pour the salsa into an 8-inch cast-iron skillet or 8-inch square baking dish.

5. To assemble the burritos, lay a slice of chicken breast on a plate. Sprinkle 2 heaping tablespoons of the shredded cheese down the middle, followed by 3 tablespoons of cooked chorizo and 3 tablespoons of eggs and any additional fillings of your choice. Roll it up tightly and place it seam side down on the salsa in the skillet or baking dish. Repeat with the rest of the ingredients. Top the burritos with the remaining cheese. Place in the oven and bake until the cheese has melted, about 8 minutes.

6. Serve warm with a dollop of sour cream and garnished with cilantro, if desired.

Starters
AND SNACKS

CHAPTER 7

Amuse-Bouche PLATTER

OPTION

EGG-FREE   NUT-FREE

Prep Time: 8 minutes

Yield: 12 servings

2 cups olives (green, black, purple, or a combination)

1 pint pickles, store-bought or homemade (page 318)

Selection of deli meats (1 pound total), such as sliced ham, pastrami, and/or prosciutto, or ½ recipe Teriyaki Jerky (page 186)

Selection of cheeses (1 pound total), such as Brie, Halloumi (see Note), sliced fresh mozzarella, sharp cheddar, and/or goat cheese

6 Prosciutto and Arugula Roll-Ups (page 198)

6 Purple Pickled Eggs (page 182) or 6 Classic Deviled Eggs (page 194) (omit for egg-free)

Crudités, such as sliced cucumber or carrot sticks

Place the olives and pickles in two separate bowls and set them on a large serving platter. Roll up the deli meats and place on the serving platter. Place the cheeses, roll-ups, pickled eggs, and crudités on the platter.

NOTE:

To grill Halloumi cheese, as shown in the photo, follow the instructions in Step 4 of Easy Tomato Soup with Grilled Cheese (page 218).

KETO

NUTRITIONAL INFO (per serving)				
calories	fat	protein	carbs	fiber
346	24g	28g	5.6g	1.6g
	62%	32%	6%	

BLT "CHIPS" AND DIP

EGG-FREE   NUT-FREE

Prep Time: 8 minutes

Yield: 6 servings

2 medium heads endive

1 cup Blue Cheese Dressing
(page 119)

2 strips bacon, cooked and
crumbled into pieces

1 small tomato, diced

1. Trim about ½ inch off the stem end of each head of endive. Remove and discard any tired outer leaves. Separate the leaves and arrange them on a large serving platter.

2. Spoon the dressing evenly into the stem, or "scoop," ends of the endive leaves. Then top the dressing with the crumbled bacon and diced tomato. This dish is best if served soon after preparing, but it can be stored in an airtight container in the fridge for up to a day.

KETO

NUTRITIONAL INFO (per serving)				
calories	fat	protein	carbs	fiber
119	10.5g	4.9g	1.9g	0.9g
	79%	16%	6%	

Italian POPPERS

EGG-FREE NUT-FREE DAIRY-FREE OPTION

Prep Time: 8 minutes

Cook Time: 10 minutes

Yield: 18 poppers (3 per serving)

18 mini sweet peppers or jalapeño peppers

FILLING:

1 (8-ounce) package mascarpone cheese or softened cream cheese (or 1 cup mashed avocado for dairy-free)

1 tablespoon chopped fresh oregano (optional)

1 teaspoon fine sea salt

½ teaspoon finely chopped garlic, or 4 cloves roasted garlic (page 134)

9 slices prosciutto, cut lengthwise into 18 (1-inch-wide) strips

Marinara sauce, warmed, for serving (optional)

This is a great appetizer to prepare up to two days ahead. As your guests arrive, all you have to do is pop them in a preheated oven. A toaster oven works great for these tasty bites.

1. Preheat the oven to 400°F.

2. Cut the stems off the peppers and make a slice down one long side of each pepper. If using jalapeños, remove the membranes and seeds with the tip of a small knife or a very small spoon. Leave a little of the membranes and seeds if you want hotter peppers.

3. In a medium bowl, mix together the ingredients for the filling.

4. Stuff the hollowed-out peppers with the filling. Wrap a slice of prosciutto around each stuffed pepper. Place on a rimmed baking sheet.

5. Bake for 10 minutes, or until the prosciutto is crispy. Let cool slightly before eating. Drizzle with marinara sauce or serve it alongside for dipping, if desired.

KETO

NUTRITIONAL INFO (per serving)				
calories	fat	protein	carbs	fiber
185	11.2g	18.5g	3.7g	1.2g
	54%	39%	7%	

Amazing CHEESE PUFFS

EGG-FREE   NUT-FREE   VEGE-TARIAN

Prep Time: 2 minutes

Cook Time: 1 minute

Yield: 2 servings

1 aged Gouda or Parmesan cheese rind, about 3½ inches wide and ½ inch thick

1 teaspoon Pizza Spice Mix (page 111) (optional)

I like to get the most out of my food, so when I'm done with a chunk of Parmesan cheese, I don't throw out the rind—instead, I use it to make this really tasty snack! It's super quick and easy to make. These tasty morsels also work great as croutons. (And by the way, leftover Parmesan cheese rinds are also great for adding flavor to soups. When I'm done with a chunk of Parmesan, I store the rind in the freezer until my next soup-making day.)

1. Cut the cheese rind into ½-inch squares. Place the squares on a microwave-safe plate about 2 inches apart. Microwave on high for 45 to 60 seconds, until the cheese rind squares puff up to about twice their size. Remove from the microwave and allow to cool completely.

2. Sprinkle with Pizza Spice Mix, if desired, or enjoy plain. The plain puffs are great in a Caesar salad made with my Caesar Dressing (page 116).

KETO

NUTRITIONAL INFO (per serving)				
Made with aged Gouda				
calories	fat	protein	carbs	fiber
130	11g	8g	0g	0g
	76%	24%	0%	

NUTRITIONAL INFO (per serving)				
Made with Parmesan				
calories	fat	protein	carbs	fiber
111	8g	10.1g	0g	0g
	64%	36%	0%	

Cheesy
FRIED RAVIOLI

NUT-FREE

Prep Time: 10 minutes

Cook Time: 10 minutes

Yield: 6 servings

1 cup coconut oil or duck fat, for frying

FILLING:

1 (8-ounce) package mascarpone cheese or cream cheese, softened (see Note)

1 large egg

½ cup grated Parmesan cheese (about 2 ounces)

½ teaspoon fine sea salt

½ teaspoon fresh ground black pepper

8 ounces thinly sliced prosciutto

There is a lovely restaurant in the town I live in called Mama Maria's. (Ha! Wouldn't that be a perfect name for my restaurant?) It's an Italian restaurant that we frequented about ten years ago, before our keto journey began, and they served amazing fried ravioli.

Craig and I often dream of what we would serve at our keto restaurant, and this fried ravioli would be on the menu. Yep, it is that good! When paired with a green salad tossed with keto dressing, this recipe makes enough for a meal for four people.

1. Heat the oil to 350°F in a deep fryer or in a 4-inch-deep (or deeper) cast-iron skillet over medium heat. The oil should be at least 2 inches deep; add more oil if needed.

2. Meanwhile, make the ravioli: In a small bowl, stir together the ingredients for the filling until well combined.

3. To assemble the ravioli: Lay one slice of prosciutto on a sheet of parchment paper so that the short end is toward you. Lay another slice over the top of the prosciutto so you make a Greek cross with four "arms" to wrap around the filling. Spoon about 1 heaping tablespoon of the filling into the center of the prosciutto cross. Fold one arm of the prosciutto over the filling. Continue folding the arms around the filling to make a square, making sure that the filling is covered well. Using your fingers, press down around the filling to even it out into a square shape. Repeat with the rest of the prosciutto and filling.

4. Working in batches, fry the ravioli in the hot oil for about 2 minutes, or until crisp on the outside. Remove from the oil and serve.

TIP:

Once the oil is cool, strain it and store it in mason jars in the fridge for future use. It can be used up to 4 times.

The ravioli can be assembled 2 days before frying and stored in the fridge for an easy dinner.

NOTE:

Mascarpone is the traditional choice here, but cream cheese works just as well.

KETO

NUTRITIONAL INFO (per serving)				
calories	fat	protein	carbs	fiber
315	25.5	22.5g	1.2g	0g
	72%	27%	1%	

Popsicle Crudités
WITH DILL DIP

EGG-FREE   NUT-FREE

Prep Time: 15 minutes, plus 30 minutes to chill

Yield: 8 servings

DILL DIP:

1 (8-ounce) package cream cheese, softened, or mascarpone cheese

1 cup sour cream or crème fraîche

2 tablespoons chopped fresh dill

2 tablespoons finely chopped green onions

½ teaspoon fine sea salt

2 tablespoons chicken bone broth, store-bought or homemade (page 132) (optional)

POPSICLE CRUDITÉS:

1 cucumber, peeled

1 cup cherry tomatoes

½ cup pitted black olives

6 small pickles, store-bought or homemade (page 318)

6 green onions

4 or 5 sprigs fresh basil

1 large red bell pepper, for the bowl

Special Equipment:
Long wooden skewers

This cute arrangement of Popsicle crudités is totally worth the time it takes to make! And it's surprisingly easy to put together. But if you're pressed for time, you can make the Simple Relish Tray instead (see Variation below).

1. To make the dill dip: In a medium mixing bowl, combine the softened cream cheese, sour cream, dill, green onions, and salt with a hand mixer until well combined. Refrigerate for at least 30 minutes to allow the flavors to meld. If the dip is too thick after chilling, stir in the broth 1 tablespoon at a time until it reaches your preferred thickness. The dip will keep for 4 days in the fridge.

2. To make the Popsicle crudités: Slice the cucumber into ¼-inch-thick rounds. Using a small flower-shaped cookie cutter, cut each slice into a flower. Place a skewer in each cucumber flower, pushing the skewer from the bottom to the top of the flower. Slice half of the tomatoes in half and place one in the center of each cucumber flower, securing with a half of a toothpick (insert the toothpick in the middle of the back of the flower). Place in a vase. Place the remaining whole tomatoes, the whole black olives, and the pickles on skewers and arrange in the vase. Add the whole green onions and basil leaves to the vase.

3. To make the bell pepper serving bowl: Cut the top of the pepper in a zigzag shape. Scoop out the seeds and membranes. Use the hollowed-out pepper as a bowl to serve the dip in.

VARIATION: SIMPLE RELISH TRAY WITH DILL DIP.

Prepare the dip following Step 1 above. Then prepare 1 cup sliced cucumbers, 1 cup cherry tomatoes, 8 stalks celery cut into thirds, and 1 cup sliced zucchini. Place the dip in medium serving bowl, set it in the center of a platter, and arrange the prepped vegetables around it.

KETO

NUTRITIONAL INFO (per serving)				
calories	fat	protein	carbs	fiber
163	16g	3.2g	2.5g	0g
	87%	7%	6%	

Tomato TULIPS

EGG-FREE NUT-FREE VEGE-TARIAN ONE POT/BOWL

Prep Time: 8 minutes

Yield: 12 servings

1 pint grape tomatoes

FILLING:

1 (8-ounce) package cream cheese, softened, or creamy goat cheese

1 tablespoon finely chopped green onions

1 tablespoon finely chopped fresh basil

½ teaspoon lemon juice

¼ teaspoon fine sea salt

3 green onions, root ends trimmed, for assembly

This is a great way to make veggies fun! My kids don't always love veggies. Micah jokes that he is a carnivore, like a T. rex! But I tell him that even in his meatloaf and chili, there are plants like parsley and oregano, as well as tomato sauce or salsa. He laughs and agrees, but that conversation got me to thinking that we eat with our eyes. So I decided to serve fun-shaped veggies at Easter.

1. Trim the stem end off each tomato with a sharp knife. Then slice each tomato from the top to about three-quarters of the way down (don't cut all the way through or it won't stay together as a flower). Turn the tomato and slice it again about three-quarters of the way down so you have four quartered cuts in each tomato. Remove the guts of the tomatoes.

2. In a medium bowl, combine the ingredients for the filling. Stir together until well blended.

3. Place the filling in a piping bag or plastic bag with a small hole cut in one corner. Squeeze the filling into each tomato shell.

4. To assemble: Place the trimmed green onions on a serving platter in a fan shape. Place the filled tomatoes at the top part of the green onions to resemble an arrangement of tulips. Enjoy!

TIP:

If you prefer to skip the step of cutting the tomatoes into flowers and filling them, serve the filling as a dip in a serving bowl with the tomatoes placed around it.

KETO

NUTRITIONAL INFO (per serving)				
calories	fat	protein	carbs	fiber
77	6.7g	2g	2.9g	0g
	77%	10%	13%	

Purple
PICKLED EGGS

NUT-FREE   DAIRY-FREE   VEGE-TARIAN

Prep Time: 15 minutes, plus 8 hours to pickle

Yield: 12 servings

12 large eggs

BRINE:

4 cups coconut vinegar or apple cider vinegar

⅓ cup Swerve confectioners'-style sweetener or equivalent amount of liquid or powdered sweetener (see page 37)

1 tablespoon pickling spice

1 teaspoon fine sea salt

2 cups thickly sliced red onions

1 cup shredded purple cabbage

Pickled eggs are perfect to pack for long road trips or camping trips!

1. Place the eggs in a large saucepan and cover with cold water. Bring the water to a boil, then immediately cover the pan and remove it from the heat. Allow the eggs to cook in the hot water for 11 minutes. After 11 minutes, drain the water and rinse the eggs with very cold water for a minute or two to stop the cooking process. Peel the boiled eggs.

2. Place the ingredients for the brine in a medium bowl and stir well to dissolve the sweetener and salt.

3. Place the peeled eggs in a sterile quart-sized mason jar. Pour the brine over the eggs in the jar. Add the red onions and cabbage. Cover and allow to pickle in the refrigerator overnight before consuming. Store in the refrigerator for up to 2 weeks.

KETO (L M H)

NUTRITIONAL INFO (per serving)				
calories	fat	protein	carbs	fiber
64	4.4g	5.6g	0.5g	0g
	62%	35%	3%	

Baked
BACON-WRAPPED PICKLES

NUT-FREE   DAIRY-FREE

Prep Time: 5 minutes

Cook Time: 30 minutes

Yield: 6 servings

6 pickle spears, store-bought or homemade (page 318)

6 slices bacon

Green Goddess Dressing (page 117), for serving

1. Preheat the oven or toaster oven to 425°F. Set a wire rack on top of a rimmed baking sheet.

2. Tightly wrap each pickle spear with a slice of bacon.

3. Place the wrapped pickles on the wire rack (inside the rimmed baking sheet). Bake for 20 to 30 minutes, until the bacon is cooked to your desired doneness. Remove from the oven and place on paper towels to drain.

4. Serve hot with Green Goddess Dressing.

KETO

NUTRITIONAL INFO (per serving)				
calories	fat	protein	carbs	fiber
106	9g	5.3g	1.1g	1.1g
	76%	20%	4%	

Classic
DEVILED EGGS

NUT-FREE DAIRY-FREE VEGE-TARIAN

Prep Time: 5 minutes

Cook Time: 15 minutes

Yield: 12 servings

12 large eggs

½ cup mayonnaise, store-bought or homemade (page 112)

2 teaspoons coconut vinegar or apple cider vinegar

2 teaspoons prepared yellow mustard

½ teaspoon fine sea salt

Smoked paprika, for garnish

TIP:

I keep a dozen hard-boiled eggs in my fridge at all times. My boys, who are five and six, love to help me in the kitchen, and peeling eggs is one of the things they can do without my constant attention so I can prepare other food.

I make these often for our hiking and beach adventures and store them in my backpacking cooler.

1. Place the eggs in a large saucepan and cover with cold water. Bring the water to a boil, then immediately cover the pan and remove it from the heat. Allow the eggs to cook in the hot water for 11 minutes. After 11 minutes, drain the water and rinse the eggs with very cold water for a minute or two to stop the cooking process. Peel the boiled eggs and cut them in half lengthwise.

2. Remove the egg yolks and place them in a bowl. Mash the yolks with a fork until they have the texture of very fine crumbles. Add the mayonnaise, vinegar, mustard, and salt and mix until evenly combined.

3. Fill the egg white halves with the yolk mixture. Sprinkle with paprika. Store any leftovers in an airtight container in the refrigerator for up to 3 days.

L M H
KETO

NUTRITIONAL INFO (per serving)				
calories	fat	protein	carbs	fiber
124	11.1g	5.6g	0.4g	0g
	81%	18%	1%	

Sriracha
DEVILED EGGS

NUT-FREE · DAIRY-FREE · VEGE-TARIAN

Prep Time: 5 minutes

Cook Time: 15 minutes

Yield: 12 servings

12 large eggs

½ cup mayonnaise, store-bought or homemade (page 112)

2 teaspoons prepared yellow mustard

1 to 2 teaspoons Sriracha (depending on desired spiciness), store-bought or homemade (page 124)

½ teaspoon fine sea salt

1 green onion, green part only, cut into ¼-inch-wide pieces, for garnish (optional)

These are similar to my Classic Deviled Eggs (page 184)—but with a kick! The Sriracha gives the filling a deep pumpkin-orange hue, making these deviled eggs perfect for a Halloween- or autumn-themed snack.

1. Place the eggs in a large saucepan and cover with cold water. Bring the water to a boil, then immediately cover the pan and remove it from the heat. Allow the eggs to cook in the hot water for 11 minutes. After 11 minutes, drain the water and rinse the eggs with very cold water for a minute or two to stop the cooking process. Peel the boiled eggs and cut them in half lengthwise.

2. Remove the egg yolks and place them in a bowl. Mash the yolks with a fork until they have the texture of very fine crumbles. Add the mayonnaise, mustard, Sriracha, and salt and mix until evenly combined.

3. Fill the egg white halves with the yolk mixture. If desired, incise four lines, running lengthwise, in the top of the filling with the tip of a knife to make a pumpkin design and place a piece of green onion at the top of the "pumpkin" for the stem. Store any leftovers in an airtight container in the fridge for up to 3 days.

L · M · H
KETO

NUTRITIONAL INFO (per serving)				
calories	fat	protein	carbs	fiber
124	11.1g	5.6g	0.4g	0g
	81%	18%	1%	

Teriyaki JERKY

EGG-FREE   NUT-FREE   DAIRY-FREE

Prep Time: 5 minutes, plus 1 hour to freeze and 2 hours to marinate

Cook Time: 6 to 8 hours

Yield: 8 servings

1 pound boneless venison or beef, preferably eye of round or rump roast

MARINADE:

½ cup coconut aminos or wheat-free tamari

3 tablespoons MCT oil or macadamia nut oil

2 teaspoons Swerve confectioners'-style sweetener or equivalent amount of liquid or powdered sweetener (see page 37)

2 teaspoons lime juice

1 tablespoon grated fresh ginger

1 teaspoon finely chopped garlic, or cloves from ½ head roasted garlic (page 134)

1 teaspoon fine sea salt

Special Equipment:
Dehydrator (optional)

Jerky tastes great and is the ultimate portable food. We often pack it on camping trips. But it is hard to find store-bought jerky that doesn't contain gluten or soy. Thankfully, making homemade jerky is extremely easy; it just takes time to dehydrate. My tip for you is to make a double batch and store it in the freezer.

1. Place the meat in the freezer for 1 hour to make it easier to slice cleanly. Slice the meat across the grain into long strips, 1 inch wide and ⅛ inch thick.

2. Combine the marinade ingredients in a large shallow bowl. Submerge the strips of meat in the marinade, cover, and marinate in the fridge for at least 2 hours or overnight. Remove the meat from the marinade and sprinkle with the salt.

3. Dehydrator method: Place the strips of meat in a dehydrator, not touching each other, and set the dehydrator to low (170°F).

4. Oven method: If you do not have a dehydrator, preheat the oven to 160°F. Place a rimmed baking sheet on the bottom of the oven (or bottom rack) to catch drips. Arrange the strips of marinated meat directly on the middle rack, not touching each other. Alternatively, place a wire rack on a rimmed baking sheet and arrange the strips of meat on the wire rack.

5. For both methods: Dehydrate the meat for 6 to 8 hours, until the jerky dries to the desired chewiness. For a chewier jerky, dehydrate for less time.

6. Store in an airtight container in the refrigerator for up to 2 weeks or in the freezer for up to a month.

KETO

NUTRITIONAL INFO (per serving)				
calories	fat	protein	carbs	fiber
84	4g	16.9g	0g	0g
	35%	65%	0%	

Dad's
TENDERLOIN BITES

OPTION
EGG-FREE NUT-FREE DAIRY-FREE

Prep Time: *10 minutes, plus 2 hours to marinate*

Cook Time: *5 minutes*

Yield: *12 servings*

MARINADE:

½ cup coconut aminos or wheat-free tamari

3 tablespoons MCT oil

2 teaspoons Swerve confectioners'-style sweetener or equivalent amount of liquid or powdered sweetener (see page 37)

1 tablespoon grated fresh ginger

1 teaspoon finely chopped garlic, or cloves from ½ head roasted garlic (page 134)

1 (1-pound) venison or beef tenderloin, cut into 2-inch cubes

1 (16-ounce) package bacon

Green Goddess Dressing (page 117), for serving (optional; omit for egg-free)

My dad and I have a very special connection. We bond over a lot of things, including a love of bow hunting, which he taught me how to do. He made this simple dish for me at his cabin ten years ago, and it is still a crowd-pleaser at parties! I modified his recipe to eliminate the sugar and soy sauce to make it keto-friendly. He now follows this recipe.

1. In a bowl, mix together the marinade ingredients. Add the tenderloin pieces, toss to coat in the marinade, cover, and place in the refrigerator to marinate for at least 2 hours or overnight.

2. Place an oven rack in the top position and preheat the oven to broil.

3. While the oven is heating up, assemble the bites: Cut the bacon slices in half crosswise. Take a piece of marinated meat and wrap it with a halved bacon slice. Secure with a toothpick and place on a rimmed baking sheet. Repeat with the rest of the meat and bacon.

4. Place the baking sheet under the broiler. Broil for 5 minutes for medium-rare or until done to your liking (they will continue to cook after you remove from the oven). Serve with Green Goddess Dressing, if desired.

PARTY TIP:

These bites can be prepared up to 2 days ahead and popped in the oven just before serving for an easy appetizer at your next keto gathering.

NOTE:

Serving the bites with Green Goddess Dressing increases the keto ratio from medium to high.

KETO

or high if served with dressing

NUTRITIONAL INFO (per serving)				
calories	fat	protein	carbs	fiber
299	18g	36g	0.4g	0g
	54%	45.5%	0.5%	

Paleo Deep-Fried MUSHROOMS

NUT-FREE   DAIRY-FREE

Prep Time: 10 minutes

Cook Time: 10 minutes

Yield: 4 servings

1 cup coconut oil or duck fat, for frying

16 thin slices prosciutto

32 whole small button mushrooms (about 1 pound)

Dairy-Free Ranch Dressing (page 118), for dipping

1. Heat the oil to 350°F in a deep fryer or in a 4-inch-deep (or deeper) skillet over medium-high heat. The oil should be at least 1½ inches deep; add more oil if needed.

2. While the oil is heating up, prepare the mushrooms: Lay a slice of prosciutto on a clean work surface. Slice it in half lengthwise. Place a mushroom in the middle of the half prosciutto slice and wrap the prosciutto tightly around the mushroom. Prosciutto is sticky, so it will stay in place. Repeat until all the mushrooms are wrapped.

3. Working in batches, fry the wrapped mushrooms by placing them in the hot oil for about 2 minutes, or until crisp on the outside. Remove from the oil and serve with the dressing.

KETO

NUTRITIONAL INFO (per serving)				
calories	fat	protein	carbs	fiber
93	7.6g	4.6g	1.8g	0.6g
	73.5%	19.5%	7%	

Primal SLIDERS

NUT-FREE   OPTION DAIRY-FREE

Prep Time: 10 minutes

Cook Time: 16 minutes

Yield: 4 servings

1 tablespoon coconut oil or duck fat (or unsalted butter if not dairy-sensitive)

1 pound 80% lean ground beef

1 teaspoon fine sea salt or Seasoned Salt (page 109)

4 lettuce leaves, ripped into 24 pieces total

24 small slices white cheddar cheese (omit for dairy-free)

24 pickle chips, store-bought or homemade (page 318)

24 olives, pitted

12 cherry tomatoes, halved

Green Goddess Dressing (page 117), for garnish

1. Heat the oil in a large sauté pan over medium heat.

2. While the oil is heating up, form the beef into 24 small patties about ⅔ ounce (1½ inches across) each. Season the sliders on both sides with the salt. Fry the patties in the skillet in batches, about 4 minutes per side for well-done or until cooked to your desired doneness.

3. While the second batch is frying, assemble the first batch of sliders: Place a burger patty on a serving platter and top it with a piece of lettuce, a slice of cheese (if using), a pickle chip, an olive, and a cherry tomato half. Secure with a toothpick. Repeat with the rest of the cooked patties and slider ingredients. Drizzle the sliders with the dressing before serving.

KETO   L   M   H

NUTRITIONAL INFO (per serving)				
calories	fat	protein	carbs	fiber
595	40g	55g	5g	1.4g
	62%	37%	1%	

Chili Lime
WINGS

Prep Time: 5 minutes

Cook Time: 25 minutes

Yield: 4 servings

2 pounds chicken wings

CHILI LIME SAUCE:

½ cup coconut oil (or softened unsalted butter if not dairy-sensitive)

1 tablespoon Thai red curry paste

2 tablespoons Swerve confectioners'-style sweetener or equivalent amount of liquid or powdered sweetener (see page 37)

¼ cup coconut aminos or wheat-free tamari

Juice of 1 lime

FOR SERVING:

Sliced green onion (optional)

Thinly sliced purple endive or radicchio (optional)

1. Preheat the oven to 425°F.

2. Spread out the wings on a rimmed baking sheet. Bake for 25 minutes, or until the chicken is cooked through and the skins are crisp.

3. While the wings are cooking, put the coconut oil, red curry paste, sweetener, and coconut aminos in a large bowl and mix well. Add the lime juice and stir to combine. When the wings come out of the oven, add them to the bowl and toss until well coated.

4. Garnish the wings with sliced green onion and serve with purple endive on the side, if desired. Serve with extra sauce for dipping.

KETO

NUTRITIONAL INFO (per serving)				
calories	fat	protein	carbs	fiber
428	35.1g	26.4g	2.6g	0g
	74%	24%	2%	

Eggs
GRIBICHE

NUT-FREE DAIRY-FREE VEGE-TARIAN

Prep Time: 5 minutes

Cook Time: 15 minutes

Yield: 4 servings

6 large hard-boiled eggs (see page 184)

¼ cup MCT oil or extra-virgin olive oil

½ teaspoon finely chopped garlic, or 4 cloves roasted garlic (page 134)

2 tablespoons chopped fresh chives

1 tablespoon capers, rinsed and chopped

1 tablespoon chopped cornichons

1 teaspoon whole-grain mustard

1 teaspoon finely chopped fresh tarragon

½ teaspoon fine sea salt

L M H
KETO

NUTRITIONAL INFO (per serving)				
as starter				
calories	fat	protein	carbs	fiber
229	20.7g	8.5g	0.9g	0g
	82%	16%	2%	

NUTRITIONAL INFO (per serving)				
as vegetarian meal				
calories	fat	protein	carbs	fiber
458	17g	17g	1.8g	0g
	82%	16%	2%	

If you are looking to make this recipe even easier, you can purchase hard-boiled eggs from a local market. Gribiche is delicious spooned over Spring Popovers (page 146) or, as shown in the photo, with slices of keto bread that have been fried in coconut oil. (You can find my recipe for keto bread on my site, MariaMindBodyHealth.com [search for "keto-adapted bread"] or in my book *The Ketogenic Cookbook*.)

Peel the hard-boiled eggs and chop them into small pieces. Using a fork, gently mix all the ingredients together in a small bowl.

NOTE:

For a full meal that serves two, divide the gribiche between 2 serving bowls and serve with 4 Spring Popovers (page 146) and a green salad tossed with the keto dressing of your choice (pages 116 to 121).

Zucchini
CHIPS

NUT-
FREE

VEGE-
TARIAN

Prep Time: 2 minutes, plus 21 minutes for the zucchini tortillas

Cook Time: 30 minutes

Yield: 4 servings

1 recipe Zucchini Tortillas (page 212)

One evening, as we were enjoying taco night with our usual accompaniment of Zucchini Tortillas (page 212), I was thinking about how many batches of tortillas I've wasted by burning them to a crisp. Yes, I thought . . . they crisped up! I realized that if I just lowered the temperature and increased the baking time, I could crisp them up without the burnt flavor. It worked great!

These chips taste great on their own, but to make them more keto, I suggest serving them with a keto dip, such as guacamole (page 136), Blue Cheese Dressing (page 119), or Olive Salsa (page 135). Or serve them with one of the following main dishes: Slow Cooker BBQ Chicken Wraps (page 207), Slow Cooker Beef Barbacoa Wraps (page 210), or Slow Cooker BBQ Pork Wraps (page 203).

1. Preheat the oven to 300°F. Line two large baking sheets with parchment paper and grease the paper well with coconut oil spray. Set aside.

2. Using a pizza cutter, cut the zucchini tortillas into tortilla chip shapes. Place on the prepared baking sheets. Bake for 20 to 30 minutes, until dark brown.

3. Remove from the oven and allow to cool a little. Once cool to the touch, remove them from the parchment and allow to cool completely. They will crisp up as they cool.

4. Store in an airtight container in the fridge for up to 4 days.

KETO

NUTRITIONAL INFO (per serving)				
calories	fat	protein	carbs	fiber
150	10.8g	10g	4.2g	1.2g
	63.5%	26.5%	10%	

Roll-Ups
AND WRAPS

CHAPTER 8

Prosciutto and Arugula
ROLL-UPS

NUT-FREE DAIRY-FREE ONE POT/BOWL

Prep Time: 8 minutes

Yield: 6 roll-ups (2 per serving)

2 cups arugula, mizuna, and/or other torn leafy lettuce

¼ cup Green Goddess Dressing (page 117) or other dairy-free keto dressing (pages 116 to 121)

12 thin slices prosciutto (about 4 ounces)

2 large hard-boiled eggs (see page 184), peeled and chopped

1 small tomato, chopped

1. Place the arugula in a medium-sized bowl and toss it with the dressing.

2. Lay a slice of prosciutto on a clean work surface with the narrow end facing you. Place a small handful of the dressed arugula along the edge of the prosciutto closest to you, then top with ½ tablespoon each of the chopped eggs and tomato. Roll up and place seam side down on a serving platter. Repeat with the remaining ingredients.

3. Store in an airtight container in the refrigerator for up to 4 days. Do not freeze.

KETO

NUTRITIONAL INFO (per serving)				
calories	fat	protein	carbs	fiber
116	9.6g	6.2g	1.2g	0g
	75%	21%	4%	

Mini Pastrami
ROLL-UPS

EGG-FREE · NUT-FREE · DAIRY-FREE (OPTION) · ONE POT/BOWL

Prep Time: 8 minutes

Yield: 8 servings (8 bite-sized pieces or 1 large roll-up per serving)

1 pound thinly sliced pastrami

8 ounces chive cream cheese (or Dairy-Free Minute "Cream Cheese" Spread, page 138, for dairy-free)

8 dill pickles, store-bought or homemade (page 318)

My boys enjoy these roll-ups so much that I often make a large batch to keep in the fridge. In fact, they'll grab a whole roll-up, saving me the task of cutting them into bite-sized pieces.

1. Lay a slice of pastrami on a clean work surface with the shorter end facing you. Evenly spread 2 tablespoons of the cream cheese over the pastrami. Place a pickle at the closest end to you, then roll the pastrami around the pickle. Slice crosswise into eight pieces, secure the pastrami ends with toothpicks, and place the mini roll-ups on a serving platter. Repeat with the remaining ingredients. (Note: To save time, leave the roll-ups whole, to make eight roll-ups total.)

2. Store in an airtight container in the refrigerator for up to 4 days. Do not freeze.

KETO

NUTRITIONAL INFO (per serving)				
calories	fat	protein	carbs	fiber
197	13.5g	14.9g	4g	1.6g
	62%	30%	8%	

Turkey
SUSHI

NUT-FREE   ONE POT/BOWL

Prep Time: 5 minutes

Yield: 3 servings

12 slices roast deli turkey (about 4 ounces)

½ cup plus 2 tablespoons mayonnaise, store-bought or homemade (page 112), or any keto-friendly dressing, such as Dairy-Free Ranch Dressing (page 118)

12 slices provolone cheese

12 thin slices tomato

1 cup arugula, micro salad greens, or torn lettuce leaves of choice

We eat with our eyes! Sure, these roll-ups can be eaten without being cut into fun sushi slices, but my kids appreciate the little extra time it takes to make food cute. Plus, I get the bonus of eating the end pieces that are not perfect sushi shapes!

1. Place a slice of turkey on a clean work surface with the short end facing you. Spread 2½ teaspoons of mayo or keto-friendly dressing on the turkey. Top with a slice of provolone cheese and then a slice of tomato. Arrange the greens across the top of the tomato.

2. Starting at the end closest to you, roll it up like a sushi roll and slice into 1-inch pieces. Store leftovers in an airtight container in the fridge for up to 4 days.

VARIATION: TURKEY ROLL-UPS.

Save yourself the step of cutting the rolled-up turkey slices into sushi-like portions and serve them whole instead. Makes 12 roll-ups (4 per serving).

SINGLE SERVING OPTION

To make a single serving, use 4 slices roast deli turkey, 2 heaping tablespoons mayonnaise or other keto-friendly dressing, 4 slices provolone cheese, 4 slices tomato, and a handful of greens.

KETO

NUTRITIONAL INFO (per serving)				
calories	fat	protein	carbs	fiber
406	31.7g	24.6g	5.4g	0.7g
	71%	24%	5%	

Philly Cheesesteak ROLL-UPS

EGG-FREE NUT-FREE

Prep Time: 8 minutes

Cook Time: 10 minutes

Yield: 12 roll-ups (2 per serving)

FILLING:

2 tablespoons coconut oil or unsalted butter

1 large green bell pepper, thinly sliced

½ cup thinly sliced onions

½ teaspoon fine sea salt

⅛ teaspoon fresh ground black pepper

12 slices roast beef (from the deli counter), cut into 6-by-2-inch strips

2 cups shredded provolone cheese (about 8 ounces)

TIP:

Instead of using a green bell pepper, use 1 cup store-bought roasted red peppers, sliced into strips. Place the onions in a microwave-safe dish with a tablespoon of coconut oil or butter and microwave on high for 1 minute, or until softened.

KETO

NUTRITIONAL INFO (per serving)				
calories	fat	protein	carbs	fiber
312	19.3g	30.5g	3.1g	0.7g
	56%	39%	4%	

To make this dish even easier, you can use a jar of marinated red bell peppers and skip the step of sautéing the green peppers in the oil (see Tip).

1. Preheat the oven to 300°F.

2. To make the filling: Heat the coconut oil in a large sauté pan over medium heat. Add the sliced green pepper and onions and cook until the pepper is soft and the onions are translucent, about 6 minutes. Season with the salt and pepper. Remove from the heat.

3. Lay a slice of roast beef on a clean work surface with the shorter end in front of you. Sprinkle about 2 tablespoons of the shredded cheese on the slice of roast beef. Place 2 tablespoons of the sautéed veggies on top of the cheese. Roll it up, starting at the short end. Place the roll seam side down in a large casserole dish. Repeat with the remaining roast beef and filling.

4. Top the roll-ups with the remaining cheese. Bake for 10 minutes, or until the cheese is completely melted. Serve warm.

5. Store leftovers in an airtight container for up to 3 days. Reheat in a 350°F oven for 4 minutes or in the microwave for 30 seconds, or until heated through.

Slow Cooker
BBQ PORK WRAPS

EGG-FREE · NUT-FREE · DAIRY-FREE · ONE POT/BOWL · SLOW COOKER

Prep Time: 5 minutes

Cook Time: 8 hours

Yield: 20 lettuce wraps (2 per serving) or 10 tortilla wraps (1 per serving)

PORK:

1 medium onion, sliced into thick rings

1 (3½-pound) boneless pork shoulder roast

5 cloves garlic, sliced

2 tablespoons paprika

1 teaspoon garlic powder

1 teaspoon chili powder

1 teaspoon fresh ground black pepper

1 teaspoon fine sea salt

2 teaspoons liquid smoke

3 cups chicken bone broth, store-bought or homemade (page 132)

WRAPS:

20 large Boston lettuce leaves or 10 Zucchini Tortillas (page 212), for wrapping

TOPPINGS (OPTIONAL):

Shredded red cabbage

Sliced or halved olives

Halved or quartered cherry tomatoes

KETO (L / M / H)

NUTRITIONAL INFO (per serving)				
calories	fat	protein	carbs	fiber
425	32.6g	27.8g	3.1g	1g
	70%	27%	3%	

1. Place the sliced onion in the bottom of a 4-quart slow cooker. Place the pork roast on top of the onion. Then add the garlic, spices, salt, liquid smoke, and broth. Cover and cook on low until the center of the meat reaches 160°F (tested with a meat thermometer), about 8 hours.

2. Transfer the meat to a cutting board and shred using two forks. Dice the cooked onion and mix into the shredded pork.

3. Serve in lettuce leaves or Zucchini Tortillas with the toppings of your choice.

4. Store leftovers in an airtight container in the refrigerator for up to 4 days.

Easy Tuna Salad
WRAPS

NUT-FREE DAIRY-FREE ONE POT/BOWL

Prep Time: 7 minutes

Yield: 4 lettuce wraps (2 per serving) or 2 tortilla wraps (1 per serving)

TUNA SALAD:

2 (3.75-ounce) cans tuna

¼ cup plus 2 tablespoons mayonnaise, store-bought or homemade (page 112)

½ teaspoon fine sea salt

⅛ teaspoon dried onion flakes or 2 tablespoons chopped fresh chives

WRAPS:

6 large Boston lettuce leaves or 3 Zucchini Tortillas (page 212)

FOR GARNISH (OPTIONAL):

1 tablespoon chopped fresh chives

6 cherry tomatoes

My dad loves to go salmon fishing and can his own salmon, which has a flavor that reminds me of canned tuna. If you prefer to use canned salmon in this recipe, it would be a great substitution (see Variation below).

I served these wraps at my son's birthday party as an easy appetizer, and they were a hit!

1. To make the tuna salad: In a large bowl, combine the tuna, mayo, salt, and onion flakes.

2. Arrange the lettuce leaves or tortillas on a cutting board.

3. Place 3 tablespoons of the tuna salad on each lettuce leaf or 6 tablespoons on each tortilla. Garnish with the fresh chives and tomatoes, if desired. Roll up the lettuce leaves or tortillas around the tuna salad and enjoy!

4. Store leftover salad in an airtight container in the refrigerator for up to 4 days.

VARIATION: EASY SALMON SALAD WRAPS.

I prefer to buy canned salmon rather than canned tuna. Canned salmon not only tastes just as good as canned tuna, but it has a better fat ratio for ketogenic eating, as well as less mercury! To make salmon wraps, simply replace the tuna with an equivalent amount of canned salmon.

KETO

NUTRITIONAL INFO (per serving)				
calories	fat	protein	carbs	fiber
441	37.2g	23.9g	0.8g	0g
	76%	22%	1%	

Sardine Salad
WRAPS

EGG-FREE · NUT-FREE · DAIRY-FREE · ONE POT/BOWL

Prep Time: 5 minutes

Yield: 8 lettuce wraps (4 per serving) or 4 tortilla wraps (2 per serving)

SARDINE SALAD:

2 tablespoons MCT oil or extra-virgin olive oil

2 tablespoons chopped green onions or fresh chives

1 tablespoon finely chopped fresh tarragon

1 tablespoon capers, rinsed

1 tablespoon lime or lemon juice

1 teaspoon whole-grain or Dijon mustard

2 (4.4-ounce) cans sardines, drained (see Note)

1 teaspoon fine sea salt

¼ teaspoon fresh ground black pepper

WRAPS:

8 large radicchio or Boston lettuce leaves or 4 Zucchini Tortillas (page 212)

Sardines are a great keto food! Using sardines with the bones in not only gives this salad a nice added crunch, it also gives you the calcium benefits from the bones.

1. To make the sardine salad: In a large bowl, combine the oil, green onions, tarragon, capers, lime juice, and mustard.

2. Lightly fold in the sardines and season with the salt and pepper.

3. Serve in radicchio leaves. Store leftover salad in an airtight container in the refrigerator for up to 4 days.

NOTE:

Check the ingredients list of the sardines. They should not be packed in canola or soybean oil.

KETO

NUTRITIONAL INFO (per serving)				
calories	fat	protein	carbs	fiber
386	28.5g	31.2g	0.9g	0g
	66.8%	32.3%	0.9%	

Slow Cooker
BBQ CHICKEN WRAPS

EGG-FREE · NUT-FREE · DAIRY-FREE · ONE POT/BOWL · SLOW COOKER

Prep Time: 10 minutes

Cook Time: 3 to 4 hours

Yield: 12 lettuce wraps (2 per serving) or 6 tortilla wraps (1 per serving)

BBQ CHICKEN SALAD:

½ onion, sliced into thick rings

2 pounds boneless, skinless chicken thighs

Fine sea salt

1 cup tomato sauce

¼ cup chicken bone broth, store-bought or homemade (page 132)

¼ cup Swerve confectioners'-style sweetener or equivalent amount of liquid or powdered sweetener (see page 37)

1 teaspoon liquid smoke

WRAPS:

12 large Boston lettuce leaves or 6 Zucchini Tortillas (page 212)

12 green onions, for tying wraps (optional)

FOR SERVING:

BBQ Sauce (page 125) (optional)

This barbecued chicken is so good that, in addition to enjoying it in wraps, we sometimes eat a plateful as is!

1. Lay the onions in a 4-quart slow cooker. Season the chicken with salt (about ⅛ teaspoon per thigh) and place on top of the onions. Pour in the tomato sauce, broth, sweetener, and liquid smoke. Cover and cook on high for 3 to 4 hours.

2. Remove the chicken from the slow cooker and transfer to a cutting board. Shred the chicken using two forks. Dice the cooked onion and stir into the shredded chicken. Return the shredded chicken and onion to the slow cooker and turn in the sauce to allow it soak up the tasty sauce.

3. Serve in Boston lettuce leaves or Zucchini Tortillas. Tie each wrap closed with a decorative piece of green onion, if desired. Serve with barbecue sauce, if desired.

4. Store leftovers in an airtight container in the refrigerator for up to 4 days.

KETO

NUTRITIONAL INFO (per serving)				
calories	fat	protein	carbs	fiber
308	18.6g	29.6g	3.2g	0.9g
	55%	39%	5%	

Slow Cooker
CHICKEN CAESAR WRAPS

NUT-FREE | OPTION DAIRY-FREE | SLOW COOKER

Prep Time: 10 minutes

Cook Time: 4 to 6 hours

Yield: 12 wraps (2 per serving)

CHICKEN:

2 pounds boneless, skinless chicken thighs

2 cups chicken bone broth, store-bought or homemade (page 132)

1 teaspoon fine sea salt

1 teaspoon fresh ground black pepper

½ cup Caesar dressing, store-bought (see Note) or homemade (page 116), plus more if desired

½ cup grated Parmesan cheese (about 2 ounces) (optional; omit for dairy-free)

¼ cup chopped fresh flat-leaf parsley

½ teaspoon fresh ground black pepper

WRAPS:

1 head romaine lettuce, leaves separated

12 green onions, for tying wraps (optional)

1. Place the chicken in a 4-quart slow cooker along with the broth, salt, and pepper. Cover and cook on low for 4 to 6 hours.

2. Remove the chicken from the slow cooker using a slotted spoon and transfer to a cutting board. (Discard the broth in the slow cooker.) Shred the chicken using two forks.

3. Place the shredded chicken in a bowl and pour the dressing over the top. Add the Parmesan cheese (if using), parsley, and pepper and stir until evenly mixed.

4. Serve wrapped in romaine leaves on a platter. Tie each wrap closed with a decorative piece of green onion, if desired.

5. Store leftovers in an airtight container in the refrigerator for up to 4 days.

NOTE:

If using store-bought Caesar dressing, check the ingredients list to make sure that it contains no soybean oil or sweetener.

L — M — H
KETO

NUTRITIONAL INFO (per serving)				
calories	fat	protein	carbs	fiber
517	35.7g	43g	3g	0.6g
	63%	34%	3%	

Bento
BOX IT!

Prep Time: 5 minutes

Yield: 1 to 4 servings (depending on amounts)

Suggestions for Bento Boxes:

Cheese curds

Salami

Olives

Pickles, store-bought or homemade (page 318)

Mini Pastrami Roll-Ups (page 199)

Turkey Sushi (page 200)

Hard-boiled eggs or Classic Deviled Eggs (page 184)

Sriracha Deviled Eggs (page 185)

Teriyaki Jerky (page 186)

Cherry tomatoes with Dill Dip (page 178)

Smoked Salmon (page 370)

Dairy-Free Milk Chocolate Protein Bars (page 154)

Strawberry Cheesecake Protein Bars (page 156)

Bananas Foster Fudge (page 353)

Many times we are looking for easy on-the-go lunches and snacks. Why not ratchet it up just a notch and pack lunches for yourself and your kids in fun bento boxes? I find it well worth the extra time to make food not just pleasurable to our taste buds but, as a bonus, a treat to look at as well. We eat with our eyes, too!

Slow Cooker

BEEF BARBACOA WRAPS

EGG-FREE NUT-FREE DAIRY-FREE ONE POT/BOWL SLOW COOKER

Prep Time: 10 minutes

Cook Time: 5 to 8 hours

Yield: 16 lettuce wraps (2 per serving) or 8 tortilla wraps (1 per serving)

BEEF BARBACOA:

1 large onion, sliced into 1-inch-thick rounds

1 (3-pound) boneless chuck roast

3 to 4 canned chipotle chiles

2 cups beef bone broth, store-bought or homemade (page 132)

⅓ cup coconut vinegar or apple cider vinegar

¼ cup lime juice

2 teaspoons finely chopped garlic, or cloves from 1 head roasted garlic (page 134)

1 teaspoon fine sea salt

1½ tablespoons chili powder

2 teaspoons dried oregano leaves

1½ teaspoons ground cumin

¼ teaspoon fresh ground black pepper

WRAPS:

16 large Boston lettuce leaves or 8 Zucchini Tortillas (page 212)

1. Place a layer of onions on the bottom of a 4-quart slow cooker. Place the roast and chiles on top of the onions. Pour the broth, vinegar, and lime juice over the roast, then add the garlic, salt, and spices to the slow cooker.

2. Cover and cook on low for 6 to 8 hours or on high for 5 to 6 hours, until the beef falls apart and can be shredded with a fork.

3. Remove the roast and transfer it to a cutting board. Shred the meat and serve in lettuce or tortilla wraps with your desired toppings.

TOPPINGS (OPTIONAL):

Shredded purple cabbage

Shredded cheddar cheese (omit for dairy-free)

Sliced olives

Diced tomato

Guacamole (page 136)

Sour cream (omit for dairy-free)

Lime wedges

TIP:

This dish is a great one to make ahead on a lazy Sunday for a weekday meal. After shredding the meat, return it to the slow cooker insert, cover, and refrigerate. When ready to consume, remove the slow cooker insert from the fridge and heat on low for 15 to 30 minutes to warm the meat through.

NOTE:

The nutritional information below is for the meat only. It does not account for any additional accompaniments. Higher-fat accompaniments such as guacamole, olives, sour cream, and cheese will help increase the fat ratio.

KETO

NUTRITIONAL INFO (per serving)				
calories	fat	protein	carbs	fiber
388	15.2g	56.5g	2.5g	0g
	37%	60%	3%	

Zucchini TORTILLAS

NUT-FREE · VEGE-TARIAN · VIDEO

Prep Time: 10 minutes

Cook Time: 15 minutes

Yield: 12 tortillas (2 per serving)

4 cups grated zucchini or combination of zucchini and yellow summer squash (about 4 medium)

½ teaspoon fine sea salt

1 cup shredded sharp cheddar cheese or grated Parmesan cheese (about 4 ounces)

1 large egg

1 tablespoon coconut flour

1 teaspoon Taco Seasoning (page 110)

We enjoy these versatile tortillas with all sorts of meals. Some of our favorite dishes to pair with them are Slow Cooker BBQ Chicken Wraps (page 207), Slow Cooker Beef Barbacoa Wraps (page 210), Slow Cooker BBQ Pork Wraps (page 203), and Taco Bar Night (page 270). I often prepare a double batch so I have leftovers for making Zucchini Chips (page 194). If you're a visual learner like me and would like to see how easy these are to make, check out the video on my site, MariaMindBodyHealth.com (type the word *video* in the search field).

1. Preheat the oven to 375°F. Line two large baking sheets with parchment paper and grease the paper well with coconut oil spray. Set aside.

2. Place the zucchini in a colander over a sink. Sprinkle with the salt and let sit for 5 minutes to draw out the moisture.

3. After 5 minutes, use your hands to squeeze out the moisture from the zucchini. Place the zucchini in a large mixing bowl with the cheese.

4. Add the egg, coconut flour, and taco seasoning and mix well with your hands.

5. Using a ⅓-cup measuring cup or your hand, scoop up six portions of the "dough" and place them on a lined baking sheet, 3 to 4 inches apart. Use your fingers to spread out each mound of dough into a 3½-inch tortilla. Repeat with the rest of the dough and second baking sheet.

6. Bake for 12 to 15 minutes, until light golden brown. Remove from the oven and let cool on the baking sheets. Once the tortillas are cool enough to touch, remove them from the parchment and enjoy!

TIP:

The recipe works great whether you use peeled or unpeeled zucchini, so to save time, you can leave the peel on. I make a double batch of tortillas to keep in the fridge for easy additions to dinners. They can be frozen, too. Store extras in an airtight container in the fridge for up to 4 days or freeze for up to 1 month. Reheat thawed tortillas in a preheated oven for 3 minutes or in the microwave for 30 seconds, or until heated through.

L — M — H
KETO

NUTRITIONAL INFO (per serving)				
calories	fat	protein	carbs	fiber
106	7.4g	6.9g	3.6g	1.3g
	62%	26%	12%	

Soups
AND SALADS

CHAPTER 9

Broccoli "Noodle" CHEESE SOUP

Prep Time: *12 minutes*

Cook Time: *18 minutes*

Yield: *6 servings as a starter, 4 servings as a meal*

1 large head broccoli with stem

2 slices bacon, chopped into ¼-inch pieces

2 tablespoons unsalted butter

¼ cup diced onions

1 teaspoon finely chopped garlic, or cloves from ½ head roasted garlic (page 134)

2 ounces (¼ cup) cream cheese

3 cups chicken or beef bone broth, store-bought or homemade (page 132)

1½ cups shredded extra-sharp cheddar cheese (about 6 ounces)

½ teaspoon fine sea salt

¼ teaspoon fresh ground black pepper

Pinch of ground nutmeg

Special Equipment:
Spiral slicer

When I made broccoli "noodles" for carbonara (page 286), I ended up with extra. So I asked myself, "What is my favorite broccoli recipe?" Answer: broccoli cheese soup! I adore that soup, and I adore noodles in soup, so I combined the two in this recipe. The noodles are made from the broccoli stem, which is just as nutrient-rich as the florets. In fact, one stem contains more vitamin C than an orange. And broccoli stems are low in calories: one stem contains 32 calories, compared to 180 calories in the equivalent amount of wheat-based pasta noodles. Plus, veggie noodles have more flavor than wheat-based noodles—and they agree with my belly!

1. Slice the broccoli florets off the stem, leaving as much of the stem intact as possible. Reserve the florets for another recipe. Trim the bottom end of the broccoli stem so that it is evenly flat.

2. Using a spiral slicer, cut the broccoli stem into noodles.

3. In a stockpot over medium heat, fry the bacon until crisp. Remove the bacon pieces and set aside, leaving the bacon drippings in the pot.

4. Add the butter, broccoli "noodles," onions, and garlic and cook until the noodles have softened, 4 to 5 minutes. Remove the noodles and onions from the pot and set aside.

5. Add the cream cheese to the pot and whisk until smooth, with no clumps of cream cheese remaining.

6. Add the broth and bring to a simmer. Add the cheddar cheese, salt, pepper, and nutmeg. Stir well to melt the cheese. Using an immersion blender, puree the soup until smooth. If you do not have an immersion blender, remove from the heat and puree in a blender, in two batches if needed (if you overfill the blender jar, it will not puree properly).

7. Pour the pureed soup into bowls and add the reserved noodles and onions. Sprinkle with the bacon pieces and serve.

KETO

NUTRITIONAL INFO (per serving)				
calories	fat	protein	carbs	fiber
232	19.2g	8.7g	2.4g	0.6g
	80%	16%	4%	

Easy Tomato Soup
WITH GRILLED CHEESE

EGG-FREE   NUT-FREE   OPTION VEGE-TARIAN

Prep Time: 8 minutes

Cook Time: 15 minutes

Yield: 4 servings

SOUP:

1 tablespoon unsalted butter or coconut oil

¼ cup finely chopped onions

1 teaspoon finely chopped garlic, or cloves from ½ head roasted garlic (page 134)

1 cup chicken bone broth, store-bought or homemade (page 132) (or vegetable broth for vegetarian)

4 ounces (½ cup) cream cheese, softened

1 (14½-ounce) can diced tomatoes, or 1 large tomato, diced (with juices)

1½ cups tomato sauce

2 teaspoons dried basil

¼ teaspoon stevia glycerite (or to taste)

¼ teaspoon fresh ground black pepper

GRILLED CHEESE:

½ pound Halloumi cheese

1 tablespoon MCT oil or melted unsalted butter

GARNISHES FOR SOUP (OPTIONAL):

¼ cup sour cream or crème fraîche

12 fresh basil leaves

When I was growing up, my standard lunch was a grilled cheese sandwich made with Wonder Bread and Campbell's tomato soup. I adored it. I love this play on my favorite childhood lunch because not only is it super simple to make, it also tastes amazing and is ketogenic!

Halloumi is a slightly rubbery and firm cheese that is delicious but on the salty side. It has a unique quality: you can grill or fry it! When heated, Halloumi gets creamy, and the saltiness declines into a robust savory morsel. It serves as the perfect "grilled cheese sandwich" without the bread!

1. To make the soup: Heat the butter in a large saucepan over medium heat. Add the onions and garlic and cook until soft, about 4 minutes, stirring often.

2. Whisk in the broth, softened cream cheese, tomatoes (including juices), tomato sauce, basil, stevia, and pepper. Simmer for 5 minutes, stirring occasionally; do not allow it to come to a boil.

3. Remove the pan from the heat and puree the soup with an immersion blender until smooth. Return the pan to low heat and cover to keep warm while you make the grilled cheese.

4. Preheat a skillet, grill pan, or panini maker to medium-high heat. Slice the chunk of cheese into ¼-inch-thick slices. Brush each side with the oil. Place in the hot skillet, grill pan, or panini maker and cook for 3 minutes per side, or until golden brown (and with grill marks if using a grill pan or panini maker).

5. Remove the cheese slices from the pan or panini maker and serve with the tomato soup. Garnish each bowl of soup with a tablespoon of sour cream and a few basil leaves, if desired.

VEGE-TARIAN OPTION

You can easily turn this soup-and-sandwich combo into a satisfying vegetarian meal simply by swapping out the chicken broth in the soup with vegetable broth.

L M H
KETO

NUTRITIONAL INFO (per serving)				
calories	fat	protein	carbs	fiber
412	33.4g	17.3g	10.9g	1.8g
	73%	17%	10%	

Simple
SALADE NIÇOISE

NUT-FREE **DAIRY-FREE**

Prep Time: 10 minutes
Yield: 6 servings

DRESSING:

¼ cup plus 2 tablespoons MCT oil

¼ cup lemon juice

½ medium shallot, finely chopped

1 tablespoon finely chopped fresh basil

1½ teaspoons finely chopped fresh thyme

1 teaspoon finely chopped fresh oregano

½ teaspoon whole-grain or Dijon mustard

Fine sea salt and fresh ground black pepper

SALAD:

2 heads red leaf lettuce, torn into bite-sized pieces, or 24 ounces spring salad mix

3 (3.75-ounce) cans tuna, drained, or 2 (8-ounce) tuna steaks, seared

6 large hard-boiled eggs (see page 184), peeled and quartered or halved

¼ cup black and/or green olives

1 (2-ounce) can anchovies (optional)

2 tablespoons capers, rinsed (optional)

Salade Niçoise is typically topped with Niçoise olives, which are small, cured black olives, and anchovies. A traditional Salade Niçoise also includes cooked green beans and potatoes, but I have omitted those for this ketogenic version. It's usually made with canned, oil-cured tuna, but you could substitute freshly grilled tuna if you prefer. Though not original to this salad, canned salmon is a great option that I sometimes use when I'm out of tuna.

I prefer Vital Choice brand canned tuna; this company selects the tuna that is lowest in mercury and packs it in BPA-free cans.

1. To make the dressing: In a medium-sized bowl, whisk together the oil, lemon juice, shallot, basil, thyme, oregano, and mustard. Season to taste with salt and pepper and set aside.

2. In a large bowl, toss the lettuce with ¼ cup of the dressing until coated. Arrange the dressed lettuce on a serving platter.

3. Coat the tuna with some of the dressing. Mound the tuna in the center of the lettuce.

4. Place the hard-boiled eggs, olives, and anchovies (if using) in mounds on the bed of lettuce.

5. Drizzle the eggs with 2 tablespoons of the dressing, sprinkle the entire salad with capers (if using), and serve immediately.

TIP:

Keep hard-boiled eggs in the fridge at all times for easy additions to meals.

L M H
KETO

NUTRITIONAL INFO (per serving)				
calories	fat	protein	carbs	fiber
393	34.9g	13.4g	5g	0.8g
	80%	14%	5%	

Chicken "Noodle" SOUP

EGG-FREE **NUT-FREE** **DAIRY-FREE** (OPTION) **ONE POT/ BOWL**

Prep Time: 10 minutes

Cook Time: 42 minutes

Yield: 4 servings

2 medium zucchini (for "noodles") or 2 (7-ounce) packages Miracle Noodles

¼ cup (½ stick) unsalted butter (or coconut oil for dairy-free)

4 boneless, skinless chicken thighs, cut into 1-inch cubes

1 cup chopped celery

¼ cup chopped onions

1½ quarts (6 cups) chicken bone broth, store-bought or homemade (page 132)

3 slices fresh ginger (optional)

1 tablespoon dried parsley

1 teaspoon fine sea salt

½ teaspoon fresh ground black pepper

½ teaspoon dried ground marjoram

1 bay leaf

Special Equipment:
Spiral slicer (optional)

1. If using zucchini to make "noodles," peel and cut the zucchini into noodle shapes using either a spiral slicer or a vegetable peeler. If using Miracle Noodles, rinse them in a colander and drain. Set the noodles aside.

2. In a stockpot, heat the butter over medium-high heat. Add the cubed chicken, celery, and onions and sauté until the veggies are soft, about 7 minutes.

3. Add the broth, ginger (if using), parsley, salt, pepper, marjoram, and bay leaf. Simmer, uncovered, for 30 minutes, or until the chicken is no longer pink inside.

4. Add the noodles: If using zucchini noodles, simmer for 5 more minutes; if using Miracle Noodles, simmer for only 1 more minute.

5. Remove from the heat, remove the bay leaf, and serve. Store in an airtight container in the refrigerator for up to 5 days. If you plan to freeze the soup, do not add the noodles (either type) until you reheat it.

KETO

NUTRITIONAL INFO (per serving)				
calories	fat	protein	carbs	fiber
309	21.2g	22g	4.9g	0.7g
	63%	29%	7%	

South of the Border SALAD

NUT-FREE   DAIRY-FREE OPTION   ONE POT/BOWL

Prep Time: 6 minutes

Cook Time: 5 minutes

Yield: 4 servings

1 pound 80% lean ground beef

2 tablespoons plus 2 teaspoons Taco Seasoning (page 110)

4 cups spring salad mix or torn lettuce leaves

4 Taco Bowls (page 271) (optional; omit for dairy-free)

½ cup salsa

½ cup diced tomatoes

½ cup sliced black olives

¼ cup sliced green onions

½ cup Taco Salad Dressing (page 121)

I keep taco seasoning in a large jar in my pantry for easy additions to meals like this one. This salad is one of my easy go-to recipes when I don't have anything else planned. It is so good!

1. Sauté the ground beef in a large skillet over medium heat, using a spatula to break up the meat into crumbles, until the meat is cooked through, about 5 minutes. Sprinkle the taco seasoning over the meat, stir, and cook for another minute.

2. Divide the lettuce among four Taco Bowls, if using, or serving bowls. Top each bowl with an equal amount of the cooked beef, salsa, tomatoes, olives, green onions, and dressing.

SINGLE SERVING OPTION

To make a single serving, use ¼ pound 80% lean ground beef, 2 teaspoons Taco Seasoning, 1 cup spring salad mix or torn lettuce leaves, 2 tablespoons salsa, 2 tablespoons diced tomatoes, 2 tablespoons sliced black olives, 1 tablespoon sliced green onions, 2 tablespoons Taco Salad Dressing, and 1 Taco Bowl (if not dairy-sensitive).

KETO

NUTRITIONAL INFO (per serving)				
calories	fat	protein	carbs	fiber
471	35g	32.5g	5.7g	1.7g
	67%	28%	5%	

Cucumber
SALAD

EGG-FREE NUT-FREE DAIRY-FREE VEGE-TARIAN

Prep Time: 5 minutes, plus 10 minutes to drain

Yield: 4 servings

2 large cucumbers, very thinly sliced

¼ cup thinly sliced red onions

1½ tablespoons fine sea salt

1 cup coconut vinegar or apple cider vinegar

¼ cup water

¼ cup MCT oil or other mild oil, such as macadamia nut or avocado oil

¼ cup Swerve confectioners'-style sweetener or equivalent amount of liquid or powdered sweetener (see page 37)

2 tablespoons chopped fresh dill, or 2 teaspoons dried

2 teaspoons grated fresh ginger (optional)

1. In a colander over a sink, toss the cucumbers and onions with the salt. Let sit and drain for 10 minutes. Press the liquid out of the vegetables and rinse well with cold water, then drain well.

2. In a medium-sized bowl, combine the vinegar, water, oil, and sweetener and stir well. Add the cucumbers and onions and toss to coat. Stir in the dill and the ginger, if desired.

KETO

NUTRITIONAL INFO (per serving)				
calories	fat	protein	carbs	fiber
161	14.2g	1.4g	7.3g	1.1g
	79%	3%	18%	

Wedge SALAD

NUT-FREE · DAIRY-FREE · ONE POT/BOWL

Prep Time: 7 minutes

Yield: 4 servings

1 head iceberg lettuce, quartered

4 tablespoons coconut vinegar or apple cider vinegar, divided

1 small tomato, diced

2 green onions, sliced, or 1 heaping tablespoon chopped red onion (or a combination of both)

2 large hard-boiled eggs (see page 184), peeled and finely chopped

2 slices bacon, cooked and crumbled

½ cup Dairy-Free Ranch Dressing (page 118)

To make this salad even easier to prepare, you can purchase hard-boiled eggs. Having a stash of cooked bacon on hand will also help you pull the salad together more quickly. I often have extra fried bacon in the fridge for easy additions to salads like this one.

1. Place the lettuce wedges cut side up on a serving platter. Pour 1 tablespoon of the vinegar onto each wedge, getting the vinegar between the leaves.

2. Sprinkle each wedge of lettuce with tomatoes, onions, chopped hard-boiled egg, and crumbled bacon, then drizzle with the ranch dressing.

KETO

NUTRITIONAL INFO (per serving)				
calories	fat	protein	carbs	fiber
204	18.4g	6.3g	4.2g	1g
	81%	12%	8%	

7-Minute
CHOPPED SALAD

NUT-FREE ONE POT/BOWL

Prep Time: 7 minutes

Yield: 4 servings

6 cups chopped romaine lettuce

4 large hard-boiled eggs (see page 184), peeled and coarsely chopped

1½ cups Greek olives, pitted

1½ cups diced ham

½ cup crumbled blue cheese (about 3 ounces)

1 large tomato, diced

1 small red onion, diced

¾ cup Blue Cheese Dressing (page 119), for serving

Impress your guests with this easy salad!

1. Arrange the romaine lettuce on a serving platter. Place the chopped hard-boiled eggs on top of the lettuce at one end of the platter.

2. Working your way across the platter, place the olives next to the eggs, followed by the ham, blue cheese, tomato, and onion. Serve with Blue Cheese Dressing.

TIP:

I store a dozen hard-boiled eggs in my fridge at all times for easy additions to meals. To make this salad even easier to prepare, you can purchase hard-boiled eggs.

KETO

NUTRITIONAL INFO (per serving)				
calories	fat	protein	carbs	fiber
331	22g	24.7g	8.4g	1.8g
	60%	30%	10%	

Fish
AND SEAFOOD

CHAPTER 10

Fish
TACOS

*Prep Time: 8 minutes, plus
13 minutes for the taco shells*

Cook Time: 20 minutes

Yield: 4 servings

FISH:

1½ teaspoons smoked paprika

1 teaspoon garlic powder

1 teaspoon onion powder

½ teaspoon fine sea salt

1½ pounds barramundi fillets, about 1 inch thick

2 tablespoons coconut oil

2 cups spring salad mix or torn lettuce leaves (optional; omit if using lettuce leaves for wraps)

8 Taco Shells (page 271) (or 8 large Boston lettuce leaves for dairy-free)

½ cup Cilantro Lime Sauce (page 115) or Green Goddess Dressing (page 117; not egg-free)

1 cup shredded purple cabbage, for garnish

You can use a different type of fish in this recipe as long as you use the same quantity and choose fillets of the same thickness (or increase or decrease the cooking time, depending on thickness). Before choosing a fish, I suggest you review the chart on page 55 that lists the fat contents of various fish, which in many cases immensely changes the nutritional profile.

1. In a small bowl, combine the smoked paprika, garlic powder, onion powder, and salt. Sprinkle the seasoning mixture over both sides of the fish fillets.

2. Heat the oil in a large, heavy-bottomed skillet over medium-high heat. Once hot, add the fish fillets (working in batches if you can't fit them all in the pan without crowding). Fry for 5 minutes per side, or until the outside is dark brown and the fish flakes apart easily.

3. Transfer the fish to a cutting board. Cut the fillets into 2-inch pieces.

4. To assemble: Place a handful of the spring salad mix (if using) in the bottom of a taco shell. Top with two or three pieces of fish and drizzle on a tablespoon of the dressing. Garnish with purple cabbage.

TIP:

To save time, try the variation for Crab Tacos (below). Or, if you do not like seafood, precooked roasted chicken from the deli will work. All you have to do is dice the chicken into bite-sized pieces and toss with the dressing.

VARIATION: CRAB TACOS.

To make this recipe even easier, use canned crab in place of the fish fillets—no frying needed! Simply use two 6-ounce cans of crabmeat in place of the fish. Drain the crab and toss it with the seasoning mixture until well coated, then jump ahead to Step 4.

KETO

NUTRITIONAL INFO (per serving)				
calories	fat	protein	carbs	fiber
385	29.5g	31.4g	1.6g	0.4g
	68%	31%	1%	

Arctic Char
WITH OLIVE SALSA

EGG-FREE   NUT-FREE   DAIRY-FREE   ONE POT/BOWL

Prep Time: 4 minutes

Cook Time: 6 minutes

Yield: 2 servings

2 (5-ounce) Arctic char fillets, about ¾ inch thick

½ teaspoon fine sea salt

¼ teaspoon fresh ground black pepper

3 tablespoons coconut oil (or unsalted butter, if not dairy-sensitive)

2 tablespoons finely chopped onions

½ scant cup Olive Salsa (page 135), for serving

1. Pat the fish dry and season it well with the salt and pepper.

2. Heat the oil in a cast-iron skillet over medium-high heat. Add the onions and cook for a few minutes, until softened. Place the fillets skin side down in the skillet. Fry for 3 minutes, or until the skin is crispy and light brown. Flip and fry another 3 minutes, or until the fish is opaque and cooked through. The exact timing will depend on the thickness of the fillets.

3. Transfer the fish to a serving platter and top each fillet with 3 heaping tablespoons of the salsa.

TIP:

Keep a separate cast-iron skillet for frying fish. When fish is heated, the fatty acids and compounds develop a strong odor and flavors that can get trapped in the pan and influence the flavor of other foods.

SINGLE SERVING OPTION

To make a single serving, use 1 (5-ounce) Arctic char fillet, about ¾ inch thick, ¼ teaspoon fine sea salt, ⅛ teaspoon fresh ground black pepper, 1½ tablespoons coconut oil or unsalted butter, 1 tablespoon finely chopped onions, and ¼ scant cup Olive Salsa.

KETO

NUTRITIONAL INFO (per serving)				
calories	fat	protein	carbs	fiber
439	33.6g	32.5g	1.1g	0g
	69%	30%	1%	

Crab-Stuffed Avocado
WITH LIME

NUT-FREE **DAIRY-FREE** **ONE POT/BOWL**

Prep Time: 5 minutes

Yield: 2 servings

¼ cup mayonnaise, store-bought or homemade (page 112)

3 tablespoons plus 1 teaspoon lime juice, divided

2 tablespoons diced onions

2 tablespoons chopped fresh cilantro

½ teaspoon ground cumin

¼ teaspoon fine sea salt

Pinch of fresh ground black pepper

1 (6-ounce) can crabmeat

1 ripe Haas avocado, halved, pitted, and peeled

Lime wedges, for serving

Green Goddess Dressing (page 117), for drizzling (optional)

1. In a medium bowl, combine the mayonnaise, 3 tablespoons of the lime juice, onions, cilantro, cumin, salt, and pepper. Gently fold in the crabmeat. Taste for seasoning and add more salt and pepper if desired.

2. Brush the avocado halves with the remaining 1 teaspoon of lime juice to prevent discoloration.

3. Place the avocado halves, cut side up, on plates. Mound the crab salad into each avocado half. Serve with lime wedges and drizzle with Green Goddess Dressing, if desired.

KETO (L M H)

NUTRITIONAL INFO (per serving)				
calories	fat	protein	carbs	fiber
434	36g	11g	12g	10g
	77%	11%	12%	

Shrimp AND GRITS

NUT-FREE

Prep Time: 2 minutes

Cook Time: 10 minutes

Yield: 4 servings

GRITS:

8 large eggs

1⅓ cups heavy cream

1 teaspoon fine sea salt

½ cup (1 stick) unsalted butter

½ cup shredded sharp cheddar cheese (about 2 ounces)

2 tablespoons coconut oil, for frying

12 precooked large shrimp, preferably with tails on

1 tablespoon chopped fresh herb of choice, for garnish (optional)

SINGLE SERVING OPTION

To make a single serving, use 2 large eggs, ⅓ cup heavy cream, ¼ teaspoon fine sea salt, 2 tablespoons unsalted butter, 2 tablespoons shredded sharp cheddar cheese, 2 teaspoons coconut oil, and 3 precooked large shrimp.

1. In a medium-sized bowl, whisk together the eggs, cream, and salt.

2. In a large saucepan, melt the butter over medium heat. Add the egg mixture to the pan and cook until the mixture thickens and small curds form, all the while scraping the bottom of the pan and stirring to keep large curds from forming. (A whisk works well for this.) This will take about 8 minutes.

3. Once the curds form and the mixture has thickened, add the cheese and stir until well combined. Cover the pan and move it to the back of the stove to keep the grits warm.

4. Heat a large skillet over high heat. Add the oil and, when very hot, season the shrimp with a sprinkle of salt and add them to the pan. Sear for about 20 seconds per side.

5. Place the grits in a serving bowl and top with the seared shrimp. Sprinkle with chopped herbs, if desired, and serve.

L M H
KETO

NUTRITIONAL INFO (per serving)				
calories	fat	protein	carbs	fiber
620	53.6g	32.2g	3.1g	0g
	77.6%	20.4%	2%	

Fish
STICKS

NUT-FREE DAIRY-FREE ONE POT/BOWL VIDEO

Prep Time: 5 minutes

Cook Time: 10 minutes

Yield: 4 servings

½ cup coconut oil or duck fat, for frying

1 pound cod fillets, about 1 inch thick

1 teaspoon fine sea salt

4 ounces sliced prosciutto

½ cup Creamy Tarragon Keto Sauce (page 122), for serving

Lemon slices, for serving

1 recipe Grilled Radicchio with Sweet-and-Sour Hot Bacon Dressing (page 312) (optional)

If you are a visual learner like me and would like to see how simple these kid-friendly fish sticks are to make, check out the video on my site, MariaMindBodyHealth.com (type the word *video* in the search field).

1. Heat the oil in a large cast-iron skillet over medium heat until it reaches 350°F. The oil should be about ½ inch deep so that it comes about halfway up the sides of the fish sticks.

2. Cut the cod fillets into sticks 2½ inches by 1 inch by 1 inch. Season all sides of the sticks with the salt. Wrap a slice of prosciutto around each fish stick; the prosciutto is sticky, so it will stay closed without needing to be secured with a toothpick.

3. Fry the fish sticks in batches to avoid overcrowding. Fry each batch for a total of 5 minutes, or until the fish is cooked through and the prosciutto is crispy, flipping halfway through.

4. Place the fish on a serving platter. Serve with the sauce, lemon slices, and Grilled Radicchio, if desired.

TIPS:

I store mason jars of strained coconut oil in the fridge to reuse for frying. I label each saved jar according to use, such as "frying fish" or "frying sweets," so my desserts do not end up tasting like leftover fish!

Try cooking with different kinds of salt, such as the black sea salt shown in the photo opposite—each has its own flavor, color, and texture and can affect a dish in subtle but interesting ways.

For easy meals, prepare a double batch of the wrapped fish sticks (complete only Step 2; do not fry them) and store in an airtight container in the fridge for up to 2 days or in the freezer for up to 1 month.

KETO

NUTRITIONAL INFO (per serving)				
calories	fat	protein	carbs	fiber
362	27.4g	29.6g	0.3g	0g
	68%	32%	0%	

Masala
MUSSELS

EGG-FREE   NUT-FREE   DAIRY-FREE   ONE POT/BOWL

Prep Time: 5 minutes

Cook Time: 10 minutes

Yield: 4 servings

¼ cup coconut oil

½ cup thinly sliced onions

1 tablespoon grated fresh ginger

1 tablespoon garam masala

1 (13½-ounce) can full-fat coconut milk

¾ cup chicken bone broth, store-bought or homemade (page 132)

1 teaspoon fine sea salt or Seasoned Salt (page 109)

3 pounds frozen mussels (on the half shell), thawed

1 tablespoon chopped fresh flat-leaf parsley (optional)

Lime wedges, for serving

I live in a beautiful area of Wisconsin right on the St. Croix River. The St. Croix is a very clean river and home to the widest variety of mussels in the entire world.

I included this recipe to serve as a teaching tool as well as an easy dinner. Many seafood options may sound like they are carb-free, but in reality, mussels, scallops, and other shellfish contain carbohydrates. To check the exact amounts of carbs in specific shellfish, see the chart on page 55.

I use frozen mussels to make this dish; they're easy to use (no cleaning necessary) and widely available. If you can find fresh mussels, feel free to use them instead of frozen if you like (see Note below).

1. Heat the coconut oil in a large, deep pot, such as a Dutch oven, over medium-high heat. Add the onions and sauté until golden brown, about 3 minutes. Add the ginger and garam masala and fry for another minute to open up the spices. Stir in the coconut milk and broth. Season with the salt.

2. Lower the heat under the pot to medium. Place the thawed mussels in the coconut milk and broth mixture to heat through, about 5 minutes.

3. Arrange the mussels in shallow bowls. Spoon some of the broth from the pot over the top and garnish with chopped parsley if desired. Serve with lime wedges.

NOTE:

If using fresh mussels, follow these steps: First, rinse and scrub them. If any are slightly open, tap on the shell. If it closes, the mussel is still alive and can be used. If it doesn't close, it's dead; throw it away. Debeard the mussels. Now they're ready to be cooked. Add the mussels to the pot (in Step 2) and steam them in the heated coconut milk and broth mixture, covered, for 6 to 8 minutes, until they open. Discard any mussels that did not open.

KETO

NUTRITIONAL INFO (per serving)				
calories	fat	protein	carbs	fiber
412	28.2g	28.8g	11.4g	7.4g
	62%	28%	11%	

King Crab Legs
WITH GARLIC BUTTER

Prep Time: *5 minutes*

Cook Time: *10 minutes*

Yield: *4 servings*

2 pounds snow or king crab clusters, thawed if frozen

½ cup unsalted butter (or MCT oil, lard, or duck fat for dairy-free)

1 tablespoon finely chopped garlic, or cloves from 1 large head roasted garlic (page 134)

⅓ cup chopped fresh flat-leaf parsley, or 1 tablespoon dried parsley

¼ teaspoon fine sea salt

½ teaspoon fresh ground black pepper

4 lemon or lime wedges, for serving (optional)

Craig and I once dined at a seafood restaurant that is well known for crab. We ordered the crab, and it came with a side of vegetable oil for dipping. I asked the waiter if I could have plain butter instead of the oil; I said I didn't mind if there was an extra charge. He went back to get some, and when he returned he said that there was no butter in the restaurant; they used only vegetable oil. I couldn't believe that a restaurant, especially a seafood restaurant, wouldn't have any butter!

1. Cut an incision, lengthwise, into the shell of each crab leg.

2. Heat the butter in a large skillet over medium heat. Add the garlic. If using raw garlic, cook until translucent; if using roasted garlic, stir and mash briefly.

3. Stir in the parsley, salt, and pepper. Continue to heat the mixture until bubbling.

4. Add the crab legs to the pan, toss to coat, and allow them to simmer in the garlic butter until completely heated, 5 to 6 minutes.

5. Transfer the crab legs to a serving platter and pour the garlic butter into 4 small bowls for dipping.

6. Serve with lemon wedges, if desired.

TIP:

To make this recipe even easier, forgo the garlic butter and just serve melted salted butter with the crab legs.

 To make a single serving, use ½ pound snow or king crab clusters, thawed if frozen; 2 tablespoons unsalted butter (or MCT oil, lard, or duck fat for dairy-free); 1 teaspoon finely chopped garlic, or cloves from ¼ head roasted garlic (page 134); 1½ tablespoons chopped fresh flat-leaf parsley (or ¾ teaspoon dried parsley); 2 pinches fine sea salt; ⅛ teaspoon fresh ground black pepper; and 1 lemon wedge, for serving (optional).

KETO

NUTRITIONAL INFO (per serving)				
calories	fat	protein	carbs	fiber
376	30.1g	21.7g	2.8g	0.6g
	72%	24%	3%	

Chicken

CHAPTER 11

Slow Cooker
CHICKEN FAJITAS

NUT-FREE · DAIRY-FREE · ONE POT/BOWL · SLOW COOKER

Prep Time: 8 minutes

Cook Time: 6 hours

Yield: 4 servings

CHICKEN:

4 bone-in, skin-on chicken thighs

2 green bell peppers, thinly sliced

½ cup thinly sliced onions

½ cup chicken bone broth, store-bought or homemade (page 132)

2 tablespoons Taco Seasoning (page 110)

FOR SERVING:

8 large Boston lettuce leaves or 4 Zucchini Tortillas (page 212; omit for dairy-free)

¼ cup chopped fresh cilantro

2 cups salsa

1 cup Simple Taco Salad Dressing (page 121)

If you have leftovers, this chicken tastes great over a salad with Simple Taco Salad Dressing (page 121) for an easy keto lunch.

1. Place the ingredients for the chicken in a 4-quart slow cooker. Cover and cook on low for 6 hours, or until the chicken is falling off the bone.

2. Shred the chicken meat with two forks; discard the bones. Place the mixture in a serving dish and serve hot with large lettuce leaves or Zucchini Tortillas. Sprinkle the chopped cilantro over the top, and serve the salsa and dressing on the side.

KETO
L — M — H

NUTRITIONAL INFO (per serving)				
calories	fat	protein	carbs	fiber
342	27g	18g	6g	2g
	72%	21%	7%	

Slow Cooker
CHIMICHURRI CHICKEN

Prep Time: 5 minutes

Cook Time: 6 hours

Yield: 6 servings with a side

1 recipe Simple Chimichurri Sauce (page 130)

6 bone-in, skin-on chicken thighs (about 2¼ pounds)

1 teaspoon fine sea salt

This dish can be made in a slow cooker or in a skillet on the stovetop (see Variation below). It's delicious either way.

1. Pour the chimichurri sauce into a 4-quart slow cooker.

2. Season the chicken with the salt, then add it to the slow cooker. Cover and cook on low for 4 to 6 hours, until the chicken is falling off the bone. Serve.

VARIATION: STOVETOP CHIMICHURRI CHICKEN.

Heat 2 tablespoons coconut oil in a large cast-iron skillet over high heat. Season the chicken with 1 teaspoon fine sea salt. When the oil is very hot, place the chicken in the pan. Fry the chicken, turning the pieces occasionally, until light brown on all sides, about 10 minutes. Pour the chimichurri sauce over the chicken. Cook, stirring often, until the sauce thickens, about 10 minutes. Reduce the heat to low and cook until the chicken is tender and no longer pink inside, 10 to 15 minutes.

KETO

NUTRITIONAL INFO (per serving)				
calories	fat	protein	carbs	fiber
505	31.4g	49.8g	1.7g	0.7g
	58%	40.5%	1.5%	

Chicken
ALFREDO

EGG-FREE · NUT-FREE · VEGE-TARIAN (OPTION) · ONE POT/BOWL · VIDEO

Prep Time: 5 minutes, plus 10 to 25 minutes for the Zoodles

Cook Time: 13 minutes

Yield: 4 servings

4 boneless, skinless chicken thighs

1 teaspoon fine sea salt

1 tablespoon coconut oil

ALFREDO SAUCE:

½ cup (1 stick) unsalted butter

1 teaspoon finely chopped garlic, or cloves from ½ head roasted garlic (page 134)

2 ounces (¼ cup) cream cheese, softened

⅓ cup chicken bone broth, store-bought or homemade (page 132)

½ cup grated Parmesan cheese (about 2 ounces)

FOR SERVING:

1 recipe Zoodles (page 308), or 2 (7-ounce) packages Miracle Noodles, prepared following package instructions

If you are a visual learner like me and would like to see how easy it is to make this dish, check out the video on my site, MariaMindBodyHealth. com (type the word *video* in the search field). You will notice in the video that I switched to a larger pot once I realized that it wasn't all going to fit. I should always listen to Julia Child's advice and start with a larger pot than I think I will need. Thankfully, I realized that I needed a larger pot before I seared the chicken!

If you swap out the chicken for mushrooms, this recipe works well as a vegetarian main dish (see Variation below).

1. Cut the chicken into 1-inch pieces and season with the salt. Heat the coconut oil in a large cast-iron skillet over medium-high heat. Once hot, sear the chunks of chicken on all sides until golden brown, about 5 minutes per side.

2. Lower the heat to medium and add the butter and garlic to the pan. Cook until the chicken is cooked through, about 5 minutes more.

3. Add the softened cream cheese to the pan and whisk until the cream cheese is melted and combined. Add the broth and Parmesan cheese and continue whisking until the sauce is smooth. Simmer for about 3 minutes to allow the flavors to develop. The flavors will open up if you simmer it longer.

4. Serve over Zoodles or Miracle Noodles.

VARIATION: MUSHROOM ALFREDO.

Replace the chicken with 1 pound button mushrooms. Cut the mushrooms in half or into quarters if large. Heat the coconut oil in a large cast-iron skillet over medium heat. Sauté the mushrooms in the oil, seasoned with the teaspoon of salt, until softened, about 7 minutes. Proceed with Step 2 to complete the recipe.

VEGE-TARIAN OPTION

Make the Mushroom Alfredo above, and replace the chicken broth with vegetable broth.

L · M · H
KETO

Chicken Alfredo

NUTRITIONAL INFO (per serving)				
calories	fat	protein	carbs	fiber
468	42.4g	21.3g	1.1g	0g
	81%	18%	1%	

Mushroom Alfredo

NUTRITIONAL INFO (per serving)				
calories	fat	protein	carbs	fiber
339	33g	9.3g	4.8g	1.1g
	86%	10%	5%	

Grilled Chicken
WITH WHITE BBQ SAUCE

Prep Time: 5 minutes, plus 1 hour to marinate

Cook Time: 20 minutes

Yield: 4 servings

MARINADE:

½ cup MCT oil

½ cup coconut vinegar or apple cider vinegar

¼ cup chopped fresh thyme, or 2 teaspoons dried thyme leaves

3 tablespoons chopped onions

1 teaspoon finely chopped garlic, or cloves from ½ head roasted garlic (page 134)

1 teaspoon fine sea salt

1 teaspoon paprika

½ teaspoon ground cumin

¼ teaspoon cayenne pepper

1 pound chicken legs

½ cup White BBQ Sauce (page 126), for serving

1. Place the ingredients for the marinade in an 8-inch square glass casserole dish and mix well. Place the chicken in the dish and turn to coat well in the marinade. Cover and place in the refrigerator to marinate for at least an hour or overnight.

2. When you're ready to grill the chicken, preheat a grill to high heat. Remove the chicken from the marinade and allow it to come to room temperature while the grill is heating up; discard the marinade.

3. If using a charcoal grill, after the briquettes are heated, move them to one side of the grill so you have both direct and indirect heat. Grease the grate so the chicken doesn't stick. Grill the chicken over direct heat until golden brown all over, about 2 minutes per side. Move the chicken to the part of the grill that doesn't have direct heat below it. If using a gas grill, reduce the heat to low. Cook the chicken for an additional 15 minutes, or until the juices run clear and the internal temperature reaches 165°F.

4. Remove from the heat and serve with the BBQ sauce.

KETO

NUTRITIONAL INFO (per serving)				
calories	fat	protein	carbs	fiber
476	41.8g	20g	5.2g	2.7g
	79%	17%	4%	

Double-Fried CHICKEN

Prep Time: 5 minutes

Cook Time: 15 minutes

Yield: 4 servings

Coconut oil, for frying

8 chicken legs

1 teaspoon fine sea salt

½ teaspoon fresh ground black pepper

8 slices prosciutto

Keto dipping sauce of choice (pages 122 to 127), for serving

I love fried chicken. This recipe creates a tasty, crispy exterior without eggs, dairy, or nuts. I like to serve fried chicken with Creamy Cilantro-Lime Pasta (page 303).

1. Heat coconut oil to 375°F in a large cast-iron skillet with sides that are at least 3 inches high. The oil should be at least 1 inch deep.

2. Season the chicken with the salt and pepper. If you do not have a thermometer, test the oil with a small piece of prosciutto to see if the oil is hot enough. If the prosciutto sizzles and shrinks, the oil is ready.

3. Place the chicken in the hot oil, working in batches if needed, and fry on all sides until golden brown and cooked through, about 7 minutes per side.

4. Remove from the skillet and wrap the prosciutto around the chicken. Don't worry if the prosciutto rips or isn't tight; it will shrink around the leg when placed in the hot oil. Place the wrapped legs back into the hot oil for 30 seconds per side, or until the prosciutto is crispy. Remove from the skillet. Serve with any keto dipping sauce.

KETO

NUTRITIONAL INFO (per serving)				
calories	fat	protein	carbs	fiber
230	18.4g	19g	0.5g	0g
	70%	29.8%	0.2%	

LAOTIAN CHICKEN AND HERBS (LARB)

EGG-FREE · NUT-FREE · DAIRY-FREE · SLOW COOKER

Prep Time: 8 minutes

Cook Time: 6 to 7 hours

Yield: 6 servings

2 pounds skin-on, bone-in chicken thighs

2 tablespoons MCT oil or untoasted, cold-pressed sesame oil

4 cloves garlic, finely chopped, or 1 head roasted garlic (page 134)

2 tablespoons finely chopped fresh ginger

2 small red chili peppers, seeded and finely chopped

4 green onions, finely chopped

¼ cup fish sauce

1 tablespoon coconut aminos or wheat-free tamari

2 tablespoons Swerve confectioners'-style sweetener or equivalent amount of liquid or powdered sweetener (see page 37)

Radicchio lettuce cups (about 2 heads), for serving

3 tablespoons chopped fresh mint, for garnish

2 tablespoons chopped fresh Thai basil, for garnish

Larb, regarded as the national dish of Laos, is a finely chopped meat salad served warm or room temperature with fresh herbs and raw vegetables. To make my life easier, I skip the mincing part and use my slow cooker to cook the meat until it is tender. Then I shred the meat, toss it in its delicious cooking liquid, and serve it in lettuce cups with fresh herbs. Easy!

1. Place all the ingredients, except the radicchio, mint, and Thai basil, in a 4-quart slow cooker, cover, and cook on low for 6 to 7 hours, until the chicken is tender and falling off the bone.

2. Remove the chicken from the slow cooker. Shred the meat with two forks; discard the bones. Return the shredded chicken to the slow cooker and toss in the juices to coat. Serve the shredded chicken in radicchio cups, garnished with the mint and basil.

L—M—H
KETO

NUTRITIONAL INFO (per serving)				
calories	fat	protein	carbs	fiber
438	28.3g	39.5g	3.6g	0.8g
	59%	36%	4%	

250 *Chicken*

Slow Cooker
"BUTTER" CHICKEN WITH NAAN

NUT-FREE · DAIRY-FREE · SLOW COOKER

Prep Time: 10 minutes

Cook Time: 6 hours

Yield: 8 servings (2 pieces of naan per serving)

BUTTER CHICKEN:

2½ pounds boneless chicken thighs, preferably with skin on

½ cup diced onions

3 tablespoons coconut oil

1 (6-ounce) jar tomato paste

1 teaspoon finely chopped garlic, or cloves from ½ head roasted garlic (page 134)

2 teaspoons turmeric powder

1 teaspoon fenugreek powder

1 teaspoon chili powder

½ teaspoon ground coriander

½ teaspoon ground cardamom

1 cup full-fat coconut milk

1 teaspoon fine sea salt

NAAN:

3 large eggs, separated

½ teaspoon cream of tartar

¼ cup unflavored egg white protein (or whey protein if not dairy-sensitive)

1 teaspoon curry powder (optional)

1 tablespoon coconut oil, for greasing the pan

Butter chicken is a well-known and all-time favorite Indian dish that is often served with naan, an oven-baked flatbread. This dairy-free version is one of my most popular recipes. A recipe tester commented: "The butter chicken was one of the best dinner recipes that I have made in a long time. I love that it is so easy to make, and my family loves that the meat becomes so tender. And the sauce is so delicious that we could have eaten it separately as soup. For a recipe that is so easy, the flavors are so complex and make me feel like I am eating out at a fancy restaurant."

My keto version of naan is fried instead of baked, but it still works great for picking up food instead of using utensils. It makes for a fun family dinner . . . unless your kids aren't yet practiced at grabbing food with bread and you are in charge of cleanup!

1. Place all the ingredients for the butter chicken in a 4-quart slow cooker. Cover and cook on low for 6 hours, or until the chicken is very tender. About 1 hour before the chicken is done, make the naan.

2. To make the naan: Using a stand mixer fitted with the whisk attachment, whip the egg whites on high speed in a clean, dry, nonreactive metal bowl until very stiff, about 3 minutes. Blend in the yolks, cream of tartar, protein powder, and curry powder (if using).

3. Heat the coconut oil in a large skillet over medium-high heat until a drop of water sizzles in the pan. Once hot, place three 3-inch circles of dough in the pan. Fry for 3 to 5 minutes per side, until golden brown. Remove from the heat. Repeat with the remaining dough, adding more coconut oil to the pan if needed.

4. Serve the chicken with naan.

5. Store leftover butter chicken in an airtight container in the fridge for up to 3 days. To reheat, place in a microwave-safe bowl and heat on medium for 1 minute, or place in an oven-safe dish and warm in a preheated 350°F oven for 5 minutes, or until heated through. Store leftover naan in an airtight container in the fridge for up to 3 days or in the freezer for up to 1 month. To reheat naan on the stovetop, place in a skillet greased with a touch of coconut oil over medium heat for a minute per side, or until warmed through, or place the naan in a preheated 350°F oven for 2 minutes.

KETO *Butter Chicken*

NUTRITIONAL INFO (per serving)				
calories	fat	protein	carbs	fiber
472	32.5g	37.4g	5.8g	0.9g
	63%	32%	5%	

KETO *Naan*

NUTRITIONAL INFO (per serving)				
calories	fat	protein	carbs	fiber
64	4.5g	5.2g	0.6g	0.5g
	64%	32.5%	3.5%	

TIP:

To cut the total cooking time for the naan in half, use two large skillets or one large griddle pan to cook 8 pieces at a time.

Chicken "Noodle" STIR-FRY

EGG-FREE · NUT-FREE · DAIRY-FREE · ONE POT/BOWL

Prep Time: 12 minutes

Cook Time: 15 minutes

Yield: 4 servings

---

4 slices bacon, diced

4 boneless, skinless chicken thighs, cut into small chunks

¼ cup diced onions

1 teaspoon finely chopped garlic, or cloves from ½ head roasted garlic (page 134)

1 teaspoon grated fresh ginger

4 cups thinly sliced cabbage (about ½ head), for "noodles," or 2 (7-ounce) packages Miracle Noodles

2 tablespoons Swerve confectioners'-style sweetener or equivalent amount of liquid or powdered sweetener (see page 37) (optional)

¼ cup coconut vinegar, apple cider vinegar, or unseasoned rice wine vinegar

½ cup coconut aminos or wheat-free tamari

Fine sea salt

Many stir-fries have a slight undertone of sweetness, which is why I added a touch of sweetener to this recipe. But if you prefer to cut out the sweetness, you can eliminate the sweetener. This dish tastes great as leftovers!

1. Fry the bacon in a large skillet over medium heat until crisp, then remove the bacon from the pan and set aside, leaving the drippings in the pan.

2. Add the diced chicken, onions, garlic, and ginger to the pan and fry over medium heat until the chicken is cooked through and golden brown on all sides, about 7 minutes. If using Miracle Noodles, rinse them in a colander and drain. Set the noodles aside.

3. Add the noodles, sweetener, vinegar, and coconut aminos. If using cabbage noodles, sauté until the cabbage is very soft, like pasta. If using Miracle Noodles, heat on low for about a minute to warm through.

4. Season with salt to taste.

SINGLE SERVING OPTION

To make a single serving, use 1 slice bacon, 1 boneless, skinless chicken thigh, 1 tablespoon diced onions, ¼ teaspoon finely chopped garlic, ¼ teaspoon grated fresh ginger, 1 cup thinly sliced cabbage or ½ (7-ounce) package Miracle Noodles, 1½ teaspoons Swerve confectioners'-style sweetener or equivalent (optional), 1 tablespoon coconut vinegar, apple cider vinegar, or rice wine vinegar, 2 tablespoons coconut aminos or wheat-free tamari, and fine sea salt to taste.

KETO

NUTRITIONAL INFO (per serving)				
calories	fat	protein	carbs	fiber
296	18.7g	25.6g	5.3g	2g
	58%	35%	7%	

Beef
AND LAMB

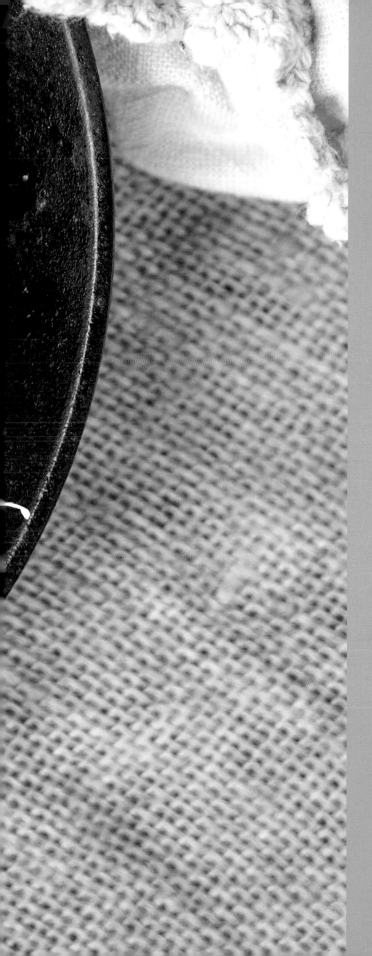

CHAPTER 12

Marinated Tenderloin
WITH BORDELAISE MUSHROOMS

EGG-
FREE   NUT-
FREE   DAIRY-
FREE

Prep Time: 5 minutes, plus 1 hour to marinate

Cook Time: 16 minutes

Yield: 4 servings

MARINADE:

2 tablespoons coarsely chopped fresh thyme leaves or other woody herb, such as rosemary

2 tablespoons MCT oil

2 tablespoons coconut vinegar or apple cider vinegar

1 teaspoon fine sea salt

2 cloves garlic, finely chopped, or cloves from ½ head roasted garlic (page 134)

4 (4-ounce) center-cut beef or venison tenderloins, trimmed and tied

2 tablespoons coconut oil (or unsalted butter if not dairy-sensitive), for frying

1 recipe Bordelaise Mushrooms (page 310)

This is an easy meal that my dad always makes in September when we bow hunt. You can use venison tenderloin if desired.

1. Combine the ingredients for the marinade in an 8-inch square baking dish. Add the tenderloins to the marinade, turning to coat. Cover and place in the refrigerator to marinate for at least 1 hour or overnight, flipping halfway through so that both sides absorb the marinade.

2. Heat the coconut oil in a large cast-iron skillet over medium-high heat. Remove the tenderloins from the baking dish; discard the marinade.

3. Place one tenderloin in the hot pan and sear for 2 minutes without disturbing; the tenderloin may stick at first but will release when ready to flip. Cook for an additional 2 minutes for medium-rare or until the meat reaches the desired doneness. Repeat with the remaining loins. Let stand for 7 minutes before slicing into medallions. Serve with Bordelaise Mushrooms.

KETO
L — M — H

NUTRITIONAL INFO (per serving)				
calories	fat	protein	carbs	fiber
344	21.1g	34.6g	0.8g	0g
	57%	42%	1%	

Grandma Nancy's
ITALIAN BEEF

EGG-FREE   NUT-FREE   DAIRY-FREE   SLOW COOKER

Prep Time: 5 minutes

Cook Time: 4 to 8 hours

Yield: 10 servings

3 cups beef bone broth, store-bought or homemade (page 132)

1 (12-ounce) jar banana peppers (with juices)

¼ cup diced onions

2 teaspoons finely chopped garlic, or cloves from 1 head roasted garlic (page 134)

2 teaspoons ground dried oregano

2 teaspoons dried basil

1 teaspoon fine sea salt

1 teaspoon fresh ground black pepper

1 (5-pound) boneless rump roast

1 cup chopped roasted red bell peppers, for garnish (optional)

My parents have a cabin on a small lake in northern Wisconsin. When we're there, we all love to spend the day fishing, swimming, and kayaking, so lunch is sort of an afterthought. My mom (Nancy) often brings a slow cooker filled with Italian beef. All we have to do is find time to stop playing and enjoy this tasty meal.

1. Place the broth, banana peppers with juices, onions, garlic, oregano, basil, salt, and pepper in a 4-quart slow cooker.

2. Place the roast on top of the broth mixture. Cover and cook on low for 8 hours or, if you're pressed for time, on high for 4 hours. (Low and slow creates a more tender and juicy roast.) The roast is done when the meat is very tender and falls apart easy. Garnish with chopped roasted red bell peppers, if desired.

KETO

NUTRITIONAL INFO (per serving)				
calories	fat	protein	carbs	fiber
331	12.1g	51g	1.5g	0.5g
	34%	63%	2%	

CASSEROLE

Prep Time: 7 minutes

Cook Time: 20 minutes

Yield: 4 servings

Bacon fat or other fat of choice, for greasing the packet

½ pound 80% lean ground beef

½ onion, thinly sliced

2 (8-ounce) packages sliced mushrooms

1 green or yellow bell pepper, seeded and cut into strips or chunks

1 medium tomato, cut into chunks

1 medium zucchini, cut lengthwise into quarters and then crosswise into quarter-moons

3 tablespoons unsalted butter (or nondairy fat for dairy-free), melted

1 teaspoon Seasoned Salt (page 109) or fine sea salt

½ teaspoon fresh ground black pepper

Easy Ketchup (page 127) or other keto sauce (pages 122 to 127), for serving

When Craig and I first married, our vacations consisted of a campsite, a tent, and our dog, Teva. On our first camping trip in the Apostle Islands in northern Wisconsin, I brought premade meals in Pyrex glass containers. As Craig put up the tent, I put a keto lasagna over the fire to heat. I went over to help with the tent when we heard a huge explosion. Craig helpfully informed me that you can't place glass over a hot fire.

So if you are looking for an easy campfire meal, try this casserole in campfire packets instead. The packets are easy to create—just line foil with unbleached parchment paper to keep aluminum from leaching into the food and tightly seal the edges. Make them before you leave home and all you have to do is heat them over your campfire.

And if you don't want to go camping? I've included methods for making this dish on the stovetop and in the oven.

1. Lay out 2 sheets of aluminum foil and 2 sheets of unbleached parchment paper that are each 12 inches square.

2. Lay one of the sheets of foil down on a counter and place one of the sheets of parchment paper on top of it. Liberally grease the parchment with bacon fat.

3. Place the meat and vegetables on the parchment paper, making sure to crumble the ground beef throughout. Drizzle with the butter and season with the Seasoned Salt and pepper.

4. Place the second sheet of parchment paper on top of the ground beef and veggie mixture, followed by the second sheet of foil. Roll the edges up all around to tightly seal the packet.

5. Start a campfire or charcoal grill well before you want to start cooking, so it has established coals by the time you begin.

6. Place the packet over the hot coals. Cook for 10 minutes, then carefully flip the packet and cook for another 10 minutes. Remove from the heat. Once the foil is cool to the touch, unwrap. Douse with your favorite keto sauce and enjoy!

KETO

NUTRITIONAL INFO (per serving)				
calories	fat	protein	carbs	fiber
301	21.9g	19.7g	8.2g	2.5g
	65%	26%	10%	

STOVETOP METHOD:

Melt the 3 tablespoons unsalted butter (or coconut oil for dairy-free) in a large skillet over medium heat. Add the rest of the ingredients and sauté until the ground beef is cooked through and veggies are tender, about 15 minutes.

OVEN METHOD:

Preheat the oven to 350°F. Grease a 9-by-13-inch baking dish with bacon fat. Place the meat and vegetables in the baking dish, making sure to crumble the ground beef throughout. Drizzle with the butter and season with the Seasoned Salt and pepper. Seal with foil and bake for 20 minutes, until the meat is cooked through and the veggies are tender.

Slow Cooker
SWEET-N-SPICY SHORT RIBS

EGG-FREE · NUT-FREE · DAIRY-FREE · SLOW COOKER

Prep Time: 5 minutes

Cook Time: 6 to 8 hours

Yield: 8 servings

1 cup beef bone broth, store-bought or homemade (page 132)

½ cup coconut aminos or wheat-free tamari

⅓ cup Swerve confectioners'-style sweetener or equivalent amount of liquid or powdered sweetener (see page 37)

¼ cup unseasoned rice vinegar

2 tablespoons Sriracha, store-bought or homemade (page 124)

1 tablespoon grated fresh ginger

2 teaspoons finely chopped garlic, or cloves from 1 head roasted garlic (page 134)

8 beef short ribs (4 pounds)

1 head green cabbage, quartered

½ teaspoon guar gum

1 tablespoon water

1 tablespoon toasted sesame oil

1. Place the broth, coconut aminos, sweetener, vinegar, Sriracha, ginger, and garlic in a 4-quart slow cooker. Stir to combine. Place the short ribs in the slow cooker, arranging them in a single layer. Lay the cabbage on top.

2. Cover and cook on low for 6 to 8 hours, until the meat is tender and easily pulls away from the bone.

3. Transfer the cabbage and short ribs to serving plates. With a large spoon or ladle, skim the fat from the cooking liquid and discard, but keep the cooking liquid in the slow cooker. Turn the slow cooker to high.

4. In a small bowl, whisk together the guar gum and water until smooth. Whisk into the cooking liquid in the slow cooker and cook on high until thickened, 2 to 3 minutes. Stir in the sesame oil. Spoon the sauce over the short ribs and cabbage and serve.

KETO

NUTRITIONAL INFO (per serving)				
calories	fat	protein	carbs	fiber
609	56g	21g	1.4g	0g
	83%	14%	1%	

Easy Corned Beef "HASH"

Prep Time: 8 minutes

Cook Time: 14 minutes

Yield: 4 servings

HERB MUSTARD VINAIGRETTE:

¼ cup plus 1 tablespoon MCT oil

¼ cup chopped fresh flat-leaf parsley

2 tablespoons coconut vinegar or apple cider vinegar

1 tablespoon finely diced onions or shallots

1 tablespoon whole-grain mustard

1½ teaspoons lemon juice

Fine sea salt and fresh ground black pepper

¼ head green cabbage

1 tablespoon coconut oil (or butter if not dairy-sensitive)

1 teaspoon finely chopped garlic, or cloves from ½ head roasted garlic (page 134)

1 (1½-pound) premade corned beef brisket, cut into bite-sized pieces

1 avocado, halved, pitted, peeled, and cut into chunks

4 poached eggs, for serving (optional; omit for egg-free)

NUTRITIONAL INFO (per serving)				
calories	fat	protein	carbs	fiber
532	46.3g	22.8g	4.1g	2.8g
	79%	18%	3%	

This "hash" has a lot of flavorful surprises, including chunks of avocado. Besides being a good addition to a keto meal, avocado has a texture that reminds me of soft potatoes. Perfect for hash! This dish would also make a perfect keto breakfast.

1. To make the vinaigrette: Place all the ingredients in a food processor and puree until smooth. Set aside.

2. To make the "hash": Slice the cabbage into noodlelike strips or small pieces. Heat the oil in a sauté pan over medium heat and sauté the cabbage and garlic until the cabbage is very tender and soft, about 8 minutes.

3. Add the corned beef and toss gently to combine and heat the beef, about 4 minutes. Gently mix in the avocado and sauté for another 2 minutes, just to warm the avocado.

4. Drizzle each serving with the vinaigrette and top with a poached egg, if desired.

Upside-Down PIZZA

EGG-FREE · NUT-FREE · OPTION VEGE-TARIAN · ONE POT/BOWL

Prep Time: 5 minutes

Cook Time: 11 minutes

Yield: 4 servings

1 (16-ounce) package cheese curds or 1 pound Halloumi cheese, cut into cubes

½ cup pizza sauce, warmed

TOPPING IDEAS:

80% lean ground beef, crumbled and cooked with Italian seasoning, or Italian sausage, crumbled and cooked (omit for vegetarian)

Bacon slices, cooked and crumbled (omit for vegetarian)

Sliced olives

Chopped bell peppers and/or sliced onions, sautéed

Chopped fresh herbs, such as basil or marjoram

Tombstone pizza began in Medford, Wisconsin, my hometown. My dad actually made pizzas at the bar where it started, and when the pizzas became popular, the owner asked him if he wanted to join the business. My dad declined and was perfectly happy following in my grandpa's footsteps in the plumbing and heating business. That story always makes me think of the "butterfly effect" and how different my life would have been if he had said yes. I'm happy he didn't, though—thanks to him, I know how to fix plumbing and lay in-floor heating!

This recipe is inspired by one of my dad's recipes, but naturally I made the crust ketogenic. Since the crust is made with cheese, I call this my upside-down pizza.

1. Place the cheese curds on a 15-inch rimmed cast-iron pizza pan. Turn the heat to medium-high and fry the cheese curds until they're golden brown on the bottom, 3 to 5 minutes. This will give you a chewy crust. For a crunchy crust, fry the curds until they're dark brown on the bottom, about 8 minutes total. Do not move the cheese curds; you want them to melt together.

2. Flip the crust and brown the other side for another 3 minutes or so.

3. Remove the pan from the heat and add the warmed sauce and desired toppings.

VARIATION: UPSIDE-DOWN MEXICAN PIZZA.

Make the cheese crust as described above, then top with salsa instead of pizza sauce and browned ground beef seasoned with taco seasoning (page 110). Garnish with olives and fresh cilantro!

VEGE-TARIAN OPTION

To make this a vegetarian meal, simply omit the meat toppings and add additional vegetarian pizza toppings of your choice, such as sliced mushrooms or diced roasted red bell peppers.

KETO

NUTRITIONAL INFO (per serving)				
calories	fat	protein	carbs	fiber
458	36.3g	28.5g	2g	0.8g
	72.5%	25.5%	2%	

Skillet
LASAGNA

EGG-FREE NUT-FREE ONE POT/BOWL

Prep Time: 3 minutes

Cook Time: 10 minutes

Yield: 4 servings

1 pound 80% lean ground beef

2 teaspoons fine sea salt

1 (24-ounce) jar marinara sauce

4 thin slices roast chicken breast (from the deli counter)

1 cup shredded mozzarella cheese (about 4 ounces), divided

1 teaspoon chopped fresh oregano, for garnish

My boys adore my lasagna. Really, they would live off lasagna if I allowed it. To meet the demand, I usually make a quadruple batch of my Protein Noodle Lasagna (from my cookbook *The Art of Healthy Eating*) and store it in the freezer. When that stash of frozen lasagna runs out, I turn to this quick skillet lasagna, which I sometimes serve over Zoodles (page 308).

I'm always dreaming up new recipes that are simple and easy to make. What is really goofy is that I almost forgot to include this one in this book, and it's a family staple!

1. In a 10-inch cast-iron skillet, brown the beef over medium-high heat, seasoning it with the salt, until cooked through, about 5 minutes, breaking up the meat with a spatula as it cooks.

2. Add the marinara sauce and stir well to combine. Push half of the sautéed beef off to one side of the skillet and place a layer of sliced chicken breast on the bottom of the skillet. Top the chicken with ½ cup of the shredded cheese. Scoop the beef on top of the deli meat to create an even layer. Top with the remaining ½ cup of cheese and sprinkle with the oregano.

3. Cover and heat on low until the cheese is melted.

KETO

NUTRITIONAL INFO (per serving)				
calories	fat	protein	carbs	fiber
311	16.1g	27.6g	13.3g	1.7g
	46.5%	35.6%	17%	

Open-Faced
HAMBURGERS ON "BUNS"

EGG-FREE NUT-FREE DAIRY-FREE

Prep Time: 10 minutes
Cook Time: 12 minutes
Yield: 4 servings

BURGERS:

1 pound 80% lean ground beef

½ teaspoon fine sea salt

½ teaspoon fresh ground black pepper

"BUNS":

4 large portobello mushroom caps (for the "buns"), stems removed (see Note)

1 tablespoon MCT oil

Fine sea salt and fresh ground black pepper

BURGER FIXINGS:

Lettuce leaves

Sliced onions and/or tomatoes

CONDIMENT IDEAS:

Keto Fry Sauce (page 123), Guacamole (page 136), or Dairy-Free Minute "Cream Cheese" Spread (page 138)

NOTE:

Save the mushroom stems for another recipe, such as Mushroom Ragu (page 300).

M
L — H
KETO

NUTRITIONAL INFO (per serving)				
calories	fat	protein	carbs	fiber
339	26.7g	20.5g	3g	0.9g
	71%	24%	4%	

For this recipe I've shared with you my secret tip for the best burgers ever (see Tips below). Really! It requires an extra step, but it's worth it. Because this book is meant to supply you with easy recipes, I've made my secret tip an optional step. One evening when you're feeling less pressed for time, give it a try. I promise, you'll love it!

1. Preheat a grill to high. If your grill isn't large enough to grill 4 portobello mushrooms and 4 hamburgers at once, preheat the oven to 425°F for the mushrooms.

2. Form the meat into 4 large patties about 1 inch thick. Season both sides with the salt and pepper. Set the patties aside while you prepare the "buns."

3. Brush the smooth side of each mushroom with the oil and season both sides with salt and pepper. Place the portobello caps on the grill (or on a rimmed baking sheet if using the oven), gill side up. Grill or bake the caps for 12 minutes. Remove from the grill or oven and place on a serving platter. To coordinate the timing of the buns and burgers, throw the patties on the grill after the caps have cooked for about 4 minutes.

4. Cook the patties to the desired doneness, about 4 minutes per side for medium-rare. Optional: Place a pan with duck fat and shallots on the grill for basting the burgers (see Tips below).

5. Top each mushroom cap with a few lettuce leaves, followed by a burger, a slice of onion and/or tomato, and the desired condiment.

TIPS:

When you set the patties on the grill, place a cast-iron skillet with a few tablespoons of duck fat (or other fat) and a tablespoon of chopped shallots on the grill next to the burgers. When the burgers are nearly done to your preference, place them in the shallot-infused hot duck fat and baste them until a nice crispy crust forms around the burger.

If you prefer, or to save time, you can wrap your hamburgers in large lettuce leaves instead of making the mushroom "buns."

SINGLE SERVING OPTION *To make a single serving, use ¼ pound ground beef, ⅛ teaspoon fine sea salt, ⅛ teaspoon fresh ground black pepper, 1 large portobello mushroom cap, stem removed, 1 teaspoon MCT oil, and the burger fixings and condiments of your choice.*

Taco Bar
NIGHT

EGG-FREE · NUT-FREE · DAIRY-FREE (OPTION) · ONE POT/BOWL

Prep Time: 10 minutes, plus 13 minutes for the taco shells

Cook Time: 6 minutes

Yield: 4 servings

1 pound 80% lean ground beef

¼ cup Taco Seasoning (page 110)

8 Taco Shells (opposite) (or 1 head Boston lettuce, separated into leaves, for dairy-free)

½ cup salsa

½ cup Guacamole (page 136)

ADDITIONAL TOPPINGS (OPTIONAL):

About ⅓ cup chopped green onions

About ⅓ cup chopped red onions

About ⅓ cup fresh cilantro leaves

About ¼ cup sliced black olives

TIP:

Skip the taco shells and just use lettuce leaves for wraps!

We adore taco bar night! One of my strategies for pulling our taco-themed dinner together quickly is to prepare the taco fixings the night before while my husband, Craig, cleans up the dinner dishes. That way all I have to do is take the bowls of prepared fixings out of the fridge and fry up the taco meat. Dinner is ready in minutes, and it takes so much stress out of my day!

1. Place the beef in a large skillet over medium heat. Sprinkle on the taco seasoning and brown the beef, stirring to break up the meat as it cooks. When the meat is cooked through, transfer it to a serving dish.

2. While the beef is browning, place the taco shells or lettuce leaves in a bowl and place the salsa and guacamole in serving dishes. Gather any additional toppings for your taco bar.

3. Assemble the tacos by filling the taco shells or lettuce leaves with a spoonful of the cooked meat and the toppings of your choice.

KETO (L M H)

NUTRITIONAL INFO (per serving)				
calories	fat	protein	carbs	fiber
354	22.4g	31.7g	5g	1.8g
	57%	36%	6%	

Taco Shells OR BOWLS

EGG-FREE NUT-FREE

Prep Time: 2 minutes

Cook Time: 11 minutes

Yield: 12 shells or bowls (1 per serving)

12 round slices provolone cheese

1. Preheat the oven or toaster oven to 375°F. (Because you need to work in small batches, this recipe is ideal for a toaster oven!) Line a baking sheet with 2 pieces of parchment paper, side by side, and grease well with coconut oil spray. If making taco shells, have on hand a skinny rolling pin (about 1 inch in diameter) or a similar-shaped cylindrical object (glass spice jars also work); if making taco bowls, have on hand two bowls 5 inches in diameter.

2. Place 2 slices of cheese on the lined baking sheet at least 2 inches apart, each on its own sheet of parchment paper. (As soon as the cheese slices are removed from the oven and begin to cool, they will harden, so it's important to bake just two at a time.) Bake for 9 to 11 minutes, or until golden brown.

3. *To make taco shells:* Wearing protective gloves, remove the pan from the oven, grab one of the pieces of parchment, and flip the bubbly cheese slice around a skinny rolling pin or similar-shaped cylindrical object. Repeat immediately with the other slice of cheese. Prop the rolling pin up so the cheese slices hang freely. Peel off the parchment paper and let the shells cool for about 5 minutes before removing them from the rolling pin.

   To make taco bowls: Wearing protective gloves, remove the pan from the oven, grab one of the pieces of parchment, and flip the bubbly cheese slice over an upside-down 5-inch bowl. Press the cheese down using your hands. Immediately repeat with the other slice of cheese. Remove the parchment from the bowls and allow to cool for 5 minutes to crisp up.

4. Repeat with remaining cheese to make a total of 12 shells or bowls. The shells/bowls will keep for 3 days in an airtight container in the fridge or for 2 weeks in the freezer.

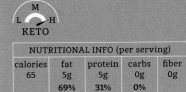

KETO

NUTRITIONAL INFO (per serving)				
calories	fat	protein	carbs	fiber
65	5g	5g	0g	0g
	69%	31%	0%	

Roasted BONE MARROW

EGG-FREE · NUT-FREE · DAIRY-FREE

Prep Time: 3 minutes

Cook Time: 25 minutes

Yield: 4 servings (2 bones per serving)

8 (2-inch) cross-cut beef or veal marrow bones

1 teaspoon fine sea salt

½ teaspoon fresh ground black pepper

SINGLE SERVING OPTION

To make a single serving, use two 2-inch marrow bones, ¼ teaspoon fine sea salt, and ⅛ teaspoon fresh ground black pepper. A toaster oven works great for this small amount.

If a meal of roasted bone marrow sounds a little crazy to you, let me list the reasons it's so good for you:

- It is one of the few natural sources of vitamin K_2, which helps reverse artery calcification, reverse Alzheimer's, and increase fertility, and which has anti-aging properties as well as many other healing properties.

- Marrow is one of the best, densest sources of fat-soluble vitamins.

- It is a great high-fat, moderate-protein source for a keto-adapted diet.

And if the health reasons alone haven't convinced you, the incredible taste and creamy texture of bone marrow will! You can enjoy it right from the bone or spread on Spring Popovers (page 146), or on my keto bread, thinly sliced and fried. (You can find a recipe for my keto bread on my site, MariaMindBodyHealth.com [search for "keto-adapted bread"] or in my book *The Ketogenic Cookbook*.) A side salad of mixed greens and chopped parsley lightly dressed with Dairy-Free Caesar Dressing (page 116) is a nice complement to the richness of marrow.

If eating straight bone marrow doesn't appeal to you, hiding it in foods is a great way to get the added benefits. Try adding it to ground beef for extra moisture, to a hearty stew, or to my Skillet Lasagna (page 266).

1. Preheat the oven to 450°F. Rinse the bones, drain, and pat dry. Season with the salt and pepper. Place them cut side up in a roasting pan.

2. Roast the bones for 15 to 25 minutes, until the marrow has puffed slightly and is warm in the center. (The exact timing will depend on the diameter of the bones; if they are 2 inches in diameter, it will take closer to 15 minutes.)

3. To test for doneness, insert a metal skewer into the center of the bone. There should be no resistance when it is inserted, and some of the marrow will have started to leak from the bones. Serve the marrow immediately with slender spoons.

KETO

NUTRITIONAL INFO (per serving)				
calories	fat	protein	carbs	fiber
500	56g	0g	0g	0g
	100%	0%	0%	

Prep Time: 10 minutes

Cook Time: 6 hours

Yield: 12 servings

BOUQUET GARNI:

2 whole cloves

1 sprig fresh thyme

1 sprig fresh rosemary

1 bay leaf

3 (1-pound) cross-cut veal shanks

2 teaspoons fine sea salt

1½ teaspoons fresh ground black pepper

½ cup coconut oil (or unsalted butter, if not dairy-sensitive)

1 small onion, cut into ½-inch pieces

1 tomato, diced

2 tablespoons tomato paste

2 cups chicken bone broth, store-bought or homemade (page 132), plus more if needed

½ cup coconut vinegar or apple cider vinegar

Special Equipment:
Cheesecloth or paper coffee filter, kitchen twine

Osso buco is a very tasty meal, so it can be tempting to overeat! And if you eat too much protein, it will take you out of ketosis. To ensure that you do not overeat protein, I suggest that you serve this dish over Zoodles (page 308) to soak up the delicious sauce and pair it with a tasty side salad with lots of keto dressing. As a bonus, enjoy the marrow from the shanks.

This elegant yet simple recipe uses a bouquet garni. Don't let those words cause you to skip this recipe. It refers to a packet of herbs and spices that infuses amazing flavor into this dish. When the dish is finished, you just pick up the bundle of herbs and remove it; this saves you the time of fishing around for and removing each sprig of thyme, clove, and bay leaf one by one.

1. To make the bouquet garni: Lay out a 6-inch square piece of cheesecloth or paper coffee filter. Place the cloves, thyme, rosemary, and bay leaf in the center and tie shut with twine. (See, that wasn't too hard!)

2. Using twine, tie the meat to the bone. This dish is so tender that it will fall off otherwise.

3. Season the shanks with the salt and pepper. Place the coconut oil and onion pieces in a 4-quart slow cooker. Place the tied shanks on top of the onions. Add the diced tomato, tomato paste, broth, vinegar, and bouquet garni. Make sure that the liquid is three-quarters up the sides of the shanks. If needed, add more broth.

4. Cover and cook on low until the meat is fork-tender, about 6 hours. Gently remove the shanks and place them on a serving platter. Remove and discard the twine.

5. Take the bouquet garni out of the pot and discard it. Pour the liquid from the pot over the shanks and serve.

TIP:

This recipe is designed to yield a large batch because it makes such great leftovers and will feed you throughout the week, depending on the size of your family.

KETO

NUTRITIONAL INFO (per serving)				
calories	fat	protein	carbs	fiber
347	17g	44.6g	2.4g	0.8g
	45%	52%	3%	

Basted
RIB-EYE STEAK

EGG-   NUT-   OPTION   ONE POT/
FREE   FREE   DAIRY-   BOWL
      FREE

Prep Time: 6 minutes

Cook Time: 8 minutes

Yield: 4 servings

1 (16-ounce) rib-eye steak, about 1¼ inches thick

1 teaspoon fine sea salt

½ teaspoon fresh ground black pepper

1 tablespoon coconut oil or duck fat

3 tablespoons unsalted butter (or more duck fat or coconut oil for dairy-free)

1 tablespoon fresh rosemary or tarragon leaves or herb of choice

1 tablespoon finely chopped onions

I adore brown butter and am always dreaming up new ways to use it. In this recipe, you sear the steak and then baste it with brown butter infused with fresh herbs, which gives the steak a rich caramel flavor and boosts its keto level. Basting the steak with an herb-infused nondairy fat, like duck fat, is an equally delicious choice if you can't consume dairy.

1. Remove the steak from the fridge about 20 minutes before you plan to cook it. Pat it dry and season with the salt and pepper.

2. Place the coconut oil in large skillet over medium-high heat. Once hot, sear the steak for 2 minutes, without moving it, then flip it over and sear it for another 2 minutes.

3. Lower the heat to medium-low and add the butter, herb, and onions. Using a spoon, constantly pour the "liquid gold" (aka butter) over the steak. Continue to baste and cook the steak for about 4 more minutes per side for medium-rare. The exact timing will depend on how thick your steak is.

4. Once cooked to your desired doneness, remove the steak from the pan and allow to rest at room temperature for 5 minutes before cutting to make sure that the juices stay in the steak. Pour the butter into a small serving dish for dipping the steak.

KETO

NUTRITIONAL INFO (per serving)				
calories	fat	protein	carbs	fiber
474	44g	21.3g	0.8g	0g
	82%	17%	1%	

Mexican
MEATLOAF CUPCAKES

NUT-FREE   ONE POT/ BOWL   VIDEO

Prep Time: 10 minutes

Cook Time: 20 minutes

Yield: 6 servings

2 pounds 80% lean ground beef

2 large eggs, beaten

2 cups shredded pepper jack or sharp cheddar cheese (about 8 ounces)

½ cup salsa

¼ cup chopped fresh cilantro (optional; see Note)

2 teaspoons Taco Seasoning (page 110)

1 teaspoon finely chopped garlic, or cloves from ½ head roasted garlic (page 134)

FOR GARNISH:

Guacamole (page 136) or sour cream

6 cherry tomatoes

We eat with our eyes, and if you make food fun, kids are likely to enjoy it, too! This recipe is a perfect example. My son Kai adores savory food. He doesn't have much of a sweet tooth, and when I asked him what he wanted for his birthday cake last year, he said meatloaf. So I made him these meatloaf cupcakes. (Because both my other son, Micah, and I have a sweet tooth, I also made my Cinnamon Swirl Cheesecake from *The Ketogenic Cookbook*, making everyone happy!) If you are a visual learner like me and would like to see how simple these savory cupcakes are to make, check out the video on my site, MariaMindBodyHealth.com (type the word *video* in the search field).

1. Preheat the oven to 350°F. Generously grease a 6-well jumbo cupcake pan with coconut oil or butter.

2. In a large bowl, use your hands to mix together the ground beef, eggs, cheese, salsa, cilantro (if using), taco seasoning, and garlic. Form the mixture into six 3-inch balls and place in the wells of the cupcake pan.

3. Bake for approximately 20 minutes, or until the internal temperature reaches 160°F.

4. Remove from the oven and top with guacamole or sour cream for the frosting and a cherry tomato!

NOTE:

I like to use fresh herbs in meat mixtures to add lots of phytonutrients. Cilantro in particular is a superfood that has tons of nutrients.

SINGLE SERVING OPTION

To make one or more single servings, have on hand six 8-ounce ramekins or cups. After forming the mixture into 3-inch balls in Step 2 above, place them in the greased ramekins or cups. Bake one or more servings as needed throughout the week for easy lunches or dinners. (A toaster oven works great here!) Garnish with guacamole or sour cream and a cherry tomato. The unbaked cupcakes will keep, covered, in the refrigerator for up to 5 days.

L   M   H
KETO

NUTRITIONAL INFO (per serving)				
calories	fat	protein	carbs	fiber
430	29.8g	39.2g	1.2g	0.6g
	63%	36%	1%	

20-Minute
GROUND LAMB CASSEROLE

EGG-FREE · NUT-FREE · DAIRY-FREE · ONE POT/BOWL · VIDEO

Prep Time: 7 minutes

Cook Time: 17 minutes

Yield: 4 servings

4 slices bacon, diced

1 pound ground lamb

¼ cup diced green bell peppers (optional)

¼ cup diced onions

1 teaspoon finely chopped garlic, or cloves from ½ head roasted garlic (page 134)

4 cups thinly sliced cabbage (about ½ head), for "noodles," or 2 (7-ounce) packages Miracle Noodles

2 cups tomato sauce

1 teaspoon fine sea salt

This super fast weeknight meal works equally well with ground beef if you don't have lamb. It tastes great as leftovers! If you are a visual learner like me and would like to see how easy this casserole is to make, check out the video on my site, MariaMindBodyHealth.com (type the word *video* in the search field).

1. Fry the bacon in a large skillet over medium heat until slightly crispy, about 5 minutes. Add the lamb, bell peppers (if using), onions, and garlic and cook, stirring often to break up the meat, until the meat is browned, about 7 minutes.

2. Add the cabbage "noodles" or Miracle Noodles and the tomato sauce. If using cabbage noodles, cover and simmer until the cabbage is very soft, like pasta, about 5 minutes. If using Miracle Noodles, heat for 1 minute, or until the noodles are warm.

3. Season with the salt and serve.

SINGLE SERVING OPTION *To make a single serving, use a small skillet and decrease the amounts to 1 slice bacon, diced, ¼ pound ground lamb, 1 tablespoon diced green bell pepper (optional), 1 tablespoon diced onions, ¼ teaspoon finely chopped garlic (or 2 cloves from a head of roasted garlic), 1 cup thinly sliced cabbage (for "noodles") or ½ (7-ounce) package Miracle Noodles, ½ cup tomato sauce, and ¼ teaspoon fine sea salt. Enjoy it right out of the pan if you like!*

L · M · H
KETO

NUTRITIONAL INFO (per serving)				
calories	fat	protein	carbs	fiber
256	17.1g	14.6g	11g	3g
	60%	23%	17%	

Grilled Lamb Chops
WITH MINT AIOLI

NUT-FREE DAIRY-FREE VIDEO

Prep Time: 5 minutes, plus 30 minutes to marinate

Cook Time: 4 minutes

Yield: 4 servings

3 tablespoons MCT oil or extra-virgin olive oil

3 tablespoons coconut vinegar or apple cider vinegar

1 teaspoon finely chopped garlic, or cloves from ½ head roasted garlic (page 134)

Leaves from 1 sprig fresh rosemary, chopped

2 teaspoons fine sea salt

8 lamb loin chops, about 1¼ inches thick

½ cup Herb Aioli made with mint (page 114), for serving

If you are a beginner cook, this recipe may sound difficult, but believe me, it is one of the easiest dinners you can make to impress your guests! If you are a visual learner like me and would like to see how simple these elegant chops are to make, check out the video on my site, MariaMindBodyHealth.com (type the word *video* in the search field).

1. In a lasagna dish or other glass dish, combine the MCT oil, vinegar, garlic, rosemary, and salt. Stir well to combine. Place the lamb chops in the marinade, cover, and place in the fridge to marinate for at least 30 minutes or overnight. When you're ready to grill the chops, remove them from the marinade and allow them to come to room temperature; discard the marinade.

2. While the chops are coming to room temperature, preheat a grill to high heat. Once the grill is hot, place the chops on the grill and cook for 2 minutes per side for medium-rare, or until the chops reach the desired doneness. If your chops are thicker than 1¼ inches, cook them longer. Remove from the grill and place on a serving platter. Allow to rest for a few minutes before slicing. Serve with mint aioli.

M
L   H
KETO

NUTRITIONAL INFO (per serving)				
calories	fat	protein	carbs	fiber
862	76g	38.2g	0.4g	0g
	80%	19%	1%	

Pork

CHAPTER 13

Broccoli
CARBONARA

NUT-FREE ONE POT/BOWL

Prep Time: 10 minutes

Cook Time: 10 minutes

Yield: 2 servings

1 large head broccoli

4 slices thick-cut bacon, cut into ¼-inch dice

¼ cup chopped onions

½ teaspoon finely chopped garlic, or 3 cloves roasted garlic (page 134)

¼ cup grated Parmesan cheese (about 1 ounce)

2 large eggs, beaten

Fine sea salt and fresh ground black pepper

Special Equipment:
Spiral slicer

1. Slice the florets off the broccoli stem, leaving as much of the stem intact as possible. (Reserve the florets for another recipe.)

2. Trim the bottom end of the broccoli stem so that it is evenly flat. Using a spiral slicer, cut the broccoli stem into "noodles."

3. Fry the bacon in a large cast-iron skillet over medium heat until crisp.

4. Remove the bacon pieces and set aside, keeping the bacon drippings in the pan.

5. Add the "noodles," onions, and garlic to the pan with the bacon drippings and cook over medium heat until the onions are translucent and the noodles are soft, about 4 minutes.

6. Return the bacon to the skillet. Stir well to combine and heat through. Add the Parmesan and toss until the cheese is melted. Add the beaten eggs and cook until the eggs are just set, tossing constantly with tongs or a large fork. Season with salt and pepper, tasting first to check the salt level, as the cheese adds quite a bit of saltiness to the dish. Serve immediately.

M
L ┃ H
KETO

NUTRITIONAL INFO (per serving)				
calories	fat	protein	carbs	fiber
216	12.3g	19g	8g	2.7g
	51%	35%	14%	

Pigs in a BACON BLANKET

EGG-FREE   NUT-FREE   DAIRY-FREE

Prep Time: 2 minutes

Cook Time: 5 minutes

Yield: 2 servings

4 slices bacon

4 hot dogs (see Note)

Easy Ketchup (page 127), for serving

NOTE:

I use Applegate's all-natural uncured beef and pork hot dogs or my own homemade venison hot dogs, which I make with natural casings after bow-hunting season. When purchasing hot dogs, avoid brands made with corn syrup or other undesirable ingredients.

I love taking my boys to the Minnesota State Fair, and I often get inspiration for recipes as we walk around and see the crazy new foods. My bacon-wrapped cheese curds recipe in *The Ketogenic Cookbook* was inspired by my first trip to the state fair with my boys years ago. The last time I was there, we came home and made these "pigs in a blanket" with bacon! This is an easy recipe to scale up or down to feed one or a crowd.

1. Preheat a large cast-iron skillet over medium heat.

2. Take a slice of bacon and secure it to one end of a hot dog with a toothpick, then spiral-wrap the bacon around the hot dog so that it covers the entire dog. Secure the other end of the bacon with another toothpick. Repeat with the rest of the bacon and hot dogs.

3. Place the wrapped dogs in the hot skillet and fry on all sides until the bacon is crisp, about 5 minutes. Remove from the skillet, remove the toothpicks, and serve with ketchup.

KETO

NUTRITIONAL INFO (per serving)				
calories	fat	protein	carbs	fiber
300	24g	19.5g	1.5g	0g
	72%	26%	2%	

Brats with
SIMPLE COLESLAW

NUT-FREE DAIRY-FREE VIDEO

Prep Time: 6 minutes

Cook Time: 10 minutes

Yield: 2 servings

4 (4-ounce) brats (see Note)

1 cup shredded or finely diced purple or green cabbage

¼ cup Dairy-Free Ranch Dressing (page 118)

2 tablespoons whole-grain or Dijon mustard, for serving

If you are a visual learner like me and would like to see how simple these brats are to make, check out the video on my site, MariaMindBodyHealth.com (type the word *video* in the search field).

1. Preheat a grill or broiler to high heat.

2. Place the brats in a pot of boiling water and boil for 8 minutes. Place the boiled brats on the grill or on a rimmed baking sheet and grill or broil for 1 to 2 minutes, or until the outsides are charred to your liking.

3. While the brats are boiling, make the coleslaw: Place the cabbage in a serving bowl and add the ranch dressing; toss to coat.

4. Place the cooked brats on a plate. Serve with the coleslaw and mustard.

NOTE:

I use all-natural brats or my own homemade venison brats, which I make with natural casings after bow-hunting season. When purchasing brats, avoid brands made with corn syrup or other undesirable ingredients.

TIP:

To make this recipe even easier and save time, purchase preshredded cabbage in a bag. Or, for a very traditional German food experience, you can serve the brats with sauerkraut. If you have some kraut on hand, all you need to do is open the jar. (For a recipe for homemade sauerkraut, see page 314.) You can also skip the step of browning the brats on the grill or under the broiler. Once they are boiled, they are fully cooked, but I prefer the taste of a grilled brat.

SINGLE SERVING OPTION

To make a single serving, use 2 brats, ½ cup shredded purple or green cabbage, 2 tablespoons Dairy-Free Ranch Dressing (page 118), and 1 tablespoon mustard.

KETO

NUTRITIONAL INFO (per serving)				
calories	fat	protein	carbs	fiber
581	47.3g	29.2g	9.9g	2.5g
	73%	20%	7%	

Sweet-n-Sour
COUNTRY-STYLE RIBS OVER ZOODLES

EGG-FREE · NUT-FREE · DAIRY-FREE · ONE POT/BOWL · SLOW COOKER

Prep Time: 6 minutes, plus 10 to 25 minutes for the Zoodles

Cook Time: 5 to 8 hours

Yield: 6 to 8 servings

1 medium onion, chopped

2 cloves garlic, crushed to a paste, or cloves from ½ head roasted garlic (page 134), crushed to a paste

½ cup coconut aminos or wheat-free tamari

⅓ cup Swerve confectioners'-style sweetener or equivalent amount of liquid or powdered sweetener (see page 37)

¼ cup coconut vinegar or apple cider vinegar

2 tablespoons tomato paste

1 tablespoon grated fresh ginger

¾ teaspoon fine sea salt

¼ teaspoon fresh ground black pepper

1 (14½-ounce) can diced tomatoes with juices

2 cups chicken or beef bone broth, store-bought or homemade (page 132)

3 pounds country-style pork spareribs, cut into individual ribs

Double recipe Zoodles (page 308), or 3 (7-ounce) packages Miracle Noodles, prepared following package instructions, for serving

1. In a 4- to 6-quart slow cooker, combine the onion, garlic, coconut aminos, sweetener, vinegar, tomato paste, ginger, salt, and pepper. Add the tomatoes and their juices and the broth; stir to combine. Add the pork spareribs and turn to coat.

2. Cover and cook until the pork is very tender—7 to 8 hours on low or 5 to 6 hours on high. (The longer cooking time will create meat that is very tender; if you prefer chewier ribs, stick to the shorter cooking time.)

3. Remove the ribs from the slow cooker, leaving the cooking liquid in the pot. Using two forks, shred the pork. Return the meat to the slow cooker and mix it into the cooking liquid. Serve over Zoodles or Miracle Noodles.

L M H
KETO

NUTRITIONAL INFO (per serving)				
calories	fat	protein	carbs	fiber
476	28.1g	45.5g	7.3g	1.4g
	54%	39%	7%	

PORK RAGU OVER PALEO POLENTA

EGG-FREE NUT-FREE OPTION DAIRY-FREE SLOW COOKER

Prep Time: 5 minutes, plus 28 minutes for the polenta

Cook Time: 5 to 8 hours

Yield: 6 servings

1 medium onion, chopped

2 tablespoons tomato paste

1 teaspoon finely chopped garlic, or cloves from ½ head roasted garlic (page 134)

1 teaspoon dried thyme leaves

1 teaspoon dried oregano leaves

¾ teaspoon fine sea salt

¼ teaspoon fresh ground black pepper

1 (14½-ounce) can diced tomatoes (with juices)

2 cups chicken or beef bone broth, store-bought or homemade (page 132)

3 pounds pork spareribs, cut into individual ribs

1 recipe Paleo Polenta (page 320), for serving

Chopped fresh flat-leaf parsley, for garnish (optional)

1. In a 4-quart slow cooker, combine the onion, tomato paste, garlic, thyme, oregano, salt, and pepper. Add the tomatoes and their juices and the broth; stir well to combine. Add the pork spareribs and turn to coat.

2. Cover and cook until the pork is very tender—7 to 8 hours on low or 5 to 6 hours on high. (The longer cooking time will create meat that is very tender; if you prefer chewier ribs, stick to the shorter cooking time.)

3. Remove the ribs from the slow cooker, leaving the cooking liquid in the pot. Using two forks, shred the pork. Return the pork to the slow cooker and mix it into the cooking liquid.

4. Divide the polenta among wide, shallow bowls and spoon the ragu over the top. Sprinkle each serving with chopped parsley, if desired, and serve immediately.

L M H
KETO

NUTRITIONAL INFO (per serving)				
calories	fat	protein	carbs	fiber
660	51g	40g	11g	4g
	69%	23%	8%	

Deconstructed
BLT WITH PORK BELLY

EGG-FREE NUT-FREE DAIRY-FREE VIDEO

Prep Time: 5 minutes

Cook Time: 16 minutes

Yield: 2 servings

1 (12-ounce) package fully cooked pork belly (see Notes)

DRESSING:

Makes ¾ cup (see Notes)

½ cup MCT oil

¼ cup coconut vinegar or apple cider vinegar

1 teaspoon fine sea salt

½ teaspoon fresh ground black pepper

½ teaspoon fish sauce

½ teaspoon stevia glycerite (or more to taste)

2 cups arugula or torn romaine lettuce

8 cherry tomatoes, halved

1 cup Guacamole (page 136), for serving (optional)

If you are a visual learner like me, check out my site, MariaMindBodyHealth.com, for a video that shows how to make this easy and tasty meal! (To find it, type the word *video* in the search field.)

1. Heat a dry skillet over high heat. Sear the pork belly on all sides, including the edges, until crisp and golden brown, about 4 minutes per side.

2. Meanwhile, make the dressing: Place all the ingredients in a jar and shake vigorously.

3. Toss the arugula with 2 tablespoons of the dressing. Place the dressed greens on a serving platter. Garnish the salad with the cherry tomato halves. Place the guacamole (if using) on the plate.

4. Remove the pork belly from the heat and slice into 1-inch medallions. Place alongside the dressed salad.

NOTES:

Vacuum-sealed packages of fully cooked pork belly are available at Trader Joe's.

This quantity of dressing is more than you need for this recipe, but it's great to have extra dressing on hand for chicken, coleslaw, or greens. It will keep for 4 days in the fridge. Shake well before using. If you don't want leftovers, simply cut the dressing recipe by three-quarters.

TIP:

If you love pork belly and want an even faster and easier way to enjoy it as part of a balanced meal, the solution is kimchi! If you have some kimchi on hand in the refrigerator (see page 316 for a recipe), you need only take the time to sear the fully cooked pork belly, slice it, and serve it with kimchi.

KETO

NUTRITIONAL INFO (per serving)				
calories	fat	protein	carbs	fiber
659	60.9g	26.6g	0.8g	0g
	83%	16%	1%	

SCHWEINSHAXEN

EGG-FREE NUT-FREE DAIRY-FREE VIDEO

Prep Time: 5 minutes

Cook Time: 2 hours 50 minutes

Yield: 6 servings

6 cloves garlic, finely chopped, or cloves from 2 heads roasted garlic (page 134)

2 tablespoons caraway seeds

2 teaspoons fine sea salt

1 teaspoon fresh ground black pepper

1 (3-pound) pork shank

FOR SERVING:

Whole-grain mustard

Sauerkraut, store-bought or homemade (page 314)

Pickles, store-bought or homemade (page 318)

My husband and I are both German, and this recipe is very close to our hearts. We had our first taste of it in Fussen, Germany, high in the mountains. It is a tasty dish often served in the fall. If you are a visual learner like me and would like to see how simple this dish is to make, check out the video on my site, MariaMindBodyHealth.com (type the word *video* in the search field).

1. Fill a large pot with water. Add the garlic, caraway seeds, salt, and pepper and bring to a boil. Place the pork shank in the boiling water, cover, and boil for 1 hour. Make sure that the water covers the whole shank during the entire cooking time; add more water if needed.

2. After 1 hour, remove the shank from the water; reserve the cooking liquid.

3. Preheat the oven to 375°F. Make lengthwise cuts in the skin of the pork shank, about 1 inch apart, all the way around. Place the shank in a roasting pan and add 2 cups of the reserved cooking liquid. Place in the oven and roast for 90 minutes.

4. Increase the oven temperature to 425°F and roast for 20 more minutes to crisp the skin. This dish is traditionally served warm (not hot) on a wooden platter with mustard, sauerkraut, and pickles.

L M H
KETO

NUTRITIONAL INFO (per serving)				
calories	fat	protein	carbs	fiber
668	45.9g	58.1g	2.3g	1g
	63%	35%	2%	

Goat Cheese Panna Cotta with
CRISPY PROSCIUTTO AND FRIED BASIL

Prep Time: 6 minutes, plus 50 minutes to set

Cook Time: 5 minutes

Yield: 2 servings as a meal, 4 servings as an appetizer

1 cup heavy cream

2 to 3 tablespoons finely chopped fresh basil

1 tablespoon Swerve confectioners'-style sweetener or equivalent amount of liquid or powdered sweetener (see page 37)

½ teaspoon fine sea salt

¼ teaspoon fresh ground black pepper

¾ teaspoon grass-fed powdered gelatin (see Tip)

2 ounces goat cheese or Brie

TOPPINGS:

2 slices prosciutto

1 tablespoon coconut oil

½ cup loosely packed fresh basil leaves

2 tablespoons shredded purple cabbage

Fine sea salt

This rich dish will have you coming back for more with its savory, salty, and slightly sweet flavor. Serve it with a simple green salad to balance its richness. When divided among four people, it makes a very good starter, too.

1. In a small saucepan, warm the cream over medium-high heat. Add the basil, sweetener, salt, and pepper and lightly stir. Continue stirring and simmer for 3 minutes, then remove from the heat.

2. Place 1 tablespoon of water in a small bowl. Sift the gelatin over the water, stir, and allow the gelatin to soften for a minute.

3. Put the cream mixture, gelatin, and goat cheese in a blender and puree until smooth. (Alternatively, blend everything together in the saucepan with an immersion blender.) Pour into two 4-ounce ramekins and refrigerate until the panna cotta has set, 30 to 50 minutes.

4. Just before serving, slice the prosciutto into thin strips. Heat the coconut oil in a skillet and fry the prosciutto with the basil leaves until crisp. Remove from the pan and drain briefly on kitchen towels, then distribute over the panna cotta. Top the prosciutto with a touch of shredded purple cabbage. Season with a pinch of salt.

TIP:

Using gelatin is an easy way to make tasty treats, but foods made with gelatin can easily get too rubbery if they sit in the fridge overnight. If you plan on making this recipe ahead of time and not serving it the same day, I suggest using ¼ teaspoon less gelatin than called for; this quantity will create the perfect creamy texture even after a day or two of resting in the fridge.

With less gelatin, the panna cotta can be made 3 days ahead, but the topping must be made right before serving.

KETO

NUTRITIONAL INFO (per serving)				
calories	fat	protein	carbs	fiber
264	21.6g	16.1g	1g	0g
	74%	24%	2%	

Sides

AND VEGETARIAN DISHES

CHAPTER 14

Mushroom RAGU

EGG-FREE   NUT-FREE   DAIRY-FREE OPTION   VEGE-TARIAN OPTION   ONE POT/BOWL

Prep Time: 8 minutes, plus 10 to 25 minutes for the Zoodles

Cook Time: 45 minutes

Yield: 4 servings

¼ cup (½ stick) unsalted butter (or MCT oil for dairy-free)

1 cup chopped onions

1 teaspoon finely chopped garlic, or cloves from ½ head roasted garlic (page 134)

1 pound portobello or button mushrooms, chopped

1 teaspoon fine sea salt

¼ teaspoon fresh ground black pepper

2 cups chicken bone broth, store-bought or homemade (page 132) (or vegetable broth for vegetarian)

½ cup tomato sauce

½ cup grated Parmesan cheese (about 2 ounces) (or nutritional yeast for dairy-free)

⅓ cup heavy cream (or full-fat coconut milk for dairy-free)

¼ cup chopped fresh basil leaves

¼ cup chopped fresh flat-leaf parsley leaves

1 recipe Zoodles (page 308) or 2 (7-ounce) packages Miracle Noodles, prepared following package instructions, for serving

When you hear the word *ragu,* it usually signifies a long cooking process and a dish made with meat. But since the star of this ragu is mushrooms, the cook time is significantly shorter. The umami taste profile from the tomato sauce and the Parmesan cheese plus the nucleotides (organic molecules that enhance umami flavor) in the mushrooms provide a mouthwatering meaty flavor without meat!

1. Heat the butter in a large cast-iron skillet or sauté pan over medium-heat. Add the onions and garlic and sauté for 5 minutes, or until the onions are translucent.

2. Add the mushrooms and season with the salt and pepper. Increase the heat to high and sauté the mushrooms until they are tender and all the liquid has evaporated, about 10 minutes.

3. Pour in the broth and tomato sauce and cook until the sauce has reduced by half, about 30 minutes. Add the Parmesan cheese and cream and stir to combine. Remove from the heat and stir in the herbs. Serve over Zoodles or Miracle Noodles.

VEGE-TARIAN OPTION *For a vegetarian meal that serves two, replace the chicken broth with vegetable broth and serve with a green salad tossed with the keto dressing of your choice (pages 116 to 121).*

L M H
KETO

NUTRITIONAL INFO (per serving)				
calories	fat	protein	carbs	fiber
246	18.5g	10.6g	9.8g	2.4g
	68%	17%	15%	

Cheesy GRITS

Prep Time: 2 minutes

Cook Time: 4 minutes

Yield: 4 servings

8 large eggs

½ cup beef bone broth, store-bought or homemade (page 132) (or vegetable broth for vegetarian)

1 teaspoon fine sea salt

½ cup (1 stick) unsalted butter

½ cup shredded sharp cheddar cheese (about 2 ounces)

Chopped fresh herbs of choice, for garnish (optional)

1. In a small bowl, whisk together the eggs, broth, and salt.

2. In a medium-sized saucepan, melt the butter over medium heat. Add the egg mixture to the pan and cook until the mixture thickens and small curds form, all the while scraping the bottom of the pan and stirring to keep large curds from forming. (A whisk works well for this task.)

3. Once curds have formed and the mixture has thickened, add the shredded cheese and stir until well combined. Remove from the heat and transfer to a serving bowl. Sprinkle with chopped herbs, if desired, and serve.

VEGE-TARIAN OPTION *For a vegetarian meal that serves two, replace the beef broth with vegetable broth and serve with a green salad tossed with the keto dressing of your choice (pages 116 to 121).*

M
L   H
KETO

NUTRITIONAL INFO (per serving)				
calories	fat	protein	carbs	fiber
408	37.8g	16.9g	1.1g	0g
	83%	16%	1%	

Creamy Cilantro-Lime PASTA

OPTION

EGG-FREE NUT-FREE DAIRY-FREE VEGE-TARIAN ONE POT/BOWL

Prep Time: 10 minutes, plus 10 to 25 minutes for the Zoodles

Yield: 4 servings

1 recipe Zoodles (page 308), or 2 (7-ounce) packages Miracle Noodles, prepared following package instructions

1 recipe Cilantro Lime Sauce (page 115)

These noodles have a little chili heat from the jalapeño in the sauce. If you don't like spicy foods, simply omit the jalapeño. If you like a lot of heat, don't bother to remove the seeds.

Place the noodles in a serving bowl. Pour the sauce over the noodles and toss to coat. Do not sauce more noodles than you plan to eat right away. Once sauced, leftover noodles get a little soggy, so store leftover noodles and sauce in separate airtight containers in the fridge for up to 5 days. Freezing is not recommended, as the dish tends to get soggy.

TIP:

For a vegetarian meal that serves 2, divide the sauced zoodles between 2 serving bowls and serve with a green salad tossed with the vegetarian keto dressing of your choice (pages 116 to 121).

L M H
KETO

NUTRITIONAL INFO (per serving)				
calories	fat	protein	carbs	fiber
388	35g	1.6g	5.7g	1.6g
	93%	2%	5%	

Pizza STICKS

Prep Time: 7 minutes

Cook Time: 20 minutes

Yield: 4 servings

CRUST:

1 (8-ounce) package cream cheese, room temperature

2 large eggs

1 teaspoon finely chopped garlic

¼ cup grated Parmesan cheese (about 1 ounce)

TOPPINGS:

1 cup pizza sauce

1 cup shredded mozzarella cheese (about 4 ounces)

Additional toppings of choice, such as ¼ cup diced green bell pepper or diced onion (optional)

2 tablespoons Pizza Spice Mix (page 111)

If you are a visual learner like me and would like to see how simple these pizza sticks are to make, check out the video on my site, MariaMindBodyHealth.com (type the word *video* in the search field).

1. Preheat the oven to 375°F. Line a 9-by-13-inch baking dish or 9-inch pie plate with parchment paper and lightly grease. (Make sure to use a dish with sides because the crust dough has the consistency of batter.)

2. In a large bowl, combine the cream cheese, eggs, garlic, and Parmesan cheese with a handheld mixer. Spread into the greased pan. Prebake for 10 minutes, or until golden brown. Allow the crust to cool for 2 minutes.

3. Ladle the pizza sauce over the crust. Top evenly with the mozzarella cheese and additional pizza toppings (if using). Sprinkle on the spice mix.

4. Bake the pizza until crisp and golden, about 10 minutes. Remove from the oven, slice into sticks, and serve.

TIP:

For a vegetarian meal that serves 2, divide the sticks between 2 plates and serve with a green salad tossed with the vegetarian keto dressing of your choice (pages 116 to 121).

KETO

NUTRITIONAL INFO (per serving)				
calories	fat	protein	carbs	fiber
372	30.8g	18.8g	6.2g	0.5g
	74%	20%	6%	

Easy as Portobello
PIZZA PIE

EGG-FREE · NUT-FREE · VEGE-TARIAN · ONE POT/BOWL

Prep Time: 4 minutes

Cook Time: 12 minutes

Yield: 2 servings

4 large portobello mushrooms

½ cup marinara sauce

1 (8-ounce) ball fresh mozzarella cheese, thinly sliced

TOPPINGS:

Chopped fresh basil leaves (reserve some for garnish)

Halved cherry tomatoes, sliced olives, diced bell peppers, and/or diced onions

1 tablespoon Pizza Spice Mix (page 111) (optional)

1. Preheat the oven to 400°F. Line a rimmed baking sheet with parchment paper.

2. Remove the stems from the mushrooms and save them for another recipe, such as Mushroom Ragu (page 300).

3. Place the mushroom caps, gill side up, on the lined baking sheet. Evenly distribute the sauce, cheese, and pizza toppings among the mushroom caps. Sprinkle with the spice mix (if using).

4. Bake for 12 minutes, or until the cheese has melted and the mushrooms are soft. Garnish with additional fresh basil leaves.

TIP:

For a vegetarian meal that serves 2, serve with a green salad tossed with the vegetarian keto dressing of your choice (pages 116 to 121).

SINGLE SERVING OPTION

To make a single serving, use 2 large portobello mushrooms, ¼ cup marinara sauce, 4 ounces fresh mozzarella, and the toppings of your choice, along with 1½ teaspoons Pizza Spice Mix, if desired. A toaster oven is ideal for making this size portion!

KETO

NUTRITIONAL INFO (per serving)				
calories	fat	protein	carbs	fiber
392	27g	27g	10g	2g
	62%	28%	10%	

Zoodles
TWO WAYS

EGG-FREE · NUT-FREE · DAIRY-FREE · VEGE-TARIAN · VIDEO

Prep Time: 5 minutes (plus 5 minutes to drain for salted, raw noodles)

Cook Time: 20 minutes (for baked noodles)

Yield: 4 servings (1 cup per serving)

2 medium zucchini, not more than 12 inches long

1 tablespoon fine sea salt (if making salted and drained zoodles)

Special Equipment:
Spiral slicer

TIP:

To enjoy zoodles throughout the week, prepare a double or triple batch of spiral-sliced zucchini by completing Steps 2 and 3. Store the raw noodles in an airtight container in the fridge for up to 5 days. Bake or salt and drain the amount of noodles you need, per Step 4 or 5, just before serving.

I like to call zucchini noodles "zoodles." I make a lot of them because I love growing zucchini in my garden, and it does take over! But if you have the space, garden-fresh zucchini is absolutely worth it.

One of the tricks to making zucchini noodles is to use zucchini that aren't too large—no more than 12 inches long and 2 inches wide. The seeds in large zucchini can make a mess out of your spiral slicer. The other trick is to remove some of the water from the zucchini noodles so that the beautiful sauce you've made doesn't become a watery mess when tossed with the noodles. The two easiest ways to do so are to salt and drain the raw zoodles or to dehydrate them in a low-temperature oven (which I prefer).

To increase the ketogenic level of this dish to high, toss the noodles with melted butter or a ketogenic sauce (see pages 122 to 130). And if you are a visual learner like me and would like to see how zoodles are made, check out the video on my site, MariaMindBodyHealth.com (type the word *video* in the search field).

1. If making baked zoodles, preheat the oven to 250°F. Place a paper towel on a rimmed baking sheet.

2. To prepare the zucchini for either method: Cut the ends off the zucchini to create nice even edges. If you desire white "noodles," peel the zucchini.

3. Using a vegetable spiral slicer, swirl the zucchini into long, thin, noodlelike shapes by gently pressing down on the handle while turning it clockwise.

4. To make baked zoodles: Spread out the zucchini noodles on the prepared baking sheet and bake for 20 minutes. Remove from the oven and serve immediately.

5. To make salted and drained noodles: Place the raw zoodles in a colander over the sink and sprinkle with the salt. Allow to sit for 5 minutes, then press to wring out the extra water. Serve immediately.

6. Zoodles are best consumed as soon as they're baked or salted and drained, so it's best to make just the amount you need (though to save time, you can spiral-slice the zucchini in advance; see Tip). If you have leftover prepared zoodles, store them unsauced in an airtight container in the refrigerator for up to 5 days. Freezing is not recommended since the zoodles tend to get soggy.

KETO — *to make HIGH, see headnote*

NUTRITIONAL INFO (per serving)				
calories	fat	protein	carbs	fiber
18	0.2g	1.4g	3.8g	1.2g
	3%	27%	70%	

**SINGLE
SERVING
OPTION**

To make a single serving of zoodles, use one small zucchini or half a medium zucchini. A toaster oven is ideal for making a single-serving batch of baked zoodles. If you're using more than one zucchini, however, you will need to use a standard-size oven and a larger rimmed baking sheet (about 18 by 13 inches or its equivalent) so that you can spread the noodles out without crowding them.

Bordelaise
MUSHROOMS

EGG-FREE NUT-FREE DAIRY-FREE

Prep Time: 5 minutes

Cook Time: 50 minutes

Yield: 4 servings

¼ cup bacon fat or duck fat (or unsalted butter if not dairy-sensitive)

2 tablespoons finely chopped shallots

1 clove garlic, finely chopped, or 4 cloves roasted garlic (page 134)

2 cups sliced button or baby bella mushrooms

1 cup beef bone broth, store-bought or homemade (page 132)

⅓ cup red wine vinegar

1 tablespoon coconut aminos

¼ teaspoon chopped fresh thyme (or to taste)

Fine sea salt and fresh ground black pepper

⅛ teaspoon guar gum

1. Melt the fat in a large skillet over medium heat. (Note: If using butter, increase the heat to high and brown the butter by whisking until the butter is frothy and brown flecks appear, then reduce the heat to low. Be careful not to burn the butter; you don't want black flecks.)

2. Stir in the shallots and garlic and cook for 3 minutes, or until the shallots are translucent. Add the mushrooms, in batches if necessary to avoid crowding, and cook until browned and softened, about 5 minutes.

3. Stir in the broth, vinegar, coconut aminos, and thyme. Increase the heat to medium-high and simmer rapidly for 5 minutes. Add salt and pepper to taste.

4. Lower the heat to medium-low and continue to cook for 30 minutes, or until the sauce has reduced by about a quarter. Sift the guar gum into the simmering sauce and whisk until thickened, about 3 minutes.

KETO
L M H

NUTRITIONAL INFO (per serving)				
calories	fat	protein	carbs	fiber
128	11.6g	1.9g	3.5g	0.7g
	82%	7%	11%	

Curry Braised CUCUMBERS

EGG-FREE · NUT-FREE · DAIRY-FREE · VEGE-TARIAN

Prep Time: 5 minutes

Cook Time: 7 minutes

Yield: 4 servings

2 (4-inch) cucumbers

2 tablespoons coconut oil

2 teaspoons turmeric powder

1 teaspoon lime juice

1 teaspoon finely chopped fresh Thai or Italian basil leaves

¼ teaspoon fine sea salt

Here is one of Julia Child's many practical cooking tips to live by: "Always start out with a larger pot than what you think you need." I often find myself wishing I'd listened to that advice! Learn from my mistakes and make sure you use a large skillet for this recipe.

1. Slice the cucumbers lengthwise into quarters. Slide the knife down the center of the cucumber quarters to remove as many seeds as you can. Dice into ½-inch pieces.

2. Place the coconut oil, turmeric, lime juice, basil, and salt in a large skillet over medium heat. Add the cucumbers and sauté for 7 minutes, or until the cucumbers are getting soft but not brown.

3. Remove from the heat and serve warm or cold. Store leftovers in an airtight container in the fridge for up to 3 days.

KETO

NUTRITIONAL INFO (per serving)				
calories	fat	protein	carbs	fiber
78	7g	0.6g	3.5g	0.6g
	80%	3%	17%	

Grilled Radicchio with
SWEET-AND-SOUR HOT BACON DRESSING

OPTION

EGG-FREE · NUT-FREE · DAIRY-FREE

Prep Time: 6 minutes

Cook Time: 20 minutes

Yield: 8 servings

2 heads radicchio

DRESSING:

4 slices bacon, finely diced

¼ cup MCT oil

3 tablespoons coconut vinegar or apple cider vinegar

1 teaspoon Swerve confectioners'-style sweetener or equivalent amount of liquid or powdered sweetener (see page 37)

Fine sea salt and fresh ground black pepper

½ cup Cilantro Lime Sauce (page 115), for serving (optional)

1. Slice each head of radicchio into quarters, leaving the stem intact in order to keep the wedges together. Rinse well under cold water for a few minutes to help cut the bitterness. Drain and pat dry.

2. Preheat a grill to medium-high heat or place a grill pan over medium-high heat.

3. While the grill or pan is heating, make the dressing: In a large sauté pan, cook the bacon slowly over medium heat until it is crisp and golden brown, 8 to 10 minutes. Leave the bacon and drippings in the pan. Add the oil, vinegar, and sweetener and bring to a boil for a minute, then remove from the heat. Season to taste with salt and pepper.

4. Drizzle the cut sides of each radicchio quarter with the dressing. Place sliced side down on the grill or grill pan and sear for 2 to 5 minutes, depending on how charred you prefer the leaves, then flip and char the other side. Remove from the heat and place sliced side up on a serving platter. Serve warm, drizzled with Cilantro Lime Sauce, if desired.

M
L H
KETO

NUTRITIONAL INFO (per serving)				
calories	fat	protein	carbs	fiber
126	11.6g	3.2g	2.1g	0g
	83%	10%	7%	

Caramelized ENDIVE

EGG-FREE NUT-FREE DAIRY-FREE VEGE-TARIAN

Prep Time: 6 minutes

Cook Time: 22 minutes

Yield: 8 servings

¼ cup duck fat or coconut oil (or unsalted butter if not dairy-sensitive)

1 teaspoon finely chopped garlic, or cloves from ½ head roasted garlic (page 134)

2 tablespoons thinly sliced shallots or finely diced onions

4 heads endive, sliced in half lengthwise

½ teaspoon fine sea salt

¼ teaspoon fresh ground black pepper

The method used in this recipe can also be used to make caramelized radicchio. Simply cut two heads of radicchio into quarters and follow the recipe as written.

1. Melt the fat in a large sauté pan over low heat. (Note: If using butter, increase the heat to high and brown the butter by whisking until the butter is frothy and brown flecks appear, then reduce the heat to low. Be careful not to burn the butter; you don't want black flecks.)

2. Add the garlic and shallots to the pan and sweat the shallots until translucent, about 2 minutes.

3. Add the endive halves to the pan, cut side down. Cook over low heat for 20 minutes, or until the endive is tender. Sprinkle on the salt and pepper and serve.

L **M** H
KETO

NUTRITIONAL INFO (per serving)				
calories	fat	protein	carbs	fiber
103	7g	3g	8g	7.8g
	60%	11%	30%	

Easy Homemade
SAUERKRAUT

EGG-FREE NUT-FREE DAIRY-FREE VEGE-TARIAN

Prep Time: 15 minutes, plus 3 to 5 days to ferment

Yield: 1½ to 2 quarts (about 1 cup per serving)

1 head green or purple cabbage

2 tablespoons fine sea salt

2 teaspoons caraway seeds (optional)

2 tablespoons Swerve confectioners'-style sweetener or equivalent amount of liquid or powdered sweetener (see page 37) (optional; see Note)

Sauerkraut is not a high-fat side, but fermented foods are a healthy addition to any diet, including a ketogenic diet. To make sauerkraut part of your keto-adapted lifestyle, just make sure to eat it with foods that are high in fat, such as brats (see page 288), as a true German like myself would.

1. Sterilize two 1-quart or eight 8-ounce mason jars. (I like to use small jars so that I can take individual portions with me for lunches.) For instructions, see "Tips for Pickling and Fermenting" on page 319.

2. Core the cabbage, remove and discard the limp outer pieces, and shred the cabbage. Place in a large bowl and sprinkle with the salt.

3. Use your hands to massage the salt into the cabbage until it starts to sweat and moisture is released into the bowl. This takes about 10 minutes. Add the caraway and sweetener (if using).

4. Divide the cabbage mixture between the sterilized mason jars. Press the mixture down to get out air bubbles. Place a sterilized weight on top of each jar to keep the cabbage submerged in the brine. (I place a measuring cup weighted down with a few clean rocks inside the mouth of the jar.)

5. Cover each jar with a piece of cheesecloth and secure the cheese-cloth in place. Set on the counter for 3 to 5 days, depending on how fermented you prefer your sauerkraut. The longer it ferments, the more pungent the flavor will become. Once it is fermented to your liking, remove the weights that are keeping the sauerkraut submerged. Cover the jars tightly and store in the fridge for up to 3 months.

NOTE:

Bavarian-style sauerkraut, which is what I grew up on, is traditionally sweet. If you prefer your sauerkraut more tangy, simply omit the sweetener.

M

L H

KETO

NUTRITIONAL INFO (per serving)				
calories	fat	protein	carbs	fiber
32	0.1g	1.4g	6.6g	2.8g
	2%	17%	82%	

Easy
KIMCHI

EGG-FREE · NUT-FREE · DAIRY-FREE · VEGE-TARIAN

Prep Time: 20 minutes, plus 3 to 5 days to ferment

Yield: 1½ to 2 quarts (about 1 cup per serving)

1 head napa cabbage

1 cup grated daikon radish (about 4 ounces)

4 green onions, chopped

2 to 3 tablespoons red pepper flakes (depending on desired heat)

2 tablespoons fine sea salt

5 cloves garlic, finely chopped

3 tablespoons grated fresh ginger

1 tablespoon fish sauce

1 teaspoon stevia glycerite (optional; see Note)

Special Equipment:
Food-grade rubber gloves

Kimchi is not a high-fat side, but fermented foods are a healthy addition to any diet, including a ketogenic diet. To make kimchi part of your keto-adapted lifestyle, just make sure to eat it with foods that are high in fat, such as seared pork belly (see page 292). Another thing you could do is mix in 2 tablespoons of Spicy Mayo (page 113) just before serving to increase the fat ratio. Think of it as a creamy, spicy slaw of sorts.

1. Sterilize two 1-quart or eight 8-ounce mason jars. (I like to use small jars so that I can take individual portions with me for lunches.) For instructions, see "Tips for Pickling and Fermenting" on page 319.

2. Core the cabbage and chop into bite-sized pieces. Place the cabbage, daikon, and green onions in a large bowl. Sprinkle with the red pepper flakes and salt.

3. Wearing food-grade rubber gloves, use your hands to massage the salt into the veggies until they start to sweat and moisture is released into the bowl. This takes about 10 to 15 minutes. Add the garlic, ginger, fish sauce, and sweetener (if using).

4. Divide the kimchi mixture between the sterilized mason jars. Press the mixture down to get out air bubbles. Place a sterilized weight on top of each jar to keep the mixture submerged in the brine. (I place a measuring cup weighted down with a few clean rocks inside the mouth of the jar.)

5. Cover each jar with a piece of cheesecloth and secure the cheesecloth in place. Set on the counter for 3 to 5 days, depending on how fermented you prefer your kimchi. The longer it ferments, the more pungent the flavor will become. Once it is fermented to your liking, remove the weights that are keeping the kimchi submerged. Cover the jars tightly and store in the fridge for up to 3 months.

NOTE:

Traditionally, kimchi is sweetened with a touch of sugar to balance the chili heat.

KETO

NUTRITIONAL INFO (per serving)				
calories	fat	protein	carbs	fiber
61	1g	3g	10g	3g
	15%	20%	65%	

Refrigerator PICKLES

EGG-FREE · NUT-FREE · DAIRY-FREE · VEGE-TARIAN

Prep Time: 5 minutes, plus 2 days to pickle

Yield: 1 quart (14 servings)

3 pickling cucumbers, about 4 inches long

3 sprigs fresh dill

2 cloves garlic, finely chopped

¼ cup thinly sliced white onions

2 cups coconut vinegar or apple cider vinegar

¼ cup Swerve confectioners'-style sweetener or equivalent amount of liquid or powdered sweetener (see page 37)

2 teaspoons fine sea salt

1 teaspoon mustard seed

¼ teaspoon celery seed

Nonchlorinated water

Did you know that most store-bought pickles have food dyes in them? Synthetic dyes can cause hyperactivity, which in turn can result in a deficiency of dopamine, which may be related to ADD. For these reasons, I like to make my own pickles.

Pickles are not a high-fat side but can be part of a ketogenic meal. Just make sure to eat pickles with foods that are high in fat, such as Pigs in a Bacon Blanket (page 287) or Mini Pastrami Roll-Ups (page 199).

1. Sterilize a 1-quart mason jar.

2. Clean the cucumbers and slice them into the desired shapes, such as lengthwise into spears or crosswise into rounds (for "chips"), or keep them whole.

3. Place the dill, garlic, and onions in the sterilized mason jar. Place the cucumbers on top of the onions, filling the jar with cucumbers to about 2 inches from the top.

4. In a glass or metal bowl, combine the vinegar, sweetener, salt, mustard seed, and celery seed. Pour into the mason jar. Add enough nonchlorinated water to cover the pickles and reach about 1 inch from the top of the jar.

5. Cover the jar tightly and let pickle in the refrigerator for 2 days before enjoying. Store in the refrigerator for up to 2 months.

TIP:

If you do buy pickles, look for brands without sugar. I suggest purchasing naturally fermented pickles, which are found in the refrigerated sections of the grocery store.

KETO

NUTRITIONAL INFO (per serving)				
calories	fat	protein	carbs	fiber
10	0.1g	0.4g	2.3g	(trace)
	1%	8%	91%	

Tips for Pickling and Fermenting:

- Sterilize your jars before using by placing them in boiling water. Pull them out of the hot water as you fill them. Wash the lids in room-temperature water.

- Use clean, clear, nonchlorinated water. Chlorine inhibits the growth of healthy bacteria and overwhelms the flavor. Even too much sulfur in well water will influence the flavor.

- Use coconut vinegar, which nutritionally exceeds other vinegars in its amino acid, vitamin, and mineral contents and is an excellent source of FOS (a prebiotic that promotes digestive health).

- Never use iodized salt when making pickled or fermented foods. The flavor of iodized salt takes over the taste of the lovely veggies and darkens the pickles.

- Use smaller salt crystals; they dissolve quicker.

- Mix and match the herbs and spices you love to create your favorite flavor profile! I like to use yellow mustard seed, celery seed, and fresh dill for pickling.

Paleo
POLENTA

EGG-FREE · NUT-FREE · OPTION DAIRY-FREE · OPTION VEGE-TARIAN

Prep Time: 6 minutes

Cook Time: 24 minutes

Yield: 4 servings

4 cups peeled and cubed eggplant (about 1 pound)

4 slices bacon, chopped

1 cup chopped onions

1 tablespoon finely chopped garlic, or cloves from 1 large head roasted garlic (page 134)

½ teaspoon fine sea salt

½ teaspoon dried ground oregano

½ cup beef bone broth, store-bought or homemade (page 132), or water, or more as needed

½ cup grated Parmesan cheese (about 2 ounces) (optional; omit for dairy-free)

I serve Slow Cooker Pork Ragu (page 291) over this polenta, as shown in the photo opposite, but it is equally delicious with chicken dishes and other pork dishes.

1. Place the eggplant cubes and bacon pieces in a large, heavy skillet over medium-high heat. Stir-fry until the bacon is fried and eggplant is extremely soft, about 10 minutes.

2. Using a slotted spoon, transfer the eggplant and bacon to a food processor; leave the bacon fat in the pan. Puree the eggplant and bacon until smooth.

3. With the skillet with the bacon fat over medium-high heat, add the onions and cook, stirring, until soft, about 3 minutes. Add the garlic and salt and cook, stirring, until fragrant, 45 seconds to 1 minute.

4. Add the eggplant puree and oregano to the skillet and stir to combine. Cook, stirring with a heavy wooden spoon, until the mixture forms a thick paste, 5 to 10 minutes, adding the broth or water 1 tablespoon at a time to keep the polenta from getting dry. Sprinkle with the cheese (if using), stir, and serve.

VEGE-TARIAN OPTION *To give this dish a smoky flavor without adding bacon, smoke the eggplant: Place the eggplant cubes on a large sheet of foil lined with unbleached parchment paper. Poke holes in the double layer of foil and parchment to allow smoke to penetrate the eggplant. Smoke in a smoker for 1 hour, following the directions for smoking eggplant on page 374. After removing the eggplant from the smoker, proceed with the recipe as written above, but in Step 1, use 1 tablespoon coconut oil to cook the eggplant. In Step 4, replace the beef broth with vegetable broth or water.*

L M H
KETO

NUTRITIONAL INFO (per serving)				
calories	fat	protein	carbs	fiber
136	9.2g	6.3g	8.3g	3.6g
	60%	17%	23%	

Desserts

A note on nuts and nut flours in desserts: Many ketogenic dessert recipes use nuts and nut flours, especially blanched almond flour. However, not only is almond flour expensive, but nuts are hard on the gut and quite high in carbohydrates. After years of working with metabolically damaged clients as well as many type 1 diabetics, I have found that eliminating carbohydrates from nuts helps clients heal faster, so I generally avoid them. (Since unsweetened almond milk doesn't contain carbs, it doesn't change blood sugar and affect ketosis the way almonds and almond flour do.) On rare occasions I do use coconut flour in this cookbook because it's very absorptive; as a result, you need only a few tablespoons for a recipe (versus a few cups of almond flour), which helps keep the level of carbohydrates down.

CHAPTER 15

Deconstructed
CRÈME BRÛLÉE

EGG-FREE NUT-FREE (OPTION) VEGE-TARIAN

Prep Time: 8 minutes, plus 25 minutes for the fat bombs

Yield: 4 servings

1 (8-ounce) package cream cheese, softened

½ cup unsweetened (unflavored or vanilla) almond milk, store-bought or homemade (page 131) (or unsweetened [unflavored or vanilla] hemp milk for nut-free)

¼ cup Swerve confectioners'-style sweetener or equivalent amount of liquid or powdered sweetener (see page 37), plus more if desired

1 teaspoon vanilla extract, or seeds scraped from 1 vanilla bean (about 6 inches long)

Pinch of fine sea salt

1 cup crushed Crispy Vanilla Fat Bombs (page 326) or Crispy Maple Bacon Fat Bombs (page 328), for garnish

Because my husband, Craig, adores crème brûlée, I've made it numerous times, but one too many of those times I ended up curdling the custard. Also, I don't have a torch, so when I tried to crisp up the topping, I put it under the broiler and often burned one edge because the heating was uneven. Which got me to thinking . . . I could break it down into easier steps and use crushed fat bombs for the topping. It's all much simpler!

1. Place the softened cream cheese, almond milk, sweetener, vanilla, and salt in a blender and puree until smooth. Taste to see if the mixture is sweet enough for you and add a little more sweetener if needed.

2. Scoop into 4 serving dishes and smooth out the tops. Top each dish with ¼ cup of the crushed fat bomb and serve.

TIP:

This custard and the crispy fat bombs can be made up to 2 days in advance for an easy but impressive dessert. Sprinkle the crushed crispy fat bombs on top just before serving to prevent them from getting soggy.

L M H
KETO

NUTRITIONAL INFO (per serving)				
calories	fat	protein	carbs	fiber
186	16g	7.3g	3.9g	0g
	77%	15%	8%	

Grand Marnier FAT BOMBS

EGG-FREE · NUT-FREE · DAIRY-FREE · VEGETARIAN

Prep Time: 6 minutes, plus 30 minutes to chill

Yield: 24 fat bombs (2 per serving)

FILLING:

1 cup coconut oil (or unsalted butter if not dairy-sensitive)

¼ cup Swerve confectioners'-style sweetener or equivalent amount of liquid or powdered sweetener (see page 37)

1 teaspoon orange extract or 4 drops orange oil

1 teaspoon Stur orange-mango-flavored liquid water enhancer (optional)

CHOCOLATE DRIZZLE:

¼ cup plus 2 tablespoons coconut oil

¼ cup plus 2 tablespoons unsweetened cocoa powder

¼ cup Swerve confectioners'-style sweetener or equivalent amount of liquid or powdered sweetener (see page 37)

1 teaspoon orange extract

⅛ teaspoon fine sea salt

Special Equipment:
2 (12-cavity) dome-shaped silicone truffle molds with 1-ounce cavities (optional)

KETO

NUTRITIONAL INFO (per serving)				
calories	fat	protein	carbs	fiber
275	31g	0g	0g	0g
	100%	0%	0%	

1. Line a 24-well mini muffin pan with mini muffin liners, or have on hand two 12-cavity truffle molds.

2. To make the filling: In a medium-sized bowl, mix together the ingredients for the filling until you have a paste. Divide the filling mixture among the prepared muffin cups, filling each well about two-thirds full. Place in the freezer until chilled, about 20 minutes.

3. Meanwhile, make the chocolate drizzle: Melt the coconut oil in a small saucepan over low heat. Stir in the cocoa powder, sweetener, orange extract, and salt until completely melted. Allow to cool slightly before using.

4. Drizzle the chocolate over the filling. Place back in the freezer to set, about 10 minutes. Store in an airtight container in the fridge for up to 1 week or in the freezer for up to 3 months.

Crispy Vanilla
FAT BOMBS

EGG-FREE NUT-FREE DAIRY-FREE VEGE-TARIAN

Prep Time: 5 minutes

Cook Time: 15 minutes

Yield: 1 cup crushed (¼ cup per serving) or 48 mini discs (12 per serving)

1 cup Swerve confectioners'-style sweetener or equivalent amount of powdered erythritol or monk fruit (see page 37)

1 teaspoon vanilla extract, or seeds scraped from 1 vanilla bean (about 6 inches long)

3 tablespoons coconut oil (or unsalted butter if not dairy-sensitive)

Crush these and use as a topping on keto ice cream or other desserts, or eat them whole as individual candies! To use as a crushed topping, it works best to bake it as a thin sheet. To make individual candies, you will need two mini muffin pans. Both methods are included below. You can use this basic recipe to make just about any flavor of fat bomb you like; some of my favorite flavor variations are below. Note that fat bombs that contain cocoa powder are thicker because the cocoa powder keeps the mixture from spreading out as readily.

1. Preheat the oven to 350°F. If planning to use the fat bomb as a crushed topping, have on hand a mini rimmed baking sheet, about 10 by 6 inches; if planning to make individual candies, have on hand two 24-well mini muffin pans.

2. In a medium-sized bowl, combine the sweetener, vanilla, and coconut oil with a fork until small crumbs form.

3. If making a sheet of the fat bomb (for use as a topping): Place the mixture in the middle of the baking sheet. There's no need to spread it out; it will melt into a thin layer in the oven.

4. If making individual candies: Divide the mixture evenly among the mini muffin wells, putting about 1 teaspoon of the mixture in each well.

5. Bake for 12 to 15 minutes, until the mixture becomes a liquid. Remove from the oven and allow to cool completely in the pan. The candy will harden as it cools.

6. Break the cooled sheet of candy into pieces or remove the cooled candies from the muffin pans. Store in an airtight container in the fridge for up to 1 month or in the freezer for up to 3 months.

VARIATIONS:

- **Crispy Raspberry Fat Bombs.** In Step 2, replace the vanilla with 1 teaspoon raspberry extract.

- **Crispy Orange/Orange-Mango Fat Bombs.** In Step 2, replace the vanilla with 1 teaspoon orange extract. To give the fat bombs an orange-mango flavor and a bolder color, add 2 teaspoons Stur orange-mango-flavored liquid water enhancer (see page 58).

- **Crispy Chocolate Fat Bombs.** In Step 2, add 3 tablespoons unsweetened cocoa powder.

- **Crispy Mocha Fat Bombs.** In Step 2, add 3 tablespoons unsweetened cocoa powder and 1 teaspoon espresso powder.

M
L   H
KETO

NUTRITIONAL INFO (per serving)				
calories	fat	protein	carbs	fiber
89	10.8g	0g	0g	0g
	100%	0%	0%	

Crispy Maple Bacon
FAT BOMBS

EGG-FREE NUT-FREE DAIRY-FREE

Prep Time: 5 minutes

Cook Time: 20 minutes

Yield: 1 cup crushed (¼ cup per serving) or 48 mini discs (12 per serving)

2 slices bacon, chopped into small pieces

1 cup Swerve confectioners'-style sweetener or equivalent amount of powdered erythritol or monk fruit (see page 37)

2 teaspoons maple extract

Use these fat bombs on Deconstructed Crème Brûlée (page 324) or eat them plain!

1. Preheat the oven to 350°F. If planning to use the fat bomb as a topping, have on hand a mini rimmed baking sheet, about 10 by 6 inches; if planning to make individual candies, have on hand two 24-well mini muffin pans.

2. In a large skillet, fry the bacon pieces over medium heat until crisp.

3. Place the bacon and 3 tablespoons of the bacon fat in a heat-safe medium-sized bowl; if you do not have 3 tablespoons of rendered bacon fat, add additional reserved bacon fat or coconut oil. Add the sweetener and maple extract and combine with a fork until small crumbs form.

4. If making a sheet of the fat bomb (for use as a topping): Place the mixture in the middle of the baking sheet. There's no need to spread it out; it will melt into a thin layer in the oven.

5. If making individual candies: Divide the mixture evenly among the mini muffin wells, putting about 1 teaspoon of the mixture in each well.

6. Bake for 12 to 15 minutes, until the mixture becomes a liquid. Remove from the oven and allow to cool completely in the pan. The candy will harden as it cools.

7. Break the cooled candy into pieces or remove the cooled candies from the muffin pans. Store in an airtight container in the fridge for up to 1 month or in the freezer for up to 3 months.

KETO

NUTRITIONAL INFO (per serving)				
calories	fat	protein	carbs	fiber
137	14.1g	2.5g	0g	0g
	93%	7%	0%	

CREAM BITES

EGG-
FREE   NUT-
FREE   VEGE-
TARIAN

*Prep Time: 5 minutes, plus
30 minutes to freeze*

Yield: 6 servings

2 cups heavy cream (see Note)

2 to 4 tablespoons Swerve
confectioners'-style sweetener
or equivalent amount of liquid
or powdered sweetener (see
page 37) (depending on desired
sweetness)

½ teaspoon vanilla extract, or
a few drops of vanilla oil

½ teaspoon orange extract, or
a few drops of orange oil

2 teaspoons grated orange zest,
for garnish (optional)

Special Equipment:
*Whipped cream canister
(optional)*

1   To use a whipped cream canister: Place all the ingredients but the zest in a whipped cream canister and operate following the manufacturer's instructions.

2. To whip using a bowl and mixer: Chill a large stainless-steel bowl and beaters in the freezer until cold. Place the cream in the cold bowl and whip, using a handheld mixer, until medium-stiff peaks form. Add the sweetener and extracts and beat to combine.

3. Scoop the whipped cream into a piping bag with a tip. Alternatively, scoop it into a large resealable plastic bag and snip ¼ inch off one of the corners of the bag.

4. Line a baking sheet with parchment paper. Squirt or pipe 2-tablespoon amounts of the whipped cream onto the paper, about ½ inch apart. Garnish with orange zest, if desired.

5. Place in the freezer until frozen, about 30 minutes.

6. Store in an airtight container in the freezer for up to 1 month, if they last that long!

NOTE:

When purchasing cream, do not buy ultra-pasteurized, which means that the cream has been subjected to very high heat. This type of cream tends not to whip up as well.

M
L   H
KETO

NUTRITIONAL INFO (per serving)				
calories	fat	protein	carbs	fiber
138	14.8g	0.8g	0.8g	0g
	96%	2%	2%	

Frozen Snickerdoodle
CREAM BITES

EGG-FREE NUT-FREE VEGE-TARIAN

Prep Time: 5 minutes, plus 30 minutes to freeze

Yield: 6 servings

2 cups heavy cream (see Note)

2 to 3 tablespoons Swerve confectioners'-style sweetener or equivalent amount of powdered erythritol or monk fruit (see page 37) (depending on desired sweetness)

1 teaspoon vanilla extract, or seeds scraped from 1 vanilla bean (about 6 inches long)

FOR GARNISH:

1 tablespoon Swerve confectioners'-style sweetener or equivalent amount of powdered erythritol or monk fruit (see page 37)

2 teaspoons ground cinnamon

Special Equipment:
Whipped cream canister (optional)

1. Line a baking sheet with parchment paper.

2. To use a whipped cream canister: Place the cream, sweetener, and vanilla in a whipped cream canister and operate following the manufacturer's instructions.

3. To whip using a bowl and mixer: Chill a large stainless-steel bowl and beaters in the freezer until cold. Place the cream in the cold bowl and whip, using a handheld mixer, until medium-stiff peaks form. Add the sweetener and vanilla and beat to combine.

4. Scoop the whipped cream into a piping bag with a tip. Alternatively, scoop it into a large resealable plastic bag and snip ¼ inch off one of the corners of the bag.

5. Squirt or pipe 2-tablespoon amounts of the whipped cream onto the lined baking sheet, about ½ inch apart.

6. In a small bowl, combine the 1 tablespoon powdered sweetener and the cinnamon. Sprinkle the "bites" liberally with the cinnamon mixture.

7. Place in the freezer for about 30 minutes, until frozen.

8. Store in an airtight container in the freezer for up to 1 month, if they last that long!

NOTE:

When purchasing cream, do not buy ultra-pasteurized, which means that the cream has been subjected to very high heat. This type of cream tends not to whip up as well.

KETO

NUTRITIONAL INFO (per serving)				
calories	fat	protein	carbs	fiber
138	14.8g	0.8g	0.8g	0g
	96%	2%	2%	

Strawberry CHEESECAKE IN JARS

Prep Time: 5 minutes, plus 2 hours to set

Cook Time: 5 minutes

Yield: 6 servings

¼ cup strong-brewed hot strawberry or hibiscus tea (see Note)

½ tablespoon grass-fed powdered gelatin (see Tips)

1 (8-ounce) package cream cheese, softened, or mascarpone cheese

1 cup unsweetened (unflavored or vanilla) almond milk, store-bought or homemade (page 131) (or heavy cream for nut-free)

¼ cup Swerve confectioners'-style sweetener or equivalent amount of liquid or powdered sweetener (see page 37) (or to desired sweetness)

1 teaspoon strawberry extract

Pinch of fine sea salt

CHOCOLATE DRIZZLE (OPTIONAL):

3 tablespoons unsalted butter or coconut oil

3 tablespoons unsweetened cocoa powder

2 tablespoons Swerve confectioners'-style sweetener or equivalent amount of liquid or powdered sweetener (see page 37) (or to desired sweetness)

½ teaspoon strawberry extract

KETO

NUTRITIONAL INFO (per serving)				
calories	fat	protein	carbs	fiber
220	21.3g	3.4g	5.4g	1.7g
	86%	5%	9%	

This dessert is so easy to make, yet it is very elegant when served in cute cups. It is sure to impress even non-keto guests.

1. Place the tea in a small heatproof bowl. Sift the gelatin over the tea and whisk until dissolved.

2. Place the cream cheese in a bowl and mix with handheld mixer until smooth and no lumps remain. Pour in the gelatin mixture, almond milk, sweetener, strawberry extract, and salt and mix until very smooth.

3. Pour into 6 cute serving cups. Cover and place in the fridge to set, about 2 hours.

4. Meanwhile, make the chocolate drizzle (if using): Melt the butter over low heat. Stir in the cocoa powder, sweetener, and extract until completely melted. Let cool to room temperature before using.

5. Pour 1 tablespoon of the chocolate drizzle over each cup just before serving. Store in the fridge until ready to serve. Serve the same day it is made.

NOTE:

If you do not have strawberry or hibiscus tea, you may substitute warm unflavored or vanilla almond milk, store-bought or homemade (page 131), or warm unflavored or vanilla hemp milk.

TIPS:

Using gelatin is an easy way to make tasty treats, but foods made with gelatin can easily get too rubbery if they sit in the fridge overnight. If you plan on making this recipe ahead of time and not serving it the same day, I suggest using ¼ teaspoon less gelatin than called for; this quantity will create a perfect creamy texture even after a day or two in the fridge.

Using less gelatin, this dessert can be made 3 days ahead and kept in the fridge.

PALETAS

EGG-FREE | NUT-FREE (OPTION) | DAIRY-FREE | VEGE-TARIAN

Prep Time: 5 minutes, plus 2 hours to freeze

Yield: 4 pops (1 per serving)

1 cup full-fat coconut milk (or heavy cream if not dairy-sensitive)

1 cup unsweetened (unflavored or vanilla) almond milk, store-bought or homemade (page 131) (or unsweetened [unflavored or vanilla] hemp milk for nut-free)

¼ cup Swerve confectioners'-style sweetener or equivalent amount of liquid or powdered sweetener (see page 37)

1 teaspoon strawberry, orange, or vanilla extract (or other flavor of choice)

1 teaspoon Stur liquid water enhancer (fruit flavor of choice; see page 58), or more to desired sweetness (optional)

Special Equipment:

4 Popsicle molds

Paletas are Latin American ice pops that are traditionally made with fruit juice and chunks of fruit. They can also be made with cream or milk—here, I've used coconut milk and almond milk, which give them a delicious creaminess.

1. In a blender, blend all the ingredients until well combined. Pour the mixture into 4 Popsicle molds.

2. Place in the freezer for at least 2 hours before serving. Store covered in the freezer for up to 1 month.

made with coconut milk

NUTRITIONAL INFO (per serving)				
calories	fat	protein	carbs	fiber
156	15.2g	1.6g	3.2g	0g
	88%	4%	8%	

made with heavy cream

NUTRITIONAL INFO (per serving)				
calories	fat	protein	carbs	fiber
114	12g	0.9g	1.3g	0g
	92%	3%	4%	

Orange Cream PUSH POPS

EGG-FREE | NUT-FREE OPTION | DAIRY-FREE OPTION | VEGE-TARIAN | VIDEO

Prep Time: 5 minutes, plus 2 hours to freeze

Yield: 4 pops (1 per serving)

1 teaspoon vanilla extract, or seeds scraped from 1 vanilla bean (about 6 inches long)

4 ounces (½ cup) cream cheese, softened (or ½ cup coconut cream for dairy-free)

1¼ cups unsweetened vanilla-flavored almond milk, store-bought or homemade (page 131) (or unsweetened vanilla-flavored hemp milk for nut-free)

¼ cup Swerve confectioners'-style sweetener or equivalent amount of liquid or powdered sweetener (see page 37)

1 teaspoon orange extract or 2 drops orange oil

¼ teaspoon fine sea salt

Special Equipment:
4 push pop molds

These are a summertime staple at our house. In the evenings, you can often find us riding bikes on country roads with the boys enjoying these push pops in the pull-behind. If you would like to see how easy they are to make, check out the video I made with my boys on my site, MariaMindBodyHealth.com (type the word *video* in the search field).

1. Place the ingredients in a blender and puree until smooth.

2. Pour the mixture into 4 push pop molds and freeze for at least 2 hours before serving. Store covered in the freezer for up to 1 month.

KETO

NUTRITIONAL INFO (per serving)				
calories	fat	protein	carbs	fiber
99	9.9g	2.1g	0.8g	0g
	90%	7.8%	2.2%	

Key Lime
CURD

	OPTION	
NUT-FREE	DAIRY-FREE	VEGE-TARIAN

Prep Time: 5 minutes

Cook Time: 10 minutes

Yield: 2¾ cups (¼ cup per serving)

1 cup Swerve confectioners'-style sweetener or equivalent amount of liquid or powdered sweetener (see page 37)

½ cup Key lime juice

4 large eggs

½ cup (1 stick) unsalted butter (or coconut oil for dairy-free)

1 tablespoon grated lime zest, for garnish (optional)

TIP:

Can be made 1 day ahead.

This Key lime curd is indispensable. I serve it straight up in individual bowls for a decadent creamy treat and also use it to make Key Lime Ice Cream (page 342) and Key Lime Lollies (page 342). If you can't find Key limes, you can substitute regular lime juice.

1. Place the sweetener, lime juice, and eggs in a medium-sized heavy-bottomed saucepan and whisk to combine. Add the butter and set over medium heat.

2. Once the butter has melted, whisk constantly until the mixture thickens and thickly coats the back of a spoon, about 10 minutes. Do not allow the mixture to come to a boil.

3. Pour the mixture through a fine-mesh strainer into a medium-sized bowl. Place the bowl in a larger bowl filled with ice water and whisk occasionally until the curd has cooled completely, about 15 minutes.

4. Serve in individual bowls, garnished with lime zest, if desired.

VARIATION: LEMON CURD.

Substitute ½ cup lemon juice for the Key lime juice and replace the lime zest with lemon zest (if using) for garnish.

L —M— H
KETO

NUTRITIONAL INFO (per serving)				
calories	fat	protein	carbs	fiber
94	9.4g	2g	0.4g	0g
	90%	8.5%	1.5%	

Key Lime
FAT BOMBS

NUT-FREE DAIRY-FREE OPTION

Prep Time: 5 minutes, plus 30 minutes to chill

Yield: 24 bites (2 per serving)

½ cup Key lime juice

2 teaspoons grass-fed powdered gelatin

1 cup Swerve confectioners'-style sweetener or equivalent amount of liquid or powdered sweetener (see page 37)

4 large eggs

½ cup (1 stick) unsalted butter (or coconut oil for dairy-free)

1 tablespoon grated lime zest, for garnish (optional)

Special Equipment:
Silicone truffle mold with large cavities about 1¼ inches in diameter (optional)

These tasty bites are based on my Key Lime Curd (page 338), but I've given them a twist by adding gelatin. The gelatin helps the bites keep their shape so you can take them with you for an easy, tasty on-the-go treat. If you can't find Key limes, you can use regular lime juice.

1. Have on hand a silicone truffle mold with 24 large cavities, or line a rimmed baking sheet with parchment paper.

2. Put the lime juice in a small bowl. Sift the gelatin into the lime juice to soften for a minute.

3. In a medium-sized heavy-bottomed saucepan, whisk together the sweetener, eggs, and lime juice mixture. Add the butter and set over medium heat.

4. Once the butter has melted, whisk constantly until the mixture thickens and thickly coats the back of a spoon, about 10 minutes. Do not allow the mixture to come to a boil.

5. Pour the mixture through a fine-mesh strainer into a medium-sized bowl. Pour the warm curd into truffle molds or dollop 2 tablespoons of the curd onto the lined baking sheet, spacing them about ½ inch apart. Top with the lime zest, if desired.

6. Place in the freezer until set, about 30 minutes. To unmold the bites from the truffle mold, bend one end of each mold to pop out each fat bomb.

7. Store in an airtight container in the fridge for up to 1 week or in the freezer for up to 1 month.

KETO

NUTRITIONAL INFO (per serving)				
calories	fat	protein	carbs	fiber
98	9.4g	3.3g	0.3g	0g
	86%	13%	1%	

Key Lime
ICE CREAM

NUT-FREE | DAIRY-FREE (OPTION) | VEGE-TARIAN

Prep Time: 5 minutes, plus 15 minutes for the curd and time to churn (varies according to machine)

Yield: 4¾ cups (⅓ heaping cup per serving)

1 recipe Key Lime Curd (page 338) (made with coconut oil for dairy-free)

2 cups heavy cream (or coconut cream for dairy-free)

Swerve confectioners'-style sweetener or equivalent amount of liquid or powdered sweetener (see page 37), to taste

1 tablespoon grated lime zest, for garnish (optional)

Special Equipment:
Ice cream maker

1. Place the curd and cream in a blender and puree until smooth. Taste and add sweetener to your liking.

2. Pour into an ice cream maker and churn, following the manufacturer's instructions, until set. Garnish with lime zest, if desired, and serve immediately, or transfer to a container and freeze for up to 1 month.

VARIATION: KEY LIME LOLLIES.

If you don't have an ice cream maker, pour the liquid from the blender into 14 Popsicle molds and freeze for at least 3 hours, or until set. Store covered in the freezer for up to 1 month.

L — M — H
KETO

NUTRITIONAL INFO (per serving)				
calories	fat	protein	carbs	fiber
212	22.7g	2g	0.4g	0g
	95%	4%	1%	

Coffee
ICE CREAM

NUT-FREE · DAIRY-FREE · VEGE-TARIAN

Prep Time: 5 minutes, plus time to churn (varies according to machine)

Yield: 2¾ cups (about ⅓ cup per serving)

¾ cup plus 2 tablespoons coconut oil (or unsalted butter if not dairy-sensitive)

½ cup strong-brewed decaf espresso or coffee, chilled

¼ cup Swerve confectioners'-style sweetener or equivalent amount of liquid or powdered sweetener (see page 37)

¼ cup MCT oil

4 large eggs

4 large egg yolks

1 teaspoon vanilla extract, or seeds scraped from 1 vanilla bean (about 6 inches long)

½ teaspoon fine sea salt

Special Equipment:
Ice cream maker

Making ice cream with MCT oil and salt may seem unusual, but they play important roles: the oil gives the ice cream a smooth texture and the salt helps keep it soft.

1. Place all the ingredients in a blender and puree until smooth.

2. Pour into an ice cream maker and churn, following the manufacturer's instructions, until set. Serve immediately or transfer to a container and freeze for up to 1 month.

VARIATION: COFFEE POPSICLES.

If you don't have an ice cream maker, pour the liquid into 8 Popsicle molds and freeze for at least 3 hours, or until set. Store covered in the freezer for up to 1 month.

KETO · L · M · H

NUTRITIONAL INFO (per serving)				
calories	fat	protein	carbs	fiber
332	35.3g	4.1g	1.1g	0g
	95%	4%	1%	

Hibiscus Berry
ICE CREAM

NUT-FREE   DAIRY-FREE   VEGE-TARIAN

Prep Time: 5 minutes, plus time to churn (varies according to machine)

Yield: 2¾ cups (about ⅓ cup per serving)

¾ cup plus 2 tablespoons coconut oil (or softened unsalted butter if not dairy-sensitive)

½ cup strong-brewed hibiscus tea, chilled

¼ cup Swerve confectioners'-style sweetener or equivalent amount of liquid or powdered sweetener (see page 37)

¼ cup MCT oil

4 large eggs

4 large egg yolks

2 teaspoons raspberry extract

½ teaspoon fine sea salt

Special Equipment:
Ice cream maker

The hibiscus tea gives this ice cream a lovely color and sweet flavor profile.

1. Place all the ingredients in a blender and puree until smooth.
2. Pour into an ice cream maker and churn, following the manufacturer's instructions, until set. Serve immediately or transfer to a container and freeze for up to 1 month.

VARIATION: HIBISCUS BERRY POPSICLES.

If you don't have an ice cream maker, pour the liquid into 8 Popsicle molds and freeze for at least 3 hours or until set. Store covered in the freezer for up to 1 month.

KETO

NUTRITIONAL INFO (per serving)				
calories	fat	protein	carbs	fiber
331	35.3g	4.1g	1.1g	0g
	95%	4%	1%	

Chai
ICE CREAM

NUT-FREE · DAIRY-FREE · VEGETARIAN · VIDEO

Prep Time: 5 minutes, plus time to churn (varies according to machine)

Yield: 2¾ cups (¼ cup per serving)

¾ cup plus 2 tablespoons coconut oil (or unsalted butter if not dairy-sensitive)

½ cup strong-brewed chai tea, chilled

¼ cup Swerve confectioners'-style sweetener or equivalent amount of liquid or powdered sweetener (see page 37)

¼ cup MCT oil

4 large eggs

4 large egg yolks

1 teaspoon vanilla extract, or seeds scraped from 1 vanilla bean (about 6 inches long)

1 teaspoon ground cinnamon

½ teaspoon fine sea salt

Special Equipment:
Ice cream maker

KETO

NUTRITIONAL INFO (per serving)				
calories	fat	protein	carbs	fiber
225	23.5g	2.8g	1.7g	0g
	94%	4%	2%	

If you are a visual learner like me, you can watch a video of me making this dessert on my site, MariaMindBodyHealth.com (type the word *video* in the search field).

1. Place all the ingredients in a blender and puree until smooth.

2. Pour into an ice cream machine and churn, per the manufacturer's instructions, until set. Serve immediately or transfer to a container and freeze for up to 1 month.

VARIATION: CHAI POPSICLES.

If you don't have an ice cream maker, pour the mixture into 8 Popsicle molds and freeze for at least 3 hours, or until set. Store covered in the freezer for up to 1 month.

Dreamy CHAI FLOAT

NUT-FREE DAIRY-FREE VEGE-TARIAN VIDEO

Prep Time: 5 minutes, plus time for the ice cream

Yield: 1 serving

¼ cup Swerve confectioners'-style sweetener or equivalent amount of liquid or powdered sweetener (see page 37)

1 cup strong-brewed hot chai tea

2 small scoops Chai Ice Cream (page 345)

1 cup carbonated water

If you are a visual learner like me and would like to see how easy this ice cream treat is to make, check out the video on my site, MariaMindBodyHealth.com (type the word *video* in the search field).

1. Dissolve the sweetener in the hot tea, then chill the tea. (This recipe calls for a fair amount of sweetener because it will be diluted with carbonated water.)

2. Place the ice cream in a tall glass. Pour the chilled sweetened chai tea over the ice cream. Fill with carbonated water to the top.

L M H
KETO

NUTRITIONAL INFO (per serving)				
calories	fat	protein	carbs	fiber
225	23.5g	2.8g	1.7g	0g
	94%	4%	2%	

Savory
PIZZA GELATO

NUT-FREE · DAIRY-FREE · VEGETARIAN

Prep Time: 7 minutes, plus time to churn (varies according to machine)

Yield: 2¾ cups (about ¼ cup per serving)

¾ cup plus 2 tablespoons coconut oil (or unsalted butter if not dairy-sensitive)

¼ cup MCT oil

4 large eggs

4 large egg yolks

½ cup pizza sauce

½ teaspoon fine sea salt

¼ teaspoon finely chopped garlic, or 2 cloves roasted garlic (page 134)

SUGGESTED PIZZA ADD-INS:

1 tablespoon fresh basil leaves, chopped

1 tablespoon fresh oregano leaves, chopped

1 cup sliced black olives

Special Equipment:
Ice cream maker

If a savory dessert sounds crazy to you, think about the tradition in some cultures to finish a meal with a cheese course. I just morphed the cheese course into a dessert that really and truly tastes like a slice of cheese pizza . . . but without the cheese! I developed this dessert in response to my clients' request for a savory "fat bomb"-type dessert or treat that would help them get into ketosis fast and that has no sweeteners so they could kick their sweet tooth.

1. In a blender, combine the coconut oil, MCT oil, eggs, egg yolks, pizza sauce, salt, and garlic and blend until very smooth.

2. Pour the mixture into an ice cream maker and churn, following the manufacturer's instructions, until almost fully churned. Gradually add the pizza add-ins of your choice and let mix until fully combined. Serve immediately or transfer to a container and freeze for up to 1 month.

KETO

NUTRITIONAL INFO (per serving)				
calories	fat	protein	carbs	fiber
225	23.9g	2.9g	0.8g	0g
	95%	4%	1%	

Egg-Free
ICE CREAM

EGG-FREE   NUT-FREE (OPTION)   VEGE-TARIAN   VIDEO

Prep Time: 5 minutes, plus time to churn (varies according to machine)

Yield: 5½ cups (½ cup per serving)

2 avocados, halved, pitted, and peeled

1 cup unsweetened (unflavored or vanilla) almond milk, store-bought or homemade (page 131) (or unsweetened [unflavored or vanilla] hemp milk for nut-free)

1 cup heavy cream

½ cup Swerve confectioners'-style sweetener or equivalent amount of liquid or powdered sweetener (see page 37)

1 tablespoon lime or lemon juice

1 teaspoon mint extract or a few drops of mint oil (or other flavored extract or oil of choice)

½ teaspoon fine sea salt

Special Equipment:
Ice cream maker

I usually flavor this ice cream with mint extract, but you can use it as a base for any flavor of egg-free ice cream you like: simply swap the mint extract or oil for another flavor. If you are a visual learner like me, you can watch a video of me making this dessert on my site, MariaMindBodyHealth.com (type the word *video* in the search field).

1. Place all the ingredients in a blender and puree until smooth.

2. Pour into an ice cream maker and churn, following the manufacturer's instructions, until set. Serve immediately or transfer to a container and freeze for up to 1 month. Once frozen, allow the ice cream to soften at room temperature for 15 minutes before serving.

VARIATION: EGG-FREE CREAMY POPSICLES.

If you don't have an ice cream maker, pour the liquid into 16 Popsicle molds and freeze for at least 3 hours, or until set. Store covered in the freezer for up to 1 month.

KETO

NUTRITIONAL INFO (per serving)				
calories	fat	protein	carbs	fiber
225	20.9g	1.9g	8.7g	6.8g
	83%	3%	14%	

ICE CREAM COATING

EGG-FREE · NUT-FREE · DAIRY-FREE · VEGE-TARIAN

Prep Time: 4 minutes

Yield: ½ cup (2 tablespoons per serving)

¼ cup plus 2 tablespoons coconut oil

¼ cup plus 2 tablespoons unsweetened cocoa powder

¼ cup Swerve confectioners'-style sweetener or equivalent amount of liquid or powdered sweetener (see page 37)

1 teaspoon vanilla extract, or seeds scraped from 1 vanilla bean (about 6 inches long)

½ teaspoon fine sea salt

This recipe reminds me of visiting Tasty Treat, the local ice cream shop, as a little girl and getting my ice cream cone covered with a crispy chocolate coating.

Melt the coconut oil in a small saucepan over low heat. Stir in the cocoa powder, sweetener, vanilla, and salt until completely melted. Allow to cool a bit before drizzling over ice cream. Store in the fridge for up to 2 weeks or in the freezer for up to 1 month.

FLAVOR VARIATIONS:

- **Peppermint Patty.** Replace the vanilla with 1 teaspoon mint extract or a few drops of mint oil.

- **Almond Joy.** Replace the vanilla with 1 teaspoon almond extract or a few drops of almond oil.

- **Creamsicle.** Omit the cocoa powder and add 1 teaspoon orange extract or a few drops of orange oil.

- **Key Lime.** Omit the cocoa powder and add 1 teaspoon lime extract or a few drops of lime oil.

VARIATION: CHOCOLATE CANDY BARS.

To make candy bars, pour the mixture into four 1-ounce-capacity chocolate bar-shaped silicone molds and place in the fridge until set, about 15 minutes. Store in the fridge for up to 2 weeks or in the freezer for up to 1 month.

L M H
KETO

NUTRITIONAL INFO (per serving)				
calories	fat	protein	carbs	fiber
139	14g	1g	3g	1.6g
	90%	2%	8%	

Butterscotch MOUSSE

EGG-FREE   NUT-FREE   VEGE-TARIAN

Prep Time: 5 minutes

Yield: 4 servings

½ cup heavy cream

4 ounces (½ cup) cream cheese, softened, or mascarpone cheese

¼ cup Swerve confectioners'-style sweetener or equivalent amount of liquid or powdered sweetener (see page 37) (or to desired sweetness)

1 teaspoon butterscotch extract

1. Chill a large stainless-steel bowl and beaters in the freezer until cold. Place the cream in the bowl and whip until firm peaks form.

2. Add the softened cream cheese, sweetener, and butterscotch extract and combine until very smooth. Divide among 4 serving cups. Store covered in the fridge for up to 5 days.

TIP:

This mousse can be made up to 5 days ahead.

KETO
L   M   H

NUTRITIONAL INFO (per serving)				
calories	fat	protein	carbs	fiber
129	12.9g	1.9g	0.9g	0g
	90%	**7%**	**3%**	

French Silk
MOUSSE

NUT-FREE DAIRY-FREE VEGE-TARIAN

Prep Time: 7 minutes, plus 2 hours to chill

Yield: 12 servings

½ cup coconut oil (or unsalted butter at room temperature if not dairy-sensitive)

¾ cup Swerve confectioners'-style sweetener or equivalent amount of liquid or powdered sweetener (see page 37)

2 (1-ounce) squares unsweetened baking chocolate, melted

1 teaspoon vanilla extract, or seeds scraped from 1 vanilla bean (about 6 inches long)

2 large eggs

1. Place the coconut oil in a mixing bowl and use a hand mixer to cream the oil.

2. Gradually beat in the sweetener until the mixture is light-colored and well blended.

3. Add the melted chocolate and vanilla and beat until combined.

4. Add the eggs, one at a time, beating on medium speed for 5 minutes after each addition.

5. Spoon the mousse into 6 serving bowls. Refrigerate for at least 2 hours before serving. Store in an airtight container in the fridge for up to 5 days.

KETO

NUTRITIONAL INFO (per serving)				
calories	fat	protein	carbs	fiber
218	21.5g	3.4g	2.8g	0.8g
	89%	6%	5%	

Gummy BEARS

Prep Time: 5 minutes, plus 2 hours to set

Yield: 50 gummy bears (10 per serving)

1 bag fruit tea, such as blueberry, cherry, or strawberry

½ cup boiling water

2 tablespoons grass-fed powdered gelatin

½ cup full-fat coconut milk

2 tablespoons Swerve confectioners'-style sweetener or equivalent amount of liquid or powdered sweetener (see page 37)

1 teaspoon fruit-flavored extract (same flavor as tea)

¼ teaspoon Now Foods brand Better Stevia Liquid Sweetener in Tropical Fruit or other flavor

Special Equipment:
Gummy bear mold (50-cavity)

My boys adore these gummy bears, so we make them often. I like to play around with different flavorings; our newest favorite is a touch of tropical fruit–flavored stevia glycerite. To find the different natural sweeteners and teas that I love to experiment with, check out the store on my site, MariaMindBodyHealth.com.

1. Steep the tea in the boiling water until very strong. Remove the tea bag, sift the gelatin into the hot tea, and stir until dissolved.

2. In a mixing bowl, combine the coconut milk, sweetener, extract, flavored stevia, and tea and gelatin mixture. Stir well to combine evenly.

3. Pour into a 50-cavity gummy bear mold and place in the fridge until set, about 2 hours. Store in an airtight container in the fridge for up to 5 days or in the freezer for up to 1 month. Thaw before consuming.

KETO

NUTRITIONAL INFO (per serving)				
calories	fat	protein	carbs	fiber
44	4.3g	0.5g	0.9g	0g
	88%	4%	8%	

Bananas Foster
FUDGE

EGG-FREE · NUT-FREE (OPTION) · VEGE-TARIAN · VIDEO

Prep Time: 5 minutes, plus 8 hours to chill

Cook Time: 8 minutes

Yield: 24 pieces (2 per serving)

1 cup (2 sticks) unsalted butter

¼ cup Swerve confectioners'-style sweetener or equivalent amount of powdered erythritol or monk fruit (see page 37)

1 (8-ounce) package cream cheese, softened, or mascarpone

1½ tablespoons unsweetened (unflavored or vanilla) almond milk, store-bought or homemade (page 131) (or unsweetened [unflavored or vanilla] hemp milk for nut-free)

1 teaspoon banana extract or a few drops of banana oil

¼ teaspoon fine sea salt

If you are a visual learner like me, you can watch a video of me making this dessert on my site, MariaMindBodyHealth.com (type the word *video* in the search field).

1. In a large saucepan, melt the butter over medium-high heat. Bring to a low boil and continue to cook, whisking often, until the butter turns a deep brown color, about 8 minutes. Do not allow it to turn black.

2. Remove from the heat and add the sweetener. Whisk well to combine.

3. Using a hand mixer on low speed, mix in the cream cheese, almond milk, banana extract, and salt until combined.

4. Line an 8-inch square baking pan with parchment paper, allowing the paper to drape over the sides for easy removal. Pour the mixture into the prepared pan and refrigerate overnight. It will thicken a lot.

5. Invert the pan over a cutting board to release the fudge. Peel away the parchment and cut the fudge into 1-inch cubes. Store in an airtight container in the fridge for up to 1 week or in the freezer for up to 1 month.

KETO (L M H)

NUTRITIONAL INFO (per serving)				
calories	fat	protein	carbs	fiber
202	21.9g	1.6g	0.5g	0g
	96%	3%	1%	

Flourless
FUDGY BROWNIES

NUT-FREE | DAIRY-FREE *OPTION* | VEGE-TARIAN

Prep Time: 5 minutes

Cook Time: 20 minutes

Yield: 18 brownies (1 per serving)

BATTER:

½ cup (1 stick) unsalted butter (or coconut oil for dairy-free)

1 cup unsweetened cocoa powder

1 cup Swerve confectioners'-style sweetener or equivalent amount of powdered erythritol or monk fruit (see page 37)

4 large eggs

1 teaspoon vanilla extract, or seeds scraped from 1 vanilla bean (about 6 inches long)

¼ teaspoon fine sea salt

FROSTING:

6 tablespoons unsalted butter, softened (or coconut oil for dairy-free)

⅓ cup Swerve confectioners'-style sweetener or equivalent amount of powdered erythritol or monk fruit (see page 37)

⅓ cup unsweetened cocoa powder

¼ cup heavy cream (or full-fat coconut milk for dairy-free)

1 teaspoon vanilla extract, or seeds scraped from 1 vanilla bean (about 6 inches long)

Coarse sea salt, for garnish

L — M — H
KETO

NUTRITIONAL INFO (per serving)				
calories	fat	protein	carbs	fiber
150	14g	3g	3g	1g
	84%	8%	8%	

My brother and I loved visiting Grandma Betty because she always greeted us with chocolate and music. Both she and my grandpa were musicians, and as a child I always asked her to sing "How Much Is That Doggy in the Window?" to me. She made the best brownies. My brother and I still joke that her secret to great brownies was smearing them with more frosting than she used on cake!

1. Preheat the oven to 325°F. Line an 8-by-4-inch loaf pan with parchment paper and grease well.

2. In a large bowl, combine all the ingredients for the batter until smooth. Pour the mixture into the prepared pan and bake for 20 minutes, or until a toothpick inserted in the center comes out clean. Allow the brownies to cool to room temperature before frosting.

3. Meanwhile, make the frosting: Place the butter, sweetener, and cocoa powder in a mixing bowl and mix with a hand mixer until smooth. Add the cream and vanilla and mix until smooth.

4. Spread the frosting over the cooled brownies and sprinkle with coarse sea salt. Cut into 18 pieces and serve at room temperature the day they are made. Once refrigerated, the brownies harden and must be warmed (see Step 5). An alternative solution is to bake them as individual servings (see Single Serving Option below).

5. If you plan on storing the brownies in the fridge for later, leave them unfrosted. Store the brownies and frosting in separate airtight containers in the fridge for up to 5 days. To serve, remove the frosting from the fridge and allow it to come to room temperature; remove the brownies from the container and warm in the microwave for 20 seconds, or until just warm. Top the brownies with the frosting and sprinkle with coarse sea salt.

SINGLE SERVING OPTION

If you find that having an entire pan of brownies around is just too tempting, try baking these brownies in individual servings, as needed. It's a great way to control portion size. Simply grease a 4-ounce ramekin and fill it two-thirds full with batter. Bake for 10 to 13 minutes, until a toothpick inserted in the middle comes out clean. Allow to cool before frosting with 2 tablespoons room-temperature frosting. Store extra batter in the fridge for up to 5 days for making freshly baked single-serving brownies. This type of small-batch baking is perfect for a toaster oven!

BUTTERMINTS

EGG-FREE · NUT-FREE · DAIRY-FREE (OPTION) · VEGE-TARIAN

Prep Time: 5 minutes, plus 1 hour to chill

Yield: 12 mints (2 per serving)

½ cup (1 stick) unsalted butter, softened (or coconut oil for dairy-free)

¼ cup Swerve confectioners'-style sweetener or equivalent amount of powdered erythritol or monk fruit (see page 37) (or more to taste)

½ teaspoon mint extract or ¼ teaspoon mint oil (or more to taste)

Pinch of fine sea salt

When I was growing up, we would often visit my great-grandparents. Our visits always included playing the piano and sucking on buttermints after our family dinner. In truth, my little brother and I always preferred chocolate or something more decadent to those buttermints, but now, whenever I make these tasty treats, I enjoy them and the memories they conjure.

1. Line a rimmed baking sheet with parchment paper.

2. Place all the ingredients in a bowl and combine with a hand mixer until smooth. Taste and add more sweetener and mint flavor to your liking.

3. Place the mixture into a piping bag or a resealable plastic bag with ¼ inch cut off one corner. Pipe ½-inch mints onto the parchment paper. Place in the fridge to set for up to 1 hour. Store in an airtight container in the fridge for up to 2 weeks or in the freezer for up to 1 month.

KETO (L M H)

NUTRITIONAL INFO (per serving)				
calories	fat	protein	carbs	fiber
136	15.3g	0.2g	0g	0g
	99%	1%	0%	

Smoked Foods

BONUS CHAPTER

Not everyone likes to be tied up in the kitchen. I know I prefer to be outside. Maybe cooking isn't your forte, but I encourage you to try smoking! Yes, it takes time, but if you dedicate a Sunday afternoon and make a large enough batch, you will have leftovers for easy weeknight meals. I often make a triple batch, and once the smoking is done I store portions in the freezer for easy dinners. On the day we'll have the meat for dinner, I put the frozen meat in the oven before going to work and set the delay timer on my oven so the meat will be finished just in time for dinner. By the time I get home, the house smells wonderful and dinner is ready!

If you are a visual learner like me, check out the video about smoking on my site, MariaMindBodyHealth.com (type the word *video* in the search field). The video is about smoking ribs, but the same principles apply to all the recipes in this section.

Smoker Options

There are several options to consider when smoking foods. Here are some tips to help you choose the best smoking setup.

Smoker Types

The first decision to make is what sort of smoker you will use. Smokers can be fueled by wood, charcoal, gas, or electricity, and each type has its pros and cons.

- **Wood smokers** give you the most flavorful results, but you must pay attention during the smoking process to keep the temperature steady and the wood chips replenished. They require the most involvement and monitoring of all the smokers.

- **Charcoal (natural, hardwood) smokers** take some work to adjust the coals to get the right temperature and keep it there. During smoking, you need to replenish the wood chips and adjust the coals to keep the temperature in the right range. But charcoal smokers do produce flavorful results.

- **Gas smokers** allow you to easily control the temperature; all you need to do is dial in the temperature you want, so they require less work during the smoking process than wood or charcoal smokers. You only have to worry about replenishing the wood chips.

- **Electric smokers** are very simple to use. There is no need to fiddle with temperatures. Just plug it in and keep the wood chips replenished, and it takes care of the temperature. Cheaper units have only one temperature setting (typically 250°F). I use a good-quality electric smoker—one that allows me to control the temperature—and this is the type I recommend for busy families. They also tend to cost less.

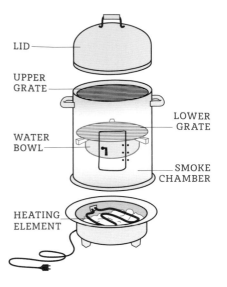

LID

UPPER GRATE

LOWER GRATE

WATER BOWL

SMOKE CHAMBER

HEATING ELEMENT

I use an electric smoker because it is easy to use and does not require a big investment (you can typically get one for less than $100). The setup is pretty easy, too. Just soak your wood chips in water for at least 30 minutes prior to smoking. Then line the lava rocks around the heating element, place the soaked wood chips on top of the lava rocks, and plug in the smoker. Fill the water bowl that came with your smoker, place the food you want to smoke to the lower and/or upper grate, and put the lid on. From that point on, all you have to do is check the wood chips and replenish them every hour or so as needed. Use the door on the side of the smoker to check and replenish the wood chips.

Wood Chips

The type of wood chips you use will determine the flavor of your end product. Here is a guide to some of the common woods used in smoking:

- **Alder wood** provides a light and sweet smoke flavor and is great for smoking poultry and fish.

- **Applewood** gives meat a slightly sweet and fruity flavor. It is especially good for smoking ham.

- **Cedar** provides a distinct aromatic flavor and is good for smoking fish and poultry.

- **Cherrywood**, like applewood, gives meat a sweet and fruity flavor. It is good for smoking turkey and chicken as well as small game birds.

- **Hickory** is commonly used for smoking in the South. It gives meats a strong smoky flavor and is great for smoking pork, chicken, and ribs. It is a classic choice for bacon.

- **Mesquite** is a very hot-burning wood that gives meat a strong smoky flavor, but it can burn too hot for some meats. It is good for smoking beef.

- **Oak** is commonly used and can be a good all-around smoking wood. But unlike the other woods, it doesn't have a distinct flavor; it can be described as more of a general-purpose flavor.

- **Pecan wood** is similar in flavor to hickory but is not as strong. It is commonly used in Gulf Coast states.

I typically use a combination of hickory and cherry or applewood, which gives a nice balance of smoky and sweet flavors. But feel free to mix and match to get the flavor you like.

Smoked
BRISKET

EGG-FREE NUT-FREE DAIRY-FREE VIDEO

Prep Time: 5 minutes, plus 30 minutes to soak the wood chips

Cook Time: 7 to 9 hours

Yield: 20 servings

1 (10-pound) beef brisket

1 cup Rib Rub (page 108)

Coconut vinegar, for sprinkling on the smoked meat before cooking

1 recipe BBQ Sauce (page 125), for serving

Special Equipment:
Smoker

4 cups wood chips of choice

1. *Optional:* For optimal flavor, the day before (or morning of the day) you plan to smoke the meat, liberally season the brisket on all sides with the rub, using your hands to rub the spices into the meat. Wrap the meat tightly with foil lined with unbleached parchment paper and seal all the edges. Refrigerate for at least 8 hours or overnight so that the flavors can permeate the meat. If you prefer to skip this step, the meat will still have a lot of flavor.

2. Thirty minutes before you smoke the meat, soak the wood chips in water and remove the meat from the fridge. If you haven't yet seasoned the brisket (per optional Step 1), place the meat on a clean cutting board and liberally season both sides with the rub. Let the brisket rest at room temperature until the smoker is ready.

3. To smoke the meat: Read the manufacturer's directions for your smoker before you begin. There are wood, electric, propane, and charcoal smokers, and each type works differently. Start the smoker and, if your smoker came with a water bowl, add water to it. When slow-cooking meat, it is essential that you have a thermometer to monitor the temperature of the smoker. When the temperature reaches 225°F to 250°F, you can start smoking the brisket.

4. Place the meat in the smoker and secure the lid so that it is airtight and no smoke escapes. Smoke the meat for 3 hours. Every so often, check the temperature and adjust the air vents to maintain a temperature of 225°F to 250°F. Add more fuel to the smoker if needed to maintain the temperature, and add more soaked wood chips if the smoke starts to dissipate.

5. After 3 hours, remove the meat from the smoker. At this point, the meat still needs to be fully cooked at a higher temperature, which is best done on a grill or in the oven. You can either cook the entire amount now or divide the meat into portions for quick and easy meals (see Tip / Single Serving Option opposite).

6. To prepare the meat for cooking: Lay the brisket on a large sheet of foil lined with unbleached parchment paper. Generously sprinkle the meat with coconut vinegar and tightly seal the foil packet closed. Note: Make sure that there are no holes in the foil or the brisket will dry out.

7. To fully cook the brisket, preheat a grill to medium (350°F) or oven to 350°F. Place the tightly wrapped brisket on the grill or in the oven for 4 to 6 hours, until the meat reaches 195°F to 205°F (if using a grill, keep the lid closed). Serve with BBQ sauce.

L M H
KETO

NUTRITIONAL INFO (per serving)				
calories	fat	protein	carbs	fiber
410	14.1g	68.8g	0g	0g
	32%	68%	0%	

TIP / SINGLE SERVING OPTION:

For easy dinners, after removing the meat from the smoker, divide the meat into family-sized or single-serving portions. Sprinkle each portion with coconut vinegar and wrap tightly in foil lined with unbleached parchment paper. Store in the fridge for up to 3 days or in the freezer for up to a month. When ready to eat, cook the meat according to Step 7. I usually remove a serving from the freezer in the morning and place it in the oven with a delay timer so the meat is finished cooking when we are ready to eat.

Smoked Beef
LONG RIBS

EGG-FREE NUT-FREE DAIRY-FREE VIDEO

Prep Time: 10 minutes, plus 30 minutes to soak the wood chips

Cook Time: 2½ hours

Yield: 12 servings

¾ cup smoked paprika

¼ cup Swerve confectioners'-style sweetener or equivalent amount of powdered stevia or erythritol (see page 37)

2 tablespoons onion powder

2 racks beef long ribs (aka beef back ribs) or other ribs (about 8 pounds)

Coconut vinegar, for sprinkling on the smoked meat before cooking

Special Equipment:
Smoker

4 cups wood chips of choice

L M H
KETO

NUTRITIONAL INFO (per serving)				
calories	fat	protein	carbs	fiber
748	61.7g	45.5g	4.4g	2.4g
	74%	24%	2%	

1. In a small bowl, stir together the paprika, sweetener, and onion powder until combined.

2. *Optional:* For optimal flavor, season the ribs the day before (or morning of the day) you plan to smoke the meat. Rinse and dry the ribs and place them on a clean cutting board. Liberally season both sides of the ribs with the rub mixture, using your hands to rub the spices into the meat. Wrap the ribs tightly with foil lined with unbleached parchment paper and seal all the edges. Refrigerate for at least 8 hours or overnight so that the flavors can permeate the meat; if you prefer to skip this step, the meat will still have a lot of flavor.

3. Thirty minutes before you're ready to smoke the meat, soak the wood chips in water and remove the ribs from the fridge and let them rest at room temperature until the smoker is ready. If you haven't yet seasoned the ribs (per optional Step 2), rinse and dry the ribs and place them on a clean cutting board. Liberally season both sides with the rub mixture, using your hands to rub the spices into the meat.

4. To smoke the meat: Read the manufacturer's directions for your smoker before you begin. There are wood, electric, propane, and charcoal smokers, and each type works differently. Start the smoker and, if your smoker came with a water bowl, add water to it. When slow-cooking meat, it is essential that you have a thermometer to monitor the temperature of the smoker. When the temperature reaches 225°F to 250°F, you can start smoking the ribs.

5. Place the meat on the smoker and secure the lid so it is airtight and no smoke escapes. Smoke the meat for 2 hours. Every so often, check the temperature and adjust the air vents to maintain a temperature of 225°F to 250°F. Add more fuel to the smoker if needed to maintain the temperature, and add more soaked wood chips if the smoke starts to dissipate.

6. After 2 hours, remove the ribs from the smoker. At this point, the meat still needs to be fully cooked at a higher temperature, which is best done on a grill or in the oven. You can either cook the entire amount now or divide the meat into portions for quick and easy meals (see Tip / Single Serving Option opposite).

7. To prepare the meat for cooking: Lay the ribs on a large sheet of foil lined with unbleached parchment paper. Generously sprinkle the meat with coconut vinegar and tightly seal the foil packet closed. Note: Make sure that there are no holes in the foil or the ribs will dry out.

8. To fully cook the meat: Preheat a grill to medium (350°F) or the oven to 350°F. Place the tightly wrapped meat on the grill or in the

oven and cook for 30 minutes, or until the meat is extremely tender (if using a grill, keep the lid closed). Remove from the grill or oven. Enjoy as is or follow Step 9 to give the meat a crispy exterior before serving.

9. *Optional:* To give the meat a crispy exterior, turn the grill or oven broiler setting to high. Remove the meat from the packet and place it on the grill or on a broiler pan and grill or broil it for 5 minutes to sear and crisp the edges.

TIP / SINGLE SERVING OPTION:

For easy dinners, after removing the ribs from the smoker, divide them into family-sized or single-serving portions. Sprinkle each portion with coconut vinegar and wrap tightly in foil lined with unbleached parchment paper. Store in the fridge for up to 3 days or in the freezer for up to a month. When ready to eat, cook the meat following Steps 8 and 9 above. I usually remove a serving from the freezer in the morning and place it in the oven with a delay timer so the meat is finished cooking when we are ready to eat.

Smoked
BABY BACK RIBS

EGG-FREE NUT-FREE DAIRY-FREE VIDEO

Prep Time: 10 minutes, plus 30 minutes to soak the wood chips

Cook Time: 4 to 5½ hours

Yield: 8 servings

4 racks baby back ribs

1 cup Rib Rub (page 108)

Coconut vinegar, for sprinkling on the smoked ribs before cooking

Special Equipment:
Smoker

4 cups wood chips of choice

1. Thirty minutes before you smoke the meat, soak the wood chips in water and remove the meat from the fridge. Place the ribs on a clean cutting board. Liberally season both sides of the ribs with the rub, using your hands to rub it into the ribs.

2. To smoke the meat: Read the manufacturer's directions for your smoker before you begin. There are wood, electric, propane, and charcoal smokers, and each type works differently. Start the smoker and, if your smoker came with a water bowl, add water to it. When slow-cooking meat, it is essential that you have a thermometer to monitor the temperature of the smoker. When the temperature reaches 225°F to 250°F, you can start smoking the ribs.

3. Place the ribs in the smoker and secure the lid so that it is airtight and no smoke escapes. Every so often, check the temperature and adjust the air vents to maintain a temperature of 225°F to 250°F. Smoke the meat for 2 to 3 hours, depending on how smoky you like your ribs; the longer you smoke, the more intense the smoke flavor will be. Add more fuel to the smoker if needed to maintain the temperature, and add more soaked wood chips if the smoke starts to dissipate.

4. After 2 to 3 hours, remove the ribs from the smoker. At this point, the meat still needs to be fully cooked at a higher temperature, which is best done on a grill or in the oven. You can either cook the entire amount now or divide the ribs into portions for quick and easy meals (see Tip / Single Serving Option opposite).

5. To prepare the ribs for cooking: Transfer the ribs to a large sheet of foil lined with unbleached parchment paper. Generously sprinkle the meat with coconut vinegar and tightly seal the foil packet closed. Note: Make sure that there are no holes in the foil or the ribs will dry out.

6. To cook the ribs: Preheat a grill to medium-low (275°F) or the oven to 275°F. Place the tightly wrapped ribs on the grill or in the oven and cook for 2 to 2½ hours, until the meat is tender. Remove the ribs from the grill or oven and take them out of the packets. Turn the grill or broiler to high. Return the ribs to the grill or oven with the meaty side toward the heat (meaty side down if using a grill, meaty side up if using the oven) and grill or broil for 5 minutes on one side to crisp the edges.

KETO

NUTRITIONAL INFO (per serving)				
calories	fat	protein	carbs	fiber
562	47.4g	31.6g	0g	0g
	76%	23%	0%	

TIP / SINGLE SERVING OPTION:

For easy dinners, after removing the ribs from the smoker, divide them into family-sized or single-serving portions. Sprinkle each portion with coconut vinegar and wrap tightly in foil lined with unbleached parchment paper. Store in the fridge for up to 3 days or in the freezer for up to a month. When ready to eat, cook the meat according to Step 6. I usually remove a serving from the freezer in the morning and place it in the oven with a delay timer so the meat is finished cooking when we are ready to eat.

Smoked
PORK SHOULDER

EGG-FREE   NUT-FREE   DAIRY-FREE   VIDEO

Prep Time: 5 minutes, plus 30 minutes to soak the wood chips

Cook Time: 6 to 7 hours

Yield: 16 servings

¾ cup smoked paprika

¼ cup Swerve confectioners'-style sweetener or equivalent amount of powdered stevia or erythritol (see page 37)

2 tablespoons onion powder

1 (8-pound) bone-in pork shoulder

Coconut vinegar, for sprinkling on the smoked meat before cooking

Special Equipment:
Smoker

4 cups wood chips of choice

This smoked pork makes great leftovers served in lettuce wraps or Zucchini Tortillas (page 212).

1. In a small bowl, stir together the paprika, sweetener, and onion powder until combined.

2. *Optional:* For optimal flavor, season the pork shoulder the day before (or morning of the day) you plan to smoke the meat. Rinse and dry the shoulder. Place it on a clean cutting board. Liberally season all sides of the shoulder with the rub mixture, using your hands to rub the spices into the meat. Wrap the shoulder tightly with foil lined with unbleached parchment paper and seal all the edges. Refrigerate for at least 8 hours or overnight so that the flavors can permeate the meat; if you prefer to skip this step, the meat will still have a lot of flavor.

3. Thirty minutes before you smoke the meat, soak the wood chips in water and remove the shoulder from the fridge and let it rest at room temperature until the smoker is ready. If you haven't yet seasoned the shoulder (per optional Step 2), rinse and dry the shoulder and place it on a clean cutting board. Liberally season all sides with the rub mixture, using your hands to rub the spices into the meat.

4. To smoke the meat: Read the manufacturer's directions for your smoker before you begin. There are wood, electric, propane, and charcoal smokers, and each type works differently. Start the smoker and, if your smoker came with a water bowl, add water to it. When slow-cooking meat, it is essential that you have a thermometer to monitor the temperature of the smoker. When the temperature reaches 225°F to 250°F, you can start smoking the pork.

5. Place the meat in the smoker and secure the lid so that it is airtight and no smoke escapes. Smoke the meat for 5 to 6 hours. Every so often, check the temperature and adjust the air vents to maintain a temperature of 225°F to 250°F. Add more fuel to the smoker if needed to maintain the temperature, and add more soaked wood chips if the smoke begins to dissipate.

6. After 5 to 6 hours (or when the internal temperature of the meat reaches 180°F to 190°F—190°F is ideal for pulled pork), remove the meat from the smoker. At this point, it still needs to be fully cooked at a higher temperature, which is best done on a grill or in the oven. You can either cook the entire amount now or divide the meat into portions for quick and easy meals (see Tip / Single Serving Option opposite).

7. To prepare the meat for cooking: Lay the pork shoulder on a large sheet of foil lined with unbleached parchment paper. Generously

L   M   H
KETO

NUTRITIONAL INFO (per serving)				
calories	fat	protein	carbs	fiber
599	46.8g	38.9g	3.3g	1.8g
	71%	27%	2%	

sprinkle the meat with coconut vinegar and tightly seal the foil packet closed. Note: Make sure that there are no holes in the foil or the shoulder will dry out.

8. To fully cook the meat: Preheat a grill to medium (350°F) or the oven to 350°F. Place the tightly wrapped meat on the grill or in the oven for and cook for 1 hour (with the lid closed if using a grill) or until the meat is extremely tender. Remove from the grill or oven. Enjoy as is or follow Step 9 to give the meat a crispy exterior before serving.

9. *Optional:* To give the meat a crispy exterior, turn the grill or oven broiler setting to high. Remove the meat from the foil and place it on the grill or on a broiler pan and grill or broil it for 5 minutes to sear and crisp the edges.

TIP / SINGLE SERVING OPTION:

For easy dinners, after removing the meat from the smoker, divide the meat into family-sized or single-serving portions. Sprinkle each portion with some coconut vinegar and tightly wrap in foil lined with unbleached parchment paper. Store in the fridge for up to 3 days or in the freezer for up to a month. When ready to eat, cook the meat according to Steps 8 and 9. I usually remove a serving from the freezer in the morning and place it in the oven with a delay timer so the meat is finished cooking when we are ready to eat.

Smoked SALMON

EGG-FREE   NUT-FREE   DAIRY-FREE   VIDEO

Prep Time: 5 minutes, plus 2 hours to marinate and 30 minutes to soak the wood chips

Cook Time: 1 hour 15 minutes to 1½ hours

Yield: 12 servings

5 pounds salmon fillets, skin on

MARINADE:

½ cup coconut aminos or wheat-free tamari

3 tablespoons MCT oil

2 teaspoons Swerve confectioners'-style sweetener or equivalent (see page 37)

3 teaspoons grated fresh ginger

2 cloves garlic, finely chopped

1 teaspoon fine sea salt

½ teaspoon ground black pepper

Special Equipment:
Smoker
4 cups wood chips of choice

NOTE:

You can use this same method to smoke other fish. My favorites are trout and Arctic char.

L   M   H
KETO

NUTRITIONAL INFO (per serving)				
calories	fat	protein	carbs	fiber
250	11.7g	36.7g	0g	0g
	42%	58%	0%	

I like to tell people, "Never say never!" I thought I'd never like salmon until I tried smoked salmon. And there's an added bonus to the great flavor that smoking imparts. Smoking, which uses low heat, is a great way to maximize the health benefit of salmon's omega-3 content. (Omega-3s are easily oxidized by heat; see sidebar, opposite.)

But whenever I ask a butcher or smoke shop what ingredients are in their smoked salmon, I find that they season it with some sort of sugar and often soy sauce, which contains wheat. That is why I love to smoke my own! Not only are you in charge of the ingredients, but you can also control how smoky you make your foods. The longer you smoke something, the more smoke flavor the end product will have.

1. Cut the salmon fillets into 4-by-3-inch pieces.

2. Mix the marinade ingredients together in a large glass or nonreactive metal bowl. Place the salmon pieces in the bowl, cover, and place in the fridge to marinate for 2 hours or overnight.

3. Thirty minutes before you smoke the salmon, place the wood chips in water to soak. Drain.

4. To smoke the salmon: Read the manufacturer's directions for your smoker before you begin. There are wood, electric, propane, and charcoal smokers, and each type works differently. Start the smoker and, if your smoker came with a water bowl, add water to it. When the temperature reaches 180°F, you can start smoking the salmon.

5. Rinse the marinade off the salmon and dry it with paper towels. Place the salmon skin side down in the smoker. Secure the lid so that it is airtight and no smoke escapes. Smoke the salmon for 30 minutes.

6. Increase the heat to 230°F and cook the salmon for an additional 45 minutes to 1 hour.

7. Remove the salmon from the smoker. Let cool and cover tightly until ready to serve. Store in the fridge for up to 10 days. If you vacuum-seal it, the smoked fish will keep for up to 3 weeks. Or you can store it in the freezer for up to a month.

SINGLE SERVING OPTION *Divide the smoked salmon into single-serving portions and freeze for up to a month for quick and easy meals.*

HOW TO GET THE MOST OUT OF YOUR OMEGA-3–RICH FOODS:

Salmon is an excellent source of omega-3s. However, it's important to understand how heat adversely affects them. Omega-3s are a type of polyunsaturated fatty acid (PUFA), which oxidizes easily. Oxidation causes inflammation in the body, which is the source of many health issues. Through a lot of research, I have come to the conclusion (and this is new and going to be a big shift in the health community) that PUFA's eicosapentaenoic acid (EPA) and, even more so, docosahexaenoic acid (DHA) are oxidized at room temperature and in the body. So in supplement form, there is a lot of oxidation occurring prior to (and after) ingestion, which causes inflammation.

The best way to think about this is that PUFAs are very unstable and easily oxidized by heat, sunlight, body heat, and so on. When you consume them, you want to get the freshest source possible, cook it as little as needed (raw is best), and get only as much as your body needs. If you eat excessive amounts, the extra will remain in your body longer, exposing it to more oxidative damage, which will cause more inflammation. This is why I no longer recommend fish oil supplements. Too much oxidation occurs prior to ingestion, and the high doses result in more oxidation in the body.

This is why smoking salmon is a great preparation: the low heat doesn't oxidize the sensitive fat!

Pan-Fried Smoked
CAULIFLOWER STEAKS

NUT-FREE · DAIRY-FREE · VEGE-TARIAN (OPTION) · VIDEO

Prep Time: 10 minutes, plus 30 minutes to soak the wood chips

Cook Time: 1 hour 10 minutes

Yield: 4 servings as side dish

1 head cauliflower

1 tablespoon MCT oil

1 teaspoon fine sea salt

½ teaspoon fresh ground black pepper

2 tablespoons coconut oil, for pan-frying

FOR SERVING:

1 cup diced fresh tomatoes or canned diced tomatoes (with juices)

1 cup Green Goddess Dressing (page 117)

Special Equipment:
Smoker
4 cups wood chips of choice

1. Thirty minutes before you smoke the cauliflower, place the wood chips in water to soak. Drain.

2. To smoke the cauliflower: Read the manufacturer's directions for your smoker before you begin. There are wood, electric, propane, and charcoal smokers, and each type works differently. Start the smoker and, if your smoker came with a water bowl, add water to it. When the temperature reaches 180°F, you can start smoking the cauliflower.

3. Using a large knife, cut the cauliflower from top to bottom into 1-inch-thick steaks. Rub with the oil and sprinkle with the salt and pepper. Place the steaks as well as any broken pieces of cauliflower on a large sheet of foil lined with unbleached parchment paper (to prevent pieces from falling into the smoker). Poke holes through the double layer of foil and parchment to allow the smoke to infuse the cauliflower.

4. Place the double layer of foil and parchment with the cauliflower in the smoker and secure the lid so that the smoker is airtight and no smoke escapes. Smoke the cauliflower for 1 hour. While the cauliflower is smoking, prepare the tomatoes and dressing for serving.

5. After 1 hour, remove the cauliflower from the smoker.

6. Heat the coconut oil in a large skillet over medium heat. Sauté the cauliflower steaks, as well as any large pieces of cauliflower that broke off, until golden brown on both sides and fork-tender, about 5 minutes per side. Fry in batches if needed to avoid crowding, and add more oil between batches if needed. Season with salt and pepper and serve on a bed of diced tomatoes, with the dressing drizzled on top.

TIP:

For a vegetarian meal that serves 2, divide the cauliflower steaks between 2 plates and serve with a green salad tossed with the vegetarian keto dressing of your choice (pages 116 to 121).

KETO · with ¼ cup *Green Goddess Dressing*

NUTRITIONAL INFO (per serving)				
calories	fat	protein	carbs	fiber
121	10.4g	1.9g	6g	3g
	77%	6%	17%	

Pan-Fried Smoked
EGGPLANT

Prep Time: *10 minutes, plus 30 minutes to soak the wood chips*

Cook Time: *1 hour 10 minutes*

Yield: *4 servings as side dish*

1 large eggplant (about 1½ pounds)

1 tablespoon MCT oil

1 teaspoon fine sea salt

½ teaspoon fresh ground black pepper

2 tablespoons coconut oil, for pan-frying

FOR SERVING:

1 cup diced fresh tomatoes or canned diced tomatoes (with juices)

1 cup Dairy-Free Ranch Dressing (page 118)

Special Equipment:

Smoker

4 cups wood chips of choice

1. Thirty minutes before you smoke the eggplant, place the wood chips in water to soak. Drain.

2. To smoke the eggplant: Read the manufacturer's directions for your smoker before you begin. There are wood, electric, propane, and charcoal smokers, and each type works differently. Start the smoker and, if your smoker came with a water bowl, add water to it. When the temperature reaches 180°F, you can start smoking the eggplant.

3. Using a large knife, cut the eggplant crosswise into 1-inch-thick rounds. Rub the eggplant on both sides with the oil and sprinkle with the salt and pepper. Place on a sheet of foil lined with unbleached parchment paper and poke holes through the double layer of foil and parchment to allow the smoke to infuse the eggplant.

4. Place the double layer of foil and parchment with the eggplant in the smoker and secure the lid so that the smoker is airtight and no smoke escapes. Smoke for 1 hour. While the eggplant is smoking, prepare the tomatoes and dressing for serving.

5. After 1 hour, remove the eggplant from the smoker.

6. Heat the coconut oil in a large skillet over medium heat. Sauté the smoked eggplant slices, working in batches to avoid crowding, until golden brown on both sides and fork-tender, about 5 minutes per side. Add more oil between batches if needed. Season with salt and pepper and serve on a bed of diced tomatoes, with the dressing drizzled on top.

TIP:

For a vegetarian meal that serves 2, divide the eggplant slices between 2 plates and serve with a green salad tossed with the vegetarian keto dressing of your choice (pages 116 to 121).

KETO

with ¼ cup Dairy-Free Ranch dressing

NUTRITIONAL INFO (per serving)				
calories	fat	protein	carbs	fiber
316	30.6g	2.2g	9.1g	4.7g
	87%	2%	11%	

Gratitude

*Gratitude unlocks the fullness of life. It turns what we have into enough, and more.
It turns denial into acceptance, chaos to order, confusion to clarity. It can turn
a meal into a feast, a house into a home, a stranger into a friend. Gratitude makes
sense of our past, brings peace for today and creates a vision for tomorrow.*

–Melody Beattie

I love the above quote about gratitude because it is a reminder that life is like ocean waves: there are ups and there are downs.

About eight years ago my husband, Craig, lost his job, which caused us to put our adoption on hold. This was a terrible time of sadness for us. There were many times I didn't want to get out of bed, but creating new recipes and sharing them on my blog was my happy place and it kept me motivated. I loved waking up early, before the sun, to read all the sweet comments people would write about a recipe I put on my blog.

I wasn't about to lie down and let this devastation get the best of me. A friend let me use her dance studio to teach yoga classes when she wasn't using it for dance. I started making punch cards for purchase and offered yoga classes at lunchtime and early in the morning on weekends. Craig came to every class, and I would end each session by reading this quote about gratitude.

Recently, a former yoga student of mine sent me a photo of an eye pillow I'd made to sell for extra money. It reminded me of just how hard those times were. I even made healthy dog treats and mittens out of old sweaters to sell. The library was our "date night"—we would pick out movies and books for entertainment because we no longer could afford to eat out.

The path this led us down—of working harder and not eating at restaurants—was not just more affordable, it was much healthier anyway! These struggles helped me be grateful for the gifts I have been given.

I want to express my gratitude to you, the reader! Without you I might still be teaching yoga classes!

I am grateful to my love and best friend, Craig, who never complains even though I often mess up the kitchen as soon as he cleans it. He has also been a huge part of this book; he made the very detailed meal plans, adding in nutritional information, as well as the charts and videos on my site, MariaMindBodyHealth.com, that supplement the material in this book.

I am grateful for my boys, Micah and Kai, who love to help me in the kitchen. Even though it takes twice as long to get dinner on the table when they help me, it is totally worth it. I was completely devastated when we had to put our adoption on hold, but I remember my mom telling me that my children just weren't born yet . . . I cry as I write this because she was totally right. These two boys were meant for me!

I am grateful for Rebecca Oberle, who is always there to help me make a dessert beautiful. She is the amazing artist behind some of the beautiful creations you see on my blog!

I am grateful for Jamie Schultz, who helped me start my blog and took photos for my self-published books; it helped me get up in the morning when I was going through the most difficult time in my life! Without you, who knows if my recipes would have been published.

I am grateful for Jimmy Moore. Jimmy, I still remember when you first contacted me to do a podcast seven years ago. I was in celebrity shock. I have always admired your work and dedication. When you contacted me to write a cookbook with you, I was in awe that I was the one you chose. You have truly been a blessing not only to me and my family, but to all dieters out there who have a trusted and respected a pioneer like you.

I also need to express my gratitude to the whole Victory Belt team. I received such amazing support and kindness from everyone at Victory Belt.

Erich, your encouragement and fun outlook made this journey sensational and totally worth the hard work! I appreciate your phone calls just to check in on me and make sure everything was going smoothly. You are very thoughtful.

Sean and Michele, I can't express how grateful I am for the time you spent helping me. I adored getting to know you both and talking to Michele on the phone about our children, our hobbies, and our strong dislike of winter!

Holly, Pam, and Erin, I can't express my appreciation for your extreme attention to detail when it comes to editing my recipes. Thank you for helping create such a beautiful book!

Bill and Haley, I am honored to have your photo on the cover of this book. I've always been a big fan of your photos and cookbooks. My first Victory Belt cookbook was your *Gather* book. I was in love with your artistry from the beginning. Thank you for taking the time to make my recipes and shoot the cover.

Susan, I am grateful for your enthusiasm and how successfully you help to promote my books! I get a smile on my face whenever I receive an e-mail from you. Your happiness shines through!

Ingredients

I've created an online store where you can find specialty ingredients used in the recipes in this book, at the best prices I have found. To access it, go to my site, MariaMindBodyHealth.com, and click on Maria's Amazon Store. Or go directly to the following URL:

astore.amazon.com/marisnutran05-20

ALMOND MILK, UNSWEETENED
Silk, www.silk.com

BBQ SAUCE
Nature's Hollow, www.natureshollow.com

BROTH, BOXED
Home Goodness, www.homegoodness.net

COCONUT FLOUR AND OIL
Tropical Traditions, www.tropicaltraditions.com

COCONUT MILK, UNSWEETENED
Tropical Traditions, www.tropicaltraditions.com

COCONUT VINEGAR
Coconut Secret, www.coconutsecret.com

EXTRACTS AND OILS
Best Flavors, www.bestflavors.com
Frontier, www.frontiercoop.com

FATS
Fatworks, www.fatworks.com

FISH SAUCE
Red Boat Fish Sauce, www.redboatfishsauce.com

GELATIN, GRASS-FED
Great Lakes Gelatin, www.greatlakesgelatin.com

GHEE
Shamim's Pantry, shamimspantry.com

GUAR GUM
NOW, www.nowfoods.com

HEMP MILK, UNSWEETENED
Pacific Foods, www.pacificfoods.com

HOT SAUCES
Marie Sharp's, www.mariesharps-bz.com

Xyla Brand Xylitol Buffalo Wing Sauce, xylitolusa.com/xylitol-condiments

JAMS
Nature's Hollow, www.natureshollow.com

JERKY AND COOKED, READY-TO-EAT MEATS
Epic Meats, www.epicbar.com
(to read more about it, go to mariamindbodyhealth.com/epic-meats-giveaway)

Sophia's Survival Food, www.grassfedjerkychews.com
(to read more about it, go to mariamindbodyhealth.com/sophias-survival-food)

Thousand Hills Cattle, www.thousandhillscattleco.com

KETCHUP
Nature's Hollow, www.natureshollow.com

LIQUID SMOKE
Wright's Liquid Smoke, www.wrightsliquidsmoke.com

LIQUID WATER ENHANCER
Stur, www.sturdrinks.com

MAYONNAISE
Primal Kitchen Mayo, www.primalblueprint.com/shop/#PB-PrimalKitchen

MCT OIL
SKINNYFat, www.caltonnutrition.com/skinnyfat
(Use coupon code $5KetoOil for $5 off)

NOODLES

Miracle Noodles, www.miraclenoodle.com

Sea Tangle Kelp Noodles, www.kelpnoodles.com

NUTS AND NUT FLOURS

Nuts.com

PICKLES

Bubbies Pickles, www.bubbies.com

POWDERED ERYTHRITOL

Sukrin Granulated and Icing Sugar, www.sukrinusa.com

Swerve, www.swervesweetener.com

Wholesome! All-Natural Zero, www.wholesomesweet.com

PROTEIN POWDERS, WHEY AND EGG WHITE

Jay Robb, www.jayrobb.com

RICE

Miracle Rice, www.miraclenoodle.com

SALAD DRESSINGS

Bragg's, www.bragg.com

SAUERKRAUT

Bubbies, www.bubbies.com

STEVIA GLYCERITE

NOW, www.nowfoods.com

TOMATO SAUCE, ORGANIC

Middle Earth Organics tomato sauces, www.tropicaltraditions.com

TUNA, CANNED

Vital Choice, www.vitalchoice.com

YACÓN SYRUP

Sunfood Superfoods, www.sunfood.com

MISCELLANEOUS

Leaf & Love Organic Zero Sugar Lemonade Boxes, www.leafandlove.com

Low Carb Adapt Bars, www.adaptyourlife.com

Mikey's Muffins, www.mikeysmuffins.com

Pure Wraps, www.thepurewraps.com

Exogenous Ketone Supplement

A ketogenic lifestyle can be enhanced with an exogenous ketone supplement. It will increase your ketone levels within minutes. My preferred supplement is KETO// OS from Pruvit. (To read more about it, go to mariamindbodyhealth.pruvitnow.com).

Books for More Information

Keto Clarity, by Jimmy Moore with Eric C. Westman, MD (Victory Belt Publishing, 2014)

The Ketogenic Cookbook, by Jimmy Moore and Maria Emmerich (Victory Belt Publishing, 2015)

Websites for More Information

Dr. Richard Bernstein, www.diabetes-book.com

Dr. William Davis, www.wheatbellyblog.com

The Eating Academy, eatingacademy.com

Jimmy Moore, www.livinlavidalowcarb.com

Recipe Websites

All Day I Dream About Food, alldayidreamaboutfood.com

Carb Wars Blog, carbwars.blogspot.com

Ditch the Carbs, ditchthecarbs.com

Fluffy Chix Cook, fluffychixcook.com

Holistically Engineered, holisticallyengineered.com

I Breathe I'm Hungry, ibreatheimhungry.com

KetoDiet App, ketodietapp.com

Low Carb Maven, lowcarbmaven.com

Low Carb Yum, lowcarbyum.com

Maria Mind Body Health, mariamindbodyhealth.com

The Nourished Caveman, thenourishedcaveman.com

Peace + Love + Low Carb, peaceloveandlowcarb.com

Sugar-Free Mom, sugarfreemom.com

More Recipes and Support for a Ketogenic Lifestyle

Track your progress and get exclusive recipes, educational materials, answers to questions, and much more on www.keto-adapted.com.

Recipe Index

Basics: Sauces, Dips, Dressings, and More

108 — Rib Rub

109 — Seasoned Salt

110 — Taco Seasoning

111 — Pizza Spice Mix

112 — Fat-Burning Immersion Blender Mayo

113 — Spicy Mayo

114 — Herb Aioli

115 — Cilantro Lime Sauce

116 — Caesar Dressing

117 — Green Goddess Dressing

118 — Dairy-Free Ranch Dressing

119 — Blue Cheese Dressing

120 — Easy French Dressing

121 — Simple Taco Salad Dressing

122 — Creamy Tarragon Keto Sauce

123 — Keto Fry Sauce

124 — Homemade Sriracha

125 — BBQ Sauce

126 — White BBQ Sauce

127 — Easy Ketchup

128 — Alfredo Sauce

129 — Minute Hollandaise

130 — Simple Chimichurri Sauce

131 — Homemade Almond Milk

132 — Simple Slow Cooker Bone Broth

134 — Slow Cooker Roasted Garlic

135 — Olive Salsa

136 — Guacamole

138 — Dairy-Free Minute "Cream Cheese" Spread

139 — Orange Marmalade

Breakfast

142 — Orange Cream Shake

144 — Crème de Menthe Shake

145 — Dairy-Free Chocolate Shake

146 — Spring Popovers

148 — Eggs in Purgatory

149 — Tex-Mex Breakfast Gravy

150 — Minute English Muffin

152 Cinnamon Roll Minute Muffins

154 Dairy-Free Milk Chocolate Protein Bars

156 Strawberry Cheesecake Protein Bars

157 Cream of No-Wheat Cereal

158 Chocolate Breakfast Custard

160 Chorizo Breakfast Patties

162 Pizza Muffins

164 Taco Breakfast Bake

166 Healthy Hash Browns

168 Green Eggs and Ham

169 Breakfast Burritos

Starters and Snacks

172 Amuse-Bouche Platter

173 BLT "Chips" and Dip

174 Italian Poppers

175 Amazing Cheese Puffs

176 Cheesy Fried Ravioli

178 Popsicle Crudités with Dill Dip

180 Tomato Tulips

182 Purple Pickled Eggs

183 Baked Bacon-Wrapped Pickles

184 Classic Deviled Eggs

185 Sriracha Deviled Eggs

186 Teriyaki Jerky

188 Dad's Tenderloin Bites

190 Paleo Deep-Fried Mushrooms

191 Primal Sliders

192 Chili Lime Wings

193 Eggs Gribiche

194 Zucchini Chips

Roll-Ups and Wraps

198 Prosciutto and Arugula Roll-Ups

199 Mini Pastrami Roll-Ups

200 Turkey Sushi

202 Philly Cheesesteak Roll-Ups

203 Slow Cooker BBQ Pork Wraps

204 Easy Tuna Salad Wraps

206 Sardine Salad Wraps

207 Slow Cooker BBQ Chicken Wraps

208 Slow Cooker Chicken Caesar Wraps

210 Slow Cooker Beef Barbacoa Wraps

212 Zucchini Tortillas

Soups and Salads

216
Broccoli "Noodle" Cheese Soup

218
Easy Tomato Soup with Grilled Cheese

220
Simple Salade Niçoise

222
Chicken "Noodle" Soup

223
South of the Border Salad

224
Cucumber Salad

225
Wedge Salad

226
7-Minute Chopped Salad

Fish and Seafood

230
Fish Tacos

232
Arctic Char with Olive Salsa

234
Crab-Stuffed Avocado with Lime

235
Shrimp and Grits

236
Fish Sticks

238
Masala Mussels

240
King Crab Legs with Garlic Butter

Chicken

244
Slow Cooker Chicken Fajitas

245
Slow Cooker Chimichurri Chicken

246
Chicken Alfredo

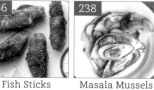
248
Grilled Chicken with White BBQ Sauce

249
Double-Fried Chicken

250
Slow Cooker Laotian Chicken and Herbs (Larb)

252
Slow Cooker "Butter" Chicken with Naan

254
Chicken "Noodle" Stir-Fry

Beef and Lamb

258
Marinated Tenderloin with Bordelaise Mushrooms

259
Grandma Nancy's Italian Beef

260
Easy Campfire Casserole

262
Slow Cooker Sweet-n-Spicy Short Ribs

263
Easy Corned Beef "Hash"

264
Upside-Down Pizza

266
Skillet Lasagna

268

Open-Faced
Hamburgers
on "Buns"

270

Taco Bar Night

272

Roasted
Bone Marrow

274

Slow Cooker
Osso Buco

276

Basted Rib-Eye
Steak

278

Mexican Meatloaf
Cupcakes

280

20-Minute
Ground Lamb
Casserole

282

Grilled Lamb
Chops with
Mint Aioli

Pork

286

Broccoli
Carbonara

287

Pigs in a
Bacon Blanket

288

Brats with
Simple Coleslaw

290

Sweet-n-Sour
Country-Style
Ribs over Zoodles

291

Slow Cooker
Pork Ragu over
Paleo Polenta

292

Deconstructed
BLT with
Pork Belly

294

Schweinshaxen

296

Goat Cheese
Panna Cotta with
Crispy Prosciutto
and Fried Basil

Sides and Vegetarian Dishes

300

Mushroom Ragu

302

Cheesy Grits

303

Creamy Cilantro-
Lime Pasta

304

Pizza Sticks

306

Easy as
Portobello
Pizza Pie

308

Zoodles
Two Ways

310

Bordelaise
Mushrooms

311

Curry Braised
Cucumbers

312

Grilled Radicchio
with Sweet-and-
Sour Hot Bacon
Dressing

313

Caramelized
Endive

314

Easy Homemade
Sauerkraut

316

Easy Kimchi

318

Refrigerator
Pickles

320

Paleo Polenta

Desserts

324 Deconstructed Crème Brûlée

325 Grand Marnier Fat Bombs

326 Crispy Vanilla Fat Bombs

328 Crispy Maple Bacon Fat Bombs

330 Frozen Orange Cream Bites

332 Frozen Snickerdoodle Cream Bites

334 Strawberry Cheesecake in Jars

336 Paletas

337 Orange Cream Push Pops

338 Key Lime Curd

340 Key Lime Fat Bombs

342 Key Lime Ice Cream

343 Coffee Ice Cream

344 Hibiscus Berry Ice Cream

345 Chai Ice Cream

346 Dreamy Chai Float

347 Savory Pizza Gelato

348 Egg-Free Ice Cream

349 Dairy-Free Chocolate Ice Cream Coating

350 Butterscotch Mousse

351 French Silk Mousse

352 Gummy Bears

353 Bananas Foster Fudge

354 Flourless Fudgy Brownies

356 Buttermints

Smoked Foods

362 Smoked Brisket

364 Smoked Beef Long Ribs

366 Smoked Baby Back Ribs

368 Smoked Pork Shoulder

370 Smoked Salmon

372 Pan-Fried Smoked Cauliflower Steaks

374 Pan-Fried Smoked Eggplant

Recipe	Page	Vege-tarian	Egg-Free	Nut-Free	Dairy-Free
Rib Rub	108	♦	♦	♦	♦
Seasoned Salt	109	♦	♦	♦	♦
Taco Seasoning	110	♦	♦	♦	♦
Pizza Spice Mix	111	♦	♦	♦	♦
Fat-Burning Immersion Blender Mayo	112	♦		♦	♦
Spicy Mayo	113	♦		♦	♦
Herb Aioli	114	♦		♦	♦
Cilantro Lime Sauce	115	♦	♦	♦	♦
Caesar Dressing	116	♦		♦	♦
Green Goddess Dressing	117	♦		♦	♦
Dairy-Free Ranch Dressing	118	♦		♦	♦
Blue Cheese Dressing	119	♦	♦	♦	
Easy French Dressing	120		♦	♦	♦
Simple Taco Salad Dressing	121	♦		♦	♦
Creamy Tarragon Keto Sauce	122	♦		♦	♦
Keto Fry Sauce	123	♦		♦	♦
Homemade Sriracha	124	♦	♦	♦	♦
BBQ Sauce	125	♦	♦	♦	♦
White BBQ Sauce	126	♦		♦	♦
Easy Ketchup	127	♦	♦	♦	♦
Alfredo Sauce	128	♦	♦	♦	
Minute Hollandaise	129	♦		♦	♦
Simple Chimichurri Sauce	130		♦	♦	♦
Homemade Almond Milk	131		♦		♦
Simple Slow Cooker Bone Broth	132		♦	♦	♦
Slow Cooker Roasted Garlic	134	♦	♦	♦	♦
Olive Salsa	135	♦	♦	♦	♦
Guacamole	136	♦	♦	♦	♦
Dairy-Free Minute "Cream Cheese" Spread	138	♦		♦	♦
Orange Marmalade	139	♦		♦	
Orange Cream Shake	142	♦	♦	♦	
Crème de Menthe Shake	144	♦	♦	♦	♦
Dairy-Free Chocolate Shake	145	♦	♦	♦	♦
Spring Popovers	146	♦		♦	♦
Eggs in Purgatory	148			♦	♦
Tex-Mex Breakfast Gravy	149		♦	♦	
Minute English Muffin	150	♦		♦	♦
Cinnamon Roll Minute Muffins	152	♦		♦	♦
Dairy-Free Milk Chocolate Protein Bars	154	♦	♦	♦	♦
Strawberry Cheesecake Protein Bars	156	♦	♦	♦	
Cream of No-Wheat Cereal	157	♦		♦	♦
Chocolate Breakfast Custard	158		♦	♦	♦
Chorizo Breakfast Patties	160		♦	♦	♦
Pizza Muffins	162	♦		♦	
Taco Breakfast Bake	164			♦	
Healthy Hash Browns	166	♦		♦	♦
Green Eggs and Ham	168			♦	♦
Breakfast Burritos	169			♦	
Amuse-Bouche Platter	172		♦	♦	
BLT "Chips" and Dip	173		♦	♦	
Italian Poppers	174		♦	♦	♦
Amazing Cheese Puffs	175	♦	♦	♦	
Cheesy Fried Ravioli	176			♦	
Popsicle Crudités with Dill Dip	178		♦	♦	
Tomato Tulips	180	♦	♦	♦	

Recipe	Page	Vegetarian	Egg-Free	Nut-Free	Dairy-Free
Purple Pickled Eggs	182	◆		◆	◆
Baked Bacon-Wrapped Pickles	183			◆	◆
Classic Deviled Eggs	184	◆		◆	◆
Sriracha Deviled Eggs	185	◆		◆	◆
Teriyaki Jerky	186		◆	◆	◆
Dad's Tenderloin Bites	188		◆	◆	◆
Paleo Deep-Fried Mushrooms	190			◆	◆
Primal Sliders	191			◆	◆
Chili Lime Wings	192		◆	◆	◆
Eggs Gribiche	193	◆		◆	◆
Zucchini Chips	194	◆		◆	
Prosciutto and Arugula Roll-Ups	198			◆	◆
Mini Pastrami Roll-Ups	199		◆	◆	◆
Turkey Sushi	200			◆	
Philly Cheesesteak Roll-Ups	202		◆	◆	
Slow Cooker BBQ Pork Wraps	203		◆	◆	◆
Easy Tuna Salad Wraps	204			◆	◆
Sardine Salad Wraps	206		◆	◆	◆
Slow Cooker BBQ Chicken Wraps	207		◆	◆	◆
Slow Cooker Chicken Caesar Wraps	208			◆	◆
Slow Cooker Beef Barbacoa Wraps	210		◆	◆	◆
Zucchini Tortillas	212	◆		◆	
Broccoli "Noodle" Cheese Soup	216		◆	◆	
Easy Tomato Soup with Grilled Cheese	218	◆	◆	◆	
Simple Salade Niçoise	220			◆	◆
Chicken "Noodle" Soup	222		◆	◆	◆
South of the Border Salad	223		◆	◆	
Cucumber Salad	224	◆	◆	◆	◆
Wedge Salad	225			◆	◆
7-Minute Chopped Salad	226			◆	
Fish Tacos	230		◆	◆	◆
Arctic Char with Olive Salsa	232		◆	◆	◆
Crab-Stuffed Avocado with Lime	234			◆	◆
Shrimp and Grits	235			◆	
Fish Sticks	236			◆	◆
Masala Mussels	238		◆	◆	◆
King Crab Legs with Garlic Butter	240		◆	◆	◆
Slow Cooker Chicken Fajitas	244			◆	◆
Slow Cooker Chimichurri Chicken	245		◆	◆	◆
Chicken Alfredo	246	◆	◆	◆	
Grilled Chicken with White BBQ Sauce	248			◆	◆
Double-Fried Chicken	249		◆	◆	◆
Slow Cooker Laotian Chicken and Herbs (Larb)	250		◆	◆	◆
Slow Cooker "Butter" Chicken with Naan	252			◆	◆
Chicken "Noodle" Stir-Fry	254		◆	◆	◆
Marinated Tenderloin with Bordelaise Mushrooms	258		◆	◆	◆
Grandma Nancy's Italian Beef	259		◆	◆	◆
Easy Campfire Casserole	260		◆	◆	◆
Slow Cooker Sweet-n-Spicy Short Ribs	262		◆	◆	◆
Easy Corned Beef "Hash"	263		◆	◆	◆
Upside-Down Pizza	264	◆	◆	◆	
Skillet Lasagna	266		◆	◆	
Open-Faced Hamburgers on "Buns"	268		◆	◆	◆
Taco Bar Night	270		◆	◆	◆
Roasted Bone Marrow	272		◆	◆	◆
Slow Cooker Osso Buco	274		◆	◆	◆
Basted Rib-Eye Steak	276		◆	◆	◆
Mexican Meatloaf Cupcakes	278			◆	

Recipe	Page	Vegetarian	Egg-Free	Nut-Free	Dairy-Free
20-Minute Ground Lamb Casserole	280		♦	♦	♦
Grilled Lamb Chops with Mint Aioli	282			♦	♦
Broccoli Carbonara	286			♦	
Pigs in a Bacon Blanket	287		♦	♦	♦
Brats with Simple Coleslaw	288			♦	♦
Sweet-n-Sour Country-Style Ribs over Zoodles	290		♦	♦	♦
Slow Cooker Pork Ragu over Paleo Polenta	291		♦	♦	♦
Deconstructed BLT with Pork Belly	292		♦	♦	♦
Schweinshaxen	294		♦	♦	♦
Goat Cheese Panna Cotta with Crispy Prosciutto and Fried Basil	296		♦	♦	
Mushroom Ragu	300	♦	♦	♦	♦
Cheesy Grits	302	♦	♦	♦	
Creamy Cilantro-Lime Pasta	303	♦	♦	♦	♦
Pizza Sticks	304	♦		♦	
Easy as Portobello Pizza Pie	306	♦	♦	♦	
Zoodles Two Ways	308	♦	♦	♦	♦
Bordelaise Mushrooms	310		♦	♦	♦
Curry Braised Cucumbers	311	♦	♦	♦	♦
Grilled Radicchio with Sweet-and-Sour Hot Bacon Dressing	312		♦	♦	
Caramelized Endive	313	♦	♦	♦	♦
Easy Homemade Sauerkraut	314	♦	♦	♦	♦
Easy Kimchi	316	♦	♦	♦	♦
Refrigerator Pickles	318	♦	♦	♦	♦
Paleo Polenta	320	♦	♦	♦	♦
Deconstructed Crème Brûlée	324	♦	♦	♦	
Grand Marnier Fat Bombs	325	♦	♦	♦	♦
Crispy Vanilla Fat Bombs	326	♦	♦	♦	♦
Crispy Maple Bacon Fat Bombs	328		♦	♦	♦
Frozen Orange Cream Bites	330	♦	♦	♦	
Frozen Snickerdoodle Cream Bites	332	♦	♦	♦	
Strawberry Cheesecake in Jars	334		♦	♦	
Paletas	336	♦	♦	♦	♦
Orange Cream Push Pops	337	♦	♦	♦	
Key Lime Curd	338	♦		♦	
Key Lime Fat Bombs	340			♦	
Key Lime Ice Cream	342	♦		♦	
Coffee Ice Cream	343	♦		♦	
Hibiscus Berry Ice Cream	344	♦		♦	♦
Chai Ice Cream	345	♦		♦	
Dreamy Chai Float	346	♦		♦	
Savory Pizza Gelato	347	♦		♦	♦
Egg-Free Ice Cream	348	♦	♦	♦	
Dairy-Free Chocolate Ice Cream Coating	349	♦	♦	♦	
Butterscotch Mousse	350	♦	♦	♦	
French Silk Mousse	351	♦		♦	♦
Gummy Bears	352		♦	♦	♦
Bananas Foster Fudge	353	♦	♦	♦	
Flourless Fudgy Brownies	354	♦		♦	♦
Buttermints	356	♦	♦	♦	♦
Smoked Brisket	362		♦	♦	♦
Smoked Beef Long Ribs	364		♦	♦	♦
Smoked Baby Back Ribs	366		♦	♦	♦
Smoked Pork Shoulder	368		♦	♦	♦
Smoked Salmon	370		♦	♦	♦
Pan-Fried Smoked Cauliflower Steaks	372	♦		♦	♦
Pan-Fried Smoked Eggplant	374	♦		♦	♦

General Index